To Rev. A.W. Sutherland.

Yours the Author

# THEY CAME FROM CAITHNESS

A Gallery of Northern Notables

*being*

Pen Portraits of Famous Caithnessians

---

*by*

D. P. THOMSON

---

# THEY CAME FROM CAITHNESS

WHEN the traveller from the south reaches Caithness, whether it be by the steep road over the Ord or by the long railway journey across the moors, he is conscious at once of a change of scene which is very marked. Trees and mountains have for the most part been left behind. The soil has become darker and the coast wilder. Place names and people's names alike are different. Fields here are divided by gorse bushes or flagstones. Ancient castles abound. Tiny harbours are tucked into odd corners of the rocky shore.

To this most northerly county tourists come in growing numbers, drawn by the twin attractions of John O' Groats and the Castle of Mey. Its population of 22,170 is almost exactly what it was 150 years ago, although in the interval it had risen to double that number. Nearly half of it is disposed in the two burghs of Wick and Thurso. On the one inhabited island of Stroma 111 people are living to-day. Just over 1 per cent. of the whole population speak Gaelic, as compared with 4,000 only 60 years ago.

"Wick," says the local guide book, "is not a Highland town. It is of purely Norse origin and still bears traces of the old Viking settlement." Created a royal burgh by James VI, in 1589, it was once the principal British centre of the herring industry. From the little harbour of Castletown alone at the close of the last century as much as 15,000 tons of Caithness paving stone would be shipped south in a single year. To-day the county depends largely on its very markedly improved agriculture.

Just how far Caithness has travelled in that direction may be seen from the pages of Dawson's "Abridged Statistical History of Scottish Counties" (1862). "Agriculture," says Dawson, "till about the commencement of the present century, was nowhere in Britain in a more degraded or semi-barbarous condition than here . . . At no very distant period the breed of cattle in Caithness was the very worst in the Highlands." All that is changed. To-day, alike on farm and small holding the evidences of improvement are to be seen on every side.

About this most northerly county two things may be said; it has had a very stormy history, and it has produced more than its share of famous men. From no town of its size in Scotland, except perhaps Earlston in Berwickshire, have so many natives of outstanding capacity gone to play their part on a wider stage than from Thurso. What is true of that parish is true only in lesser degree of other parts of the shire. Strong, hardy, self-reliant, opinionated, and at times somewhat domineering men, some of these may have been, but of the mark they have made on the world there can be no question.

Here in these pages it is with the contribution Caithness has made to the work of the Church at home and abroad that I am concerned. From the many I might have chosen to illustrate my theme I have had to make a selection, leaving out some I fain would have included, such as David Steven of Bower, Dr Swanson of Swatow and the father of Alexander Mackay of Uganda. What I have written, will, I hope, be taken as the sincere if inadequate tribute of a stranger who comes to work for a short time in the county. To the resources of my own extensive library I am grateful to have been allowed to add those of the Wick Library, with its fine Caithness Collection.

D. P. THOMSON.

Barnoak, Crieff, Perthshire,
   27th July, 1954.

## CHAPTER I

# THE APOSTLE OF THE NORTH

JOHN MACDONALD'S father was the catechist of Reay, the most westerly parish in the County of Caithness, a man universally esteemed by the people among whom he worked. It was said of him that " so richly replenished was his mind and memory with Scripture that he would repeat it exactly as if he were reading, and any mistake made by one on quoting a passage in his hearing would be instantly detected."[1]

Of John Macdonald himself it is written : "A green spot at the foot of Ben Freicheadan, near Brawlbin, marks the site of the house where he first saw the light." That was in November, 1779, in the middle of that stormy period which was to culminate in the French Revolution of ten years later.

The parish of Reay was vacant and so the services of a neighbouring minister had to be sought for baptism. The good man was found out on the moors, attired in sporting costume, a typical representative of the northern clergy of his day. Scorning to seek a more conventional background, he broke the ice of a neighbouring pool with the butt end of his gun, " and fetching water from the opening sprinkled it on the face of the infant as he repeated the solemn words of consecration."[2] It was a fit introduction to the fellowship of the Church for one whose career was to be so romantic and so memorable, and whose contribution so outstanding !

During his first five years the boy was brought up by a widow who had been present at his birth. " Each night before putting him to bed," says Donald Beaton,[1] " she knelt beside him, and in an audible voice prayed for the child." Throughout his boyhood, youth and manhood, the memory of these prayers was with John Macdonald, and in later years he would frequently refer to what that first gracious influence had meant to him.

From the age of five to eight he was under his father's care before going to school, " a smart, active little fellow, with quick black eyes, and a face which a cheerful smile seldom failed to brighten, dressed in the kilt, bare-footed and bare-headed, the active if not careful herd of his father's cows."[2]

Early a leader among the boys, he became known on entering his teens, says Dr Kennedy of Dingwall, his biographer, " as the cleverest scholar in the parish school, and he was in consequence often employed by the neighbouring farmers in making up their accounts." With the assistance of a neighbouring craftsman he is said to have added a room to his father's cottage to which he could retire with both his bed and his books, and in which he could

1 D. Beaton—" Noted Ministers Of The Northern Highlands " (1929. Northern Counties Publishing Co. 285 pp.).
2 John Kennedy—" The Apostle Of The North : The Life And Labours Of The Rev. John Macdonald, D.D., of Ferintosh (1932. Northern Counties Publishing Co. 343 pp.).

find the solitude he needed for concentration, if not yet for meditation and prayer.

Narrowly escaping the attentions of the recruiting sergeant, he left for College in Aberdeen at the age of eighteen, still a stranger to that transforming grace of which in later years he was to become so powerful a preacher. It was by the seashore, in a time of deep spiritual conflict, with the thought of suicide not far away, that John Macdonald found the light, between his first and second college sessions.

" Under the pressure of despair," says Dr Kennedy,[1] " and at the suggestion of the tempter, he advanced within the sweep of the great billows that were breaking wildly on the shore. Ere the advancing wave reached him, a ray of Gospel light pierced the darkness in which his soul was shrouded. Rushing at once from the danger which he had rashly provoked, and climbing up into a quiet cave in the rock hard by, he was there and then enabled to commit his soul to Christ. He went to the shore that day in the grasp of the destroyer; he returned from it in the arms of the Saviour." The man who found peace so hardly was to become the guide and counsellor of many as they sought the light of Christ.

Finishing his college course at Aberdeen with distinction in Mathematics, and going on later from Arts to Divinity, John Macdonald was licensed by the Presbytery of Caithness on 2nd July, 1805. Throughout the following winter he worked as missionary in the Achrany and Halladale district of his native county, later to become still more celebrated by Finlay Cook, a remarkable tribute to whose influence and ministry in the North is inscribed on the beautiful red granite obelisk which stands outside the Free Church of Reay. In September of 1806 he was ordained at Berriedale, having been married the previous January. A few months later he was inducted to a Gaelic charge in Edinburgh, and in 1813 he was translated to the Parish of Urquhart in Easter Ross, where of which he was to remain minister until his death. It was with that Ferintosh district of the Black Isle that his name was ever afterwards to be identified —and it was as " Dr John Macdonald of Ferintosh, The Apostle of the North," that he was to become known to succeeding generations of his fellow countrymen.

In all the ecclesiastical annals of Scotland there is no parallel to the influence this man exerted and to the place he made for himself in the affections of his fellow Highlanders.

" The proudest and most powerful chieftains of the Celtic race," says Dr Robert Buchanan,[2] the historian of the Disruption, and himself one of the outstanding leaders of the Free Church of Scotland, " never possessed such a mastery over the clans which

1 " The Apostle Of The North."
2 Robert Buchanan—" The Ten Years' Conflict : The History Of The Disruption Of The Church Of Scotland " (1852. New Ed. Blackie & Son. 2 Vols. 975 pp.).

the fiery cross or the wild pibroch summoned into the field, in the fierce days of feudal strife, as belonged in these more peaceful modern times, to this humble servant of Christ. From Tarbat Ness to the Outer Hebrides, from the Spey to the Pentland Firth, the fact needed but to be known that John Macdonald had come, and was about to preach the Word, in order that the country for twenty miles around should gather at his call. Ten thousand people have often been swayed as one man—stirred, into enthusiasm or melted into sadness, by this mighty and faithful preacher's voice."

"John Macdonald," says Dr John Macinnes,[1] the scholarly minister of Halkirk, " the man upon whom the Highland people spontaneously bestowed the title ' The Apostle of the North,' was probably the greatest Gaelic preacher since St Columba. He evangelised his fellow countrymen from within the Church. In him, the new and aggressive Evangelicalism of the early 19th century is in close touch and sympathy with the 18th century Fathers of the Northern Highlands."

Ferintosh, it must truthfully be said, saw comparatively little of its minister, despite the great Communion gatherings which have made " The Burn " there so famous as an open air shrine of hallowed memory, and there were not a few murmurings in consequence. John Macdonald was not a pastor; he was an evangelist. In a day when there were neither " Special Missions " nor " Special Missioners," he found his vocation and his opportunity at the great Communion gatherings, which were held once a year or once in every two years in every parish in the Highlands, and to which thousands came from a wide district round about.

"Perhaps no minister of modern times," says Donald Beaton,[2] " was more owned as the means of converting souls. While in Edinburgh, he took a deep and active interest in the great revival at Muthill. Soon after his removal to Ferintosh a movement took place among his own people. After that the Word was much blessed on both sides of Loch Tay and in Glen Lyon; and he frequently visited the district and preached with great power and success. The fruits of the revival of religion there are visible to this day. There were great spiritual movements in Ross-shire, the revivals in Kilsyth and Dundee took place and in all these Dr Macdonald took his share of the work. Wherever he heard of the Lord's cause prospering he made a point of being there to help it forward."

Far further afield than Dundee or Kilsyth this great evangelist travelled. Four times in as many years he made the long and difficult journey to S. Kilda, the inhabitants of which he found

1 " The Evangelical Movement In The Highlands Of Scotland : 1688 to 1800 " (1951. Aberdeen University Press. 299 pp.).
2 Donald Beaton—" Noted Ministers Of The Northern Highlands."

sunk in superstition and barbarism. There, on his last visit, he had the joy of seeing church, manse and school erected. At least once he crossed to Ireland on an extended mission, mastering the Erse dialect and preaching boldly among the Roman Catholics of the South-West.

In spite of his frequent transgression of the ecclesiastical proprieties this man was held in warm regard as well as great esteem by his brother ministers. Even those who differed from him widely in outlook and in spirit bade him welcome to their homes; perhaps his popularity made it difficult for them to do otherwise! Much, however, he owed to his "kind, genial and brotherly disposition, which displayed itself so pleasantly in the family circle, his interesting conversation, and especially his fund of anecdote, making him a favourite with old and young."

In the ecclesiastical controversies of his time, John Macdonald took little part, for his strength, as he well knew, lay elsewhere. His sympathies, however were fully with the Non-Intrusion cause, and when the Disruption came in 1843, and the Free Church was formed, his influence was one of the dominating factors in the situation in the Highlands. Selected to preach the first sermon at Tanfield Hall, where the Free Church was founded, he was associated, as Gaelic Moderator, with Dr McFarlane of Greenock at the famous Inverness General Assembly two years later. Right up till the time of his death, which occurred on 18th April, 1849, he continued his evangelising labours, nor did his popularity in any way diminish.

"Short in stature," says Dr Kennedy,[1] " his complexion dark; his physical frame compact, instinct with animation, and showing no trace of ailment or infirmity; his face, with features well defined and regular, showing no peculiarity that weakened the force of its impression as a whole; a brow broad and high; and eyes quick of glance, kept expressive by an active intellect, and ever beaming with fresh love and cheerfulness—those who knew him cannot forget how he seemed and moved while he was yet among them. There was no man in his day who had a clearer view of the system of revealed truth, and a more extensive acquaintance with the mind of God in His Word; who could state with greater precision the doctrines of the Gospel; indicate their mutual connections, and define their places in the system with more exactness; and who could apply the truth more skilfully to the consciousness and the work of the Christian life."

"To Dr Macdonald preaching was no toil. He was so devoted to it, and became so dependent for his happiness in his work as an evangelist, that the day of which he wearied most was the day on which he did not preach." Yet it was he who said, " I never went to the pulpit without fear, and I never left it without shame." That, perhaps, was the secret of his power.

1 "The Apostle Of The North."

## CHAPTER II

# BY PRECEPT AND EXAMPLE

IT was Janet Sinclair's lot to begin her life as the daughter of a very notable man, one of the most remarkable Scotland has produced,[1] and to lose her mother at the age of four, when her sister, Hannah, was only a year older.

Born in London, on 17th April, 1781, she and Hannah were taken north to make their home with their grandmother at Thurso Castle after their mother's death. A Scotswoman of the old school, Sir John Sinclair's mother was the daughter of Lord Strathnaver—a shrewd, energetic, gifted woman, proud of her ancient lineage, and determined to leave no stone unturned in the education and upbringing of her famous son's motherless lassies. Taken to the Parish Church in Thurso every Sunday, they were examined carefully on the sermons they heard there, and in addition were required each to repeat a Psalm and to know the answer to at least one question in the Shorter Catechism! What their training consisted of at this stage we are not told—it was obviously of less importance!

The years of childhood in Thurso were among the most formative of all. In addition to their grandmother the children had the care of an aunt, and a much-loved English nurse, to whose homely warm-hearted counsels and simple Bible lessons they owed more, perhaps, than anything else.

There followed three years of the Canongate in Edinburgh, then boarding-school, in London, under the care of the same Mrs Crisp who had been their mother's headmistress. The girls were fifteen and sixteen respectively when they returned again to Edinburgh, this time to come powerfully under the influence of Dr Walter Buchanan,[2] the noted divine, who was then Minister of the Canongate Parish Church. In the interval, their father had married again, his second wife being a daughter of Lord Macdonald, eminent for her beauty and accomplishments, for her sweetness of disposition and benevolence of spirit.

Of the two motherless girls, Hannah was essentially the student, and the book she was to write in later years, entitled "A Letter On The Principles Of The Christian Faith," had a very wide circulation. The copy that lies open in front of me

---

[1] A man of indomitable spirit and inexhaustible energy, Sir John Sinclair, Bt., of Thurso, is remembered to-day as the originator of the "The Statistical Account of Scotland " (the 3rd series of which is now being published), a work of great fascination and value which has no exact parallel in any part of the world. Founder and first President of the Board of Agriculture, he carried through the most far-reaching reforms in the farming system of the country. The list of his publications fills thirty pages and numbered among his correspondents were more than half the famous men of Europe.

[2] Walter Buchanan, D.D., Minister of the Canongate Church Edinburgh, 1789—1832, and Editor of " The Religious Monitor."

represents the 14th edition, and is dated 1821, or less than three years after the original publication.

Janet, or Jessie, as she was better known, was much more lively than her elder sister. Nimble of step, fair in colour, and with open features of a very pleasing quality (to use the phraseology of these days!) she had a remarkable command of the pencil and showed considerable musical ability. Resolved to become religious and to read the Bible together for their mutual edification and profit, these two sisters found among their father's books the volume that was to change their whole outlook and to leave a permanent mark upon them. This was the famous evangelical masterpiece of the day—"A Practical View of Christianity," by William Wilberforce, the emancipator of the slaves. Devouring it eagerly, they found in its pages the Gospel in a way in which they had never known it before, and to that hour they both dated the saving change to which they were ever afterwards to bear witness.

If it was Wilberforce who taught them what has been called " the religion of receiving and relying," it was from Dr Buchanan's preaching, and from his character and conversation, that they learned how to grow in faith, in understanding and in usefulness. Always when in Edinburgh, until her death, Lady Janet, as she became, went back to the Canongate Church to pay her tribute of gratitude and thanksgiving.

It was on 13th June, 1799, at the age of eighteen, that she was married to her second cousin, who, six years later, became Sir James Colquhoun of Luss, and at Rossdhu, on the shore of Loch Lomond, that for the larger part of each year she henceforth made her home. Sir James, who had served in the Army and was M.P. for Dumbartonshire, was a man of retiring disposition, devoting himself almost entirely after his father's death to the management of his large estates. Prejudiced at first against Evangelical religion, his wife soon won him round. In Dr John Stuart, the Parish Minister of Luss, they had a mentor famed for his wonderful garden, his scientific and literary attainments, and his great achievement in the perfecting of the Gaelic translation of the Bible.

Soon after her marriage, Janet Colquhoun began to keep a diary, and in the pages of her biography,[1] it has been transcribed at considerable length. Sustained without interruption for something like forty years, it makes extraordinarily interesting reading.

It is as the mother of five children that she unbears her heart most fully. To her two boys, when they were very young, she wrote what she thought might be her last letter, full of solicitude

1 James Hamilton—"A Memoir of Lady Colquhoun" (1845. 4th Edition. James Nisbet & Co., London. 312 pp.).

6

in every line for their spiritual well-being, their growth in grace, and their eternal destiny.

"Are you living to God?" she asks, "Are you trusting in Christ for salvation and obeying His commands To promote this my every thought regarding you has been subservient. Were I assured of this I should feel comparatively easy as to everything else. This is the one thing needful. There is no impediment on God's part . . . I feel a hope that you will be blessings to the circle in which you move, and that you will glorify God in your conduct through life. What higher honour can you aspire to? . . . In the choice of a wife seek for one who fears and loves God, and I will venture to assure you of happiness with her."

To her three young daughters she wrote with the same directness and urgency.

" When deprived of an earthly parent, to whom should you go but to your Heavenly Father? Believe me, there is in Him enough to make up for every loss, and much more than enough to satisfy every desire. Fall down on your knees before Him. Entreat Him to receive you. Entreat Him to be to you what He has been to your mother. Entreat Him to guide and instruct and sanctify you. And entreat Him through the merits and righteousness of Jesus Christ, which if you ask are yours. Read the Bible carefully, and with a desire to be instructed by it. And pray for a blessing on it. Read also other good books, many of which I leave behind me. Never neglect fervent prayer. Do not mourn for me, as those who have no hope. Look up! I am safe. I am happy, unspeakably happy. You may follow! "

A woman who could write like that had something to say to a wider circle, and it is no surprise to learn that Lady Colquhoun became an authoress, although it was not until the death of her father and her husband, both of whom had urged it, that she allowed her name to appear on the title page of her books. After her death all five were gathered into a single volume,[1] forming a collection such as had come from the pen of no woman of the Scottish Church up to that date.

Lady Colquhoun was, as might have been expected, a bountiful giver, a tireless worker, and a fearless witness. More unusual than any of these qualities, and more impressive in many ways than her Sabbath School Classes and Tract Distribution, her

---

[1] The titles are :—" Thoughts On The Religious Profession Of The Higher Classes Of Society "; " Impressions Of The Heart, Relative To The Nature And Excellence Of Genuine Religion "; " The Kingdom Of God, Containing A Brief Account Of Its Properties, Trials, Privileges And Duration "; " The World's Religion, As Contrasted With Genuine Christianity," and, more moving than any of these, " Despair And Hope, As Exemplified In The Death Of A Poor Cottager." It will be seen that they cover a wide range, embracing the fields of doctrinal, experimental, devotional and practical religion. The omnibus volume is entitled " The Works Of Lady Colquhoun Of Luss " (1852. James Nisbet & Co., London. 462 pp.).

prison visitation and her valued and devoted Home Mission work, was the fact that she had the capacity to win the confidence, as well as the affection of women of all classes, encouraging her younger friends to tell her " all that was in their heart," in the knowledge that they were as sure of kindly sympathy as of wise advice, and that their confidence would not be betrayed.

The friend and benefactor of innumerable good causes, she had the needs of Ireland and India laid specially on her heart. Never did she allow her rank or position to put her out of touch with the common people. " When the Free Church of Luss was being built," says her biographer, " she noted that one of the pews had a private door, and was also much larger and more elevated than the rest. ' For whom was that intended ? ' she asked the carpenter. ' For your Ladyship and family,' was the answer. She immediately directed that the private door should be removed and the pew made like its neighbours, ' for in the House of God,' she said, ' there ought to be no distinctions.' " One could wish that that spirit were more common !

" Tall and dignified," says Dr James Hamilton,[1] who knew her better than most men, " with an ample and intellectual forehead, and with beautiful Grecian features lighted up by a fine complexion and an eye mildly penetrating, there was something peculiarly prepossessing in the youthful appearance of Lady Colquhoun. A total absence of affectation superadded the charm of a sweet unconsciousness. Her elevated mind and graceful manners were instinct with feminine refinement and inherent nobility; and although in later years her complexion faded and her figure stooped, there came the more brightly forth the reassuring gentleness, the delicate consideration and the tact in ensuring happiness, which are among the loveliest attributes of the Christian lady."

" I have never left Lady Colquhoun," said her own minister,[1] " without feeling my affections purified, my heart warmed, and my spirit raised in humble thankfulness to God for His goodness, and in earnest desire to be conformed to His image, and to do all things to His glory. This, I am persuaded, was the result of the peculiar character of her piety, which was alike devoid of that asceticism which contracts the affections, and that enthusiasm which impairs the judgment."

" She was never highly elevated and never unduly depressed," wrote her half-brother, Sir George Sinclair, of Ulbster,[1] to his niece. " Though always dignified, her manner was often playful. She did not extract from others a strict and undeviating observance of the rules which she laid down for her own guidance, and although uncompromising as to all principles of grave importance,

1 Memoir of Lady Colquhoun.

she was always inclined to the side of lenity and indulgence when she differed from others in matter of minor moment."

" I have never," he adds, " seen any character so blameless and harmless, and without rebuke : so free from infirmities, and so adorned by virtues. She lived much **with** her Saviour in prayer, which is the surest resource for being enabled to live **like** Him in daily conversation."

Among the " Women Of The Scottish Church," who have served Christ down the centuries, Janet Sinclair, Lady Colquhoun of Luss, must be ranked very high. Her books are still read, but her Christian character and spirit constituted her greatest contribution. Hers was a life laid down in glad devotion at the Master's feet and lived from first to last to His Glory.

<br>

CHAPTER III

## A PILLAR OF THE AULD KIRK

IN the Church of Scotland Offices, at 121 George Street, Edinburgh, there hangs above the table at which a Chairman or Convener of Committee sits, in Room 34, on the second floor, in the Home Board Department, a large-size oil painting of a former generation. It is the portrait of a Wick man—The Very Rev. Kenneth M'Leay Phin, D.D., Moderator of the General Assembly of his Church in 1877, and Convener for many years of both its Business and Home Mission Committees, a " bonnie fechter," stories about whom will be found in many ministerial biographies of the period.

The name was originally " Thin," and the father was an Earlston man, who in his youth, as a " Burgher " student, had sat at the feet of the great Dr Lawson, of Selkirk, the " Olympian of the Secession," the future Principal John Lee of Edinburgh University being one of his many distinguished classmates.

Ordained to the Parish of Wick in 1813, Rev. Robert Phin had married a daughter of the local Provost, but she and his only daughter were taken early, leaving the minister and young Kenneth alone in the big manse. " On the day of his funeral," says the " John o' Groat Journal," " hundreds of persons crowded the Kirkhill . . . . Every demonstration of respect was evinced on this occasion by all ranks and denominations to the memory of the kind-hearted minister; and the various shops and warehouses in and about the town were shut."

That was in March, 1840. Just over a year later, having completed his course of training at Edinburgh University and been licensed by the Presbytery of Caithness some time before, Kenneth M. Phin was ordained to his one and only charge in the

Border town of Galashiels, a few miles west of his father's birth-place, his near neighbour in the Secession Church at Selkirk being Professor Lawson's son, George.

Here on the banks of the Gala Water—a mile above where it joins the Tweed, and within easy hail of the Abbotsford, Melrose and Dryburgh—there lived and laboured among their people from 1714 to 1907, a succession of parish ministers more interesting, more colourful, and more remarkable for character and individuality, for influence and for achievement, than those two centuries can boast in any other community of the size in Scotland.[1] It was into this notable succession that Phin entered, and in it he was to take his own distinctive place.

" Beloved as a minister, reverenced as a pastor, and universally respected as a man," this son of the manse from Wick fulfilled a pastorate of almost thirty years in that busy Border town. Amid his outside duties, which multiplied steadily with the years, Kenneth Phin never allowed himself to neglect the work of his own parish. He is said to have known by name every child in his large congregation.

Home Missions, however, were his dominant interest, and in the year 1870 he resigned his charge to give his whole strength to the work to which he had put his hand as Convener of the General Assembly's Home Mission Committee. Long before that he had made his mark in the Supreme Court of the Church.

" It sometimes happens in the physical world," says Principal Story, of Glasgow University, in his " Life of Dr Robert Lee,"[2] " that an exceptional visitation affects the whole character of a season, and so stamps itself upon the memories of men that, for a long time after, they speak of that season as associated with the special phenomenon which marked it off from all others. That, they will say, was the season of the great drought, of the dreadful floods, of the cholera, of the cattle plague, of the comet.

" Were we, in like manner, to distinguish the summer and autumn which followed the General Assembly of 1866, we would speak of them as the season of Phin; meaning thereby that in the ecclesiastical firmament the star of Mr Phin was at this time in the ascendant, and seemed, for a short period, to swell to the size of an orb of the first magnitude. Mr Phin's injunction to be loyal to the Westminster Confession was on the table of every Presbytery; Mr Phin's note of alarm was re-echoed in many a simple-minded country parish; Mr Phin's policy was discussed in half the newspapers of Scotland; Mr Phin's exuberant loyalty to the standards of the Church burst forth afresh at a meeting of the Commission of Assembly in August, and with the cry — ' The

1 cf. D. P. Thomson—" Those Ministers of Galashiels " (1946).

2 Robert H. Story—" Life and Remains of Robert Lee, D.D." (1870).

Word of God itself is in danger,' stirred up the smouldering fires of the *odium theologicum.*"

Convener of the General Assembly's Army and Navy Chaplains' Committee for quarter of a century, it was Dr Phin who succeeded on obtaining from the British Government recognition of the just claims of Presbyterian soldiers and sailors to the services of their own ministers. A doughty champion of the Establishment, he had entered the lists in 1850, with a vigorous pamphlet against Sir George Sinclair, of Ulbster, who had gone over to the Free Kirk in Thurso, entitled " The Church And Her Accuser In The Far North." More than thirty years later he was to follow this with " Fanaticism In The North " (1882).

Convener of the Home Mission Committee of the Church for the last 20 years of his life, and of the Business Committee of the General Assembly for eight of these, Kenneth M'Leay Phin died on 12th January, 1888, having been Moderator eleven years before.

Not everybody liked " this strenuous ecclesiastic! " " There was Dr Phin," says Donald Macmillan, in his " Life of Professor Hastie "[1] " then almost an extinct volcano, who as Convener of the Business Committee had bullied the House for many years, but whose day of power was on the wane. I can still see him jumping up from his chair, stamping the platform, waving his arms, and shouting down some youthful enthusiast who dared to dispute his word and authority. . . Intellectually, he belonged to the dark ages; there was no light in him, and any new movement towards freedom he would promptly suppress."

If that be thought somewhat severe, let it be remembered that " Moses Peerie," [2] who is thought to have been Principal Story himself, wrote in his *Nugæ Ecclesiasticæ*:

> There's nane wi' sic a start can spring,
> Rampaging to the floor;
> There's nane fae sic a leathern throat,
> Can gie sae lood a roar!

It is to Dr A. K. H. Boyd of St Andrews that we turn first for a judicial appraisal of this admittedly controversial figure in the ecclesiastical arena.

" I said a kind word of the removal of Dr Phin," he writes,[3] " long a prominent Assembly speaker, and a useful doer of Church work. He was not a preacher, and he had given up the living of Galashiels to devote himself to the management of our Home Mission. He had no liking at all for hymns, or organs, or read prayers. But he was a wise man, and bowed his head to the the inevitable course of events which he was quite powerless to

1 Donald Macmillan—"The Life Of Professor Hastie " (1926).
2 "Memoir Of Principal Robert Herbert Story, D.D., LL.D., by His Daughter" (1909)
3 A. K. H. Boyd—"Twenty-five Years At St Andrews " (1892).

resist. . . . It was when Phin was Moderator that Archbishop Tait[1] came to the General Assembly, sitting for a space beside the Commissioner. The Assembly rose to receive the Archbishop; an almost unprecedented mark of respect."

The final estimates are perhaps at once the most generous and the most fair.

" This great calamity which has befallen our Church makes me very sad," wrote Professor A. H. Charteris, to his friend William Robertson,[2] when the news of Phin's death came, " I would rather have lost the fight to him than miss him from the battlefield. He was the last of the men I looked up to thirty years ago when I began life in the ministry; and now one thinks of the generous man, the bold champion, and the antiquely courteous Christian gentleman, so big and strong and kind."

" We 3rd Year Divinity students met him much in our Tolbooth Mission work," wrote Dr W. S. Bruce of Banff, from the vantage ground of old age.[3] " By 1877 he had come to lead the General Assembly, and to exercise a wide influence in the Church. In the chair his fine appearance, his ready aptitude for business, and his commanding presence gave him complete control. His ever wistful and kindly eyes and his rosy cheeks were striking features, conveying the idea of a very happy and affable personality. . . In private he had an extraordinary charm, although he had little small talk. Home Missions absorbed him; he really lived and died for the Church of Scotland's well-being. Men have worn stars and got large pensions from the Church who never did so much as Kenneth Phin for the good of the nation and the Church."

1 Archbishop of Canterbury.
2 Hon. Arthur Gordon—" The Life Of Archibald Hamilton Charteris, D.D., LL.D."
   (1912).
3 W. S. Bruce—" Reminiscences Of Men And Manners During The Past Seventy
   Years " (1929).


CHAPTER IV

# A BUILDER OF BRIDGES

IT was on Sunday, 30th July, 1870, that the new Free Church of Thurso was opened for public worship, the preacher in the forenoon being Rev. Walter Ross Taylor, who had that most northerly town for nearly forty years. In the afternoon and evening of that day it was his only son, Walter Ross Taylor of Kelvinside Free Church, Glasgow, who officiated—the thirty-two-year-old minister of a Church Extension charge in the west end of the city, just opposite the Botanic Gardens.

Fourteen years later the father was to be Moderator of the General Assembly of the Free Church of Scotland; and in October, 1900, his son, occupying the same high office, was to lead the Union procession down the Mound, from the Assembly Hall in Edinburgh, and along Princes Street to the Waverley Market, where, in the presence of 7000 people, he was to constitute the first General Assembly of the United Free Church. It is a record probably without parallel in the annals of a small country town!

Born in Tain, on 11th November, 1805, ten years before Waterloo, the father's portrait has been finely sketched in Auld's[1] "Memorials of Caithness Ministers." Eldest son of the Sheriff of Cromarty, he lived to the ripe old age of 90, journeying south to Edinburgh in the year of his death to see one of the bairns he had baptised in Thurso—the distinguished Principal William Miller of the Madras Christian College in India—installed in the Moderatorial Chair of his Church, making three from that Thurso congregation within the space of less than twenty years.

A graduate of Edinburgh University and a student of New College, Walter Ross Taylor, Jun., was to make his first notable Assembly appearance as the protagonist of William Robertson Smith, the famous Old Testament scholar, then on the last of his trials for heresy. His opponent on that occasion was his own former Professor and Principal, the redoubtable Dr Robert Rainy. It was as "Rainy's henchman" that he was later to be known, although by no means always in agreement with him, and as "Rainy's successor" that men were to look to him in the closing months of his life.

To the end, however, Ross Taylor remained a champion of freedom of thought and of utterance, standing by both George Adam Smith and Marcus Dods, when they were in danger of going the way of Professor Robertson Smith.

"The best and most effective speech of the seven hour debate" (on the Adam Smith case), says the historian of the United Free Church Assembly, "was that of Dr Ross Taylor, who brushed aside all irrelevancies and side issues, and went straight to the point. The book under review[2] did not subvert their belief in the Bible as the revelation of God, but stoutly maintained it. His speech was punctuated by hearty applause all through, and its effect was obviously to clear many doubtful minds."

Four years later, Ross Taylor was to secure the election of Marcus Dods to the Principalship of New College, Edinburgh, calling on the Assembly for a "deliberate, strong and majestic

1 Archibald Auld—"Memorials of Caithness Ministers, &c." (1911. W. F. Henderson, Edinburgh. 392 pp.).
2 George Adam Smith—"Modern Criticism And The Preaching Of The Old Testament."

action " in the face of what he described as " the bitterness and maliciousness of those calumnies against a scholar of more than European reputation."

His was certainly not his father's standpoint. One wonders what the old man would have thought about it all, doughty champion of the orthodoxies as he remained to the end!

Beginning his ministry in what was then the quiet country village of East Kilbride, the younger Walter Ross Taylor was called in 1868 to the recently started Church extension charge of Kelvinside, Glasgow. Here he was to remain until the end of his ministry, nearly forty years later.

Occupying what has been described as " perhaps the finest church site in Glasgow," the building was a very striking one in the French and Italian style. The congregation, however, was deeply in debt and showed no signs of growth. The first short ministry had not been by any means a success. A preacher of note [1]Mr Traill may have been, but he lacked the physique needed for the building of a new charge.

Now everything began to change, the congregation responding from the start to the youthful and vigorous personality of its new minister. Within ten years its membership had gone up from 282 to 785, and from then it never looked back, a daughter Church being opened in Partick in spite of the set-back experienced in the failure of the City of Glasgow Bank in 1878, by which so many of the members were affected. It remains to-day one of the strongest causes in the west end of the city.

It was not, however, as a preacher or a pastor that the man from Thurso was to make his mark, but as an ecclesiastical states-man and a far-sighted Church leader. Called to the Convenership of the important Sustentation Fund Committee of the Free Church in 1890, as Rainy's successor, he rapidly came to the front in both Presbytery and General Assembly. Rainy was an Edinburgh man, and his lieutenant had to be from Glasgow. With the passing of the shrewd and capable Dr Adam,[2] it was on the minister of Kelvinside that the mantle inevitably descended, and from that day until his death, Ross Taylor was an acknow-ledged leader of his denomination, and one of Scotland's best known and most distinguished Churchmen.

Two supreme services the Church owed to this man — the creation of the Central Fund, on which the ministers of its weaker congregations depended for their stipends, as earlier they had looked to the separate and distinctive Sustentation and Augmenta-tion Funds of the Free and U.P. kirks, and the contribution he made to the causes of reconciliation and re-union.

1 Rev. William Traill, late of Elgin (South Church).
2 Rev. John Adam, D.D. (Died 1890).

A delegate of his Church to the General Presbyterian Alliance at Toronto in 1892, Dr Ross Taylor went to South Africa ten years later with Dr Archibald Scott, of St George's Parish Church, Edinburgh, deputed by their respective Assemblies to do what they could to mitigate the inevitable bitterness occasioned among the membership of the Dutch Reformed Church as a result of the Boer War. They are said to have succeeded to a remarkable degree in their mission of conciliation.

Before the close of the Union Assembly of 1900, Walter Ross Taylor had moved a motion regretting the separation that had come about, and expressing the hope that there might still be a continuance together in the work of Christ in the land. Unhappily, however, on this vital issue the minister of Kelvinside stood alone among the leaders. About half-way through the long-drawn-out period of litigation over the property of the Free Church which followed the Union, there came, says William W. Smith,[1] a moment when an amicable and immediate settlement might have been possible. It was in vain that Ross Taylor pled with his fellow churchmen.

" It is more than a probability," says Smith,[1] " that had the United Free Church leaders followed the counsel of the one man who saw further than the rest, the disasterous and wasteful situation that inevitably resulted from the decision of the House of Lords two years later would not have come to pass."

" In the testing time which followed," says the same writer, " the spirit of reasonableness and courtesy shown by Dr Taylor marked him clearly out in the public eye from others who were associated with him in prominent positions in the United Free Church. The members of the second Royal Commission were so impressed by his evidence and by the tone in which it was given that it materially influenced their decision as to the equitable division of the property of the Church." Indeed it is the verdict of " The Dictionary of National Biography " that Dr Taylor was " largely responsible for the passing of the Act of Parliament in 1905."

The closing years of his life were given to the cause of re-union, and despite the fact that in the 1906 Assembly of the United Free Church he could only secure 100 votes in support of a motion in favour of " an earnest effort on the part of the Presbyterian Churches to come to an agreement," he announced his intention of devoting the remainder of his strength to the furtherance of this cause.

It was in December, 1907, that Walter Ross Taylor died. Less than six months later the General Assemblies of both the

1 William W. Smith—" Kelvinside Church, Botanic Gardens: 1859-1934 " (1937. Blackie & Son, Ltd. 192 pp.).

great Scottish Churches agreed to appoint committees to explore the situation, and from that hour the cause of union never really looked back, the consummation coming twenty-one years later. In this as in other matters the Thurso man was ahead of his times, but his work had not been in vain. The World Council of The Churches, meeting at Evanston this summer, is something in which his whole heart would have rejoiced.

CHAPTER V

## ROSS OF COWCADDENS

H E was born near the shores of Loch Rangag in Caithness[1] and his ministry of sixteen years in Rothesay made a deep mark on the life of that famous Clyde resort, but it is with the Cowcaddens district of Glasgow that his name and fame are associated. It was as " Ross of Cowcaddens " that he earned the admiration and regard of a generation by no means wanting either in great figures or in colourful personalities. Among them all he made his niche and won his place, and it is to his son, J. M. E. Ross, who became the gifted and much-loved editor of " The British Weekly "—himself a preacher and writer of distinction—that we owe the story of his father's life.[2]

William Ross was a miller's son, and his father was one of " The Men " — outstanding laymen of their church — in whose house service was held two Sundays out of three, the minister coming the third to a meeting-house not far away. The mother was a singularly gracious woman, as tactful as she was benevolent, gentle, loving and trusted. The home was one given to hospitality and many a famous preacher found shelter within its walls. Finlay Cook was there often—one of the most noted men in the North. The bookshelves were well stocked, Bunyan, Boston and William Guthrie rubbing shoulders with one another, with perhaps Dugald Buchanan the first favourite.

When William was still a small boy the family moved to the Lybster district. There, before leaving for Moray House in Edinburgh, Ross became a pupil teacher and a temperance worker. He was to finish his first course of training " with special qualifications and authority to teach Gaelic," and from Moray House was to go on to Edinburgh University and New College. As a student he gave several hours a day to private teaching to help to pay his way through, acted as precentor under Dr Thomas McLauchlan in St Columba's Church, and as Secretary to the Highland Com-

1 In the Parish of Latheron.
2 J. M. E. Ross—" William Ross Of Cowcaddens : A Memoir " (1905. Hodder & Stoughton. 328 pp.).

mittee of the Free Church of Scotland. There cannot have been very many leisure hours!

Turning down offers of a Professorship at Nagpur in India and a Grammar School Headmastership in New Zealand, William Ross chose, out of three calls addressed to him as a probationer for the ministry, that of Chapelhill, Rothesay, and within a very short time of his arrival and ordination was making both his views and his influence felt in the town. With a congregation that was growing steadily in membership he was active from the first in the twin causes of evangelism and temperance, both of which were to remain so near his heart to the end. D. L. Moody, the famous evangelist, he managed to lure down to Rothesay for a day, and throughout the whole island of Bute he made the temperance cause a force to be reckoned with. Identifying himself early with the Independent Order of Good Templars, he rapidly became in succession Chaplain of the Scottish Lodge, Right Worthy Grand Templar, and finally Grand Worthy Chief Templar of the World.

Seventy-seven countries were represented in the movement at that time and it boasted four hundred thousand members. Rothsay was long to remember and speak of the day, in 1877, when a special steamer brought 2000 regalia-clad Good Templars to the town to pay honour to their " Chief," the young minister of Chapelhill, and to hold a great congratulatory demonstration in the public park of the town. Temperance work took William Ross across the Atlantic again and again, as it did to Norway and Sweden, and even to Australia and New Zealand.[1] The record of his journeys in that interest alone is almost breath-taking.

Ross, however, was more than a temperance enthusiast and an evangelist; he was a Celtic scholar of some distinction. At New College he had taken prizes in the Gaelic Class and while still at Rothesay he acted as Secretary of the joint Church of Scotland and Free Church Committee on the revision of the Gaelic Bible. A member of the Royal Irish Academy and of the Celtic Society of Montreal, he had been appointed an Inspector of Schools under the Gaelic School Society in 1865, while still a student, and through the larger part of his ministry he conducted a Gaelic Class in the Free Church Theological College in Glasgow. An unsuccessful candidate for the Celtic Chair at Edinburgh University, when it was founded in 1882, he continued to build up a splendid library of books on Celtic literature, and had dreams of works of his own on the Celtic race, grammar and Church, which like so much else in this field that he had planned to do, never materialised.

Happy as he was in Rothesay, William Ross felt keenly that the Church had never realised the importance of her Home

1 His brother, John, who donated the Ross Institute in Halkirk, had emigrated to New Zealand.

17

Missionary enterprise, and when the call came to take up work in the crowded district of Cowcaddens, just below the Forth and Clyde Canal, in Glasgow, he felt he could not say no. Ross began his great work in the city with certain clear-cut convictions. He believed that every Church ought to be an evangelistic agency, and that the Church building itself was the place to use for the purpose. While he remained at Cowcaddens whatever else might be going on in the halls there was an evangelistic meeting or service in the Church every night of the week. Twice a year there was a special mission, supplemented by a long summer campaign in the open air. The only way to get at the people of these crowded tenement and slum areas, he believed, was to keep at them, and so far as aggressive evangelism and temperance propaganda were concerned, he gave neither them nor his congregation any rest.

The district for which he was responsible formed a rough triangle round the Church, itself a finely-situated and well-equipped building — a landmark still in that part of the city. These streets were systematically combed house by house. " Better to plough a small field than to scratch a whole acre," was a favourite motto of Ross's. His lot was cast among the poorest of the poor, but, says his son, he never regretted it. 450 were added to the membership of the Church in his first year; 1000 in his first three years. And looking back over his eleven years' work he was able to say that 24,000 people had been conversed with personally about the things that mattered. Ross was nothing if not thorough!

He might have become a great preacher, says his biographer, adding as he did to Celtic fire and imagination " an unusual power of easy and fluent speech, freshness of outlook and individuality of standpoint." Pressure of work, however, made that impossible, and too often he gave himself insufficient time to prepare. First and foremost he was an evangelist, with a power of personal appeal and a winning and wooing note that found a response in many a heart. This man had his own methods. For the social side of the Church's work he had no time at all, but he ran what was virtually an amateur surgery, and he gave himself without stint to the care of little children and to the ministry of intercession.

His young wife had died very early in their married life, leaving him with the infant son, who became his biographer, and he made no attempt to fill the vacant place. " Men of the Pauline spirit," he was known to say, " will always be more or less lonely." Of a deeply sympathetic nature, he knew both what to give and what to with-hold.

"He was one of the very few men," wrote a grateful recipient of his ministry,[1] "who could both sympathise and inspire, one of the very few even among good men, who did not leave you weaker for their absence . . . The great aim and passion of his life was the bringing of every man, woman and child he met into direct communication with the living Christ." That is as notable a tribute as can be paid by one man to another.

William Ross died in March of 1904, his later years being given, at the pressing request of the leaders of his Church, to itinerant evangelistic work, especially in the Highlands of Scotland.

Nothing quite like his funeral procession has ever been seen in Glasgow. The children of Cowcaddens led; the United Free Church Presbytery of Glasgow followed; office-bearers and friends brought up the rear. In the centre of the city the police had to stop all traffic in the vicinity of the station. At Rothesay, where he was laid to rest, a great concourse of people was waiting when the vessel carrying the coffin steamed slowly into the harbour. His day's work was done, but his name will not be forgotten. He has added one rich chapter to the annals of evangelism in Scotland.

## CHAPTER VI

## MILLER OF MADRAS

"THE most famous of all the Free Church institutions abroad," wrote Dr Norman L. Walker in 1895,[2] "are the Christian College at Madras and that of Lovedale in Kaffraria." The great success of the former is due in a very large measure to its Principal, Dr Miller. "The Madras Christian College," said Dr Gustav Warneck, the German historian, in his "History of Protestant Missions" (1901), "now presided over by Miller, has about 1800 students, and ranks as the most excellent of all the higher educational institutions of India." Miller was a Thurso man, and Lovedale was shortly to get, as its second head, another Caithnessian, James Henderson from Watten. It is a record such as few counties can challenge!

Born on 13th January, 1838, William Miller was one of three brothers, who grew up in this most northerly of all British towns under the inspiring ministry of Dr Walter Ross Taylor, one of the greatest theologians of his day, and the acknowledged leader of his Church in the North. "The Doctor" was to be Moderator of the Free Church General Assembly in 1884, Miller himself in

1 William Ross of Cowcaddens.
2 Norman L. Walker—"Chapters From The History Of The Free Church Of Scotland" (1895 Oliphant, Anderson & Ferrier. 364 pp.).

1896. His older brother, John, became a well-known and success-ful farmer at Scrabster, near the home of his boyhood; his younger brother, Alexander, who gifted its fine library to the Miller Institution in his native town, ministered for years in Buckie, and was for long the Foreign Mission Convener of his Church.

William Miller went East after a brilliant career at Marischal College, Aberdeen, and New College, Edinburgh, followed by a short assistantship to Dr Candlish, the famous minister of Free St George's, Edinburgh. Madras, to which he was appointed, is the most important city in southern India, " the home[1] of the great Hindu temples—and the region in which Christianity first took root, and where it exhibits its most marked development. From the Bengal border to Cape Comorin it stretches south for 1000 miles. Slightly bigger than the United Kingdom, it has a population of 38 million, 35 million of whom are Hindus."

Founded 100 years earlier, Madras itself became, under Clive, " the centre of the East in the struggle between France and Britain that brought India into the Empire." Here, where Lally planted one of his batteries in his attempt to capture the fort— " on the gallantry and resolution of whose defenders hung for years the fate that for weal or woe was to bind Britain and India together in one united whole "—stands to-day the Madras Christian College, beside it the High Court of Judicature, " perhaps the finest building erected by the British Government in India."

Missionary work in that area had been begun long before the Scottish Churches awakened to their responsibility overseas. In 1835 two Church of Scotland chaplains had opened a school for the education in English of a hitherto untouched group. Two years later John Anderson came out from Kirkpatrick Durham, in Dumfriesshire, to take charge of the work, and in 1843, along with all his fellow missionaries, he transferred his allegiance to the new Free Church of Scotland. The work grew rapidly, but Anderson, a man of outstanding capacity, was dogged through-out by ill-health, and in 1855 he died, leaving no successor. It was to this somewhat unenviable situation that Miller came out seven years later.

Five years before he landed the University of Madras had been founded. " It was in these circumstances," says one of his sucessors,[1] " in the midst of a feeling either antagonistic or indifferent to religious training, confronted by an Institution which was languishing and a College which enjoyed the advantage of Government prestige, that Mr Miller entered on his work in Madras, and faced the problem which the introduction of University education there set to the Church."

1 G.Pittendreigh, D.D.

"The year just closing," we are told,[1] "had been a disasterous one, the staff having by disease and death become perilously weak, and the school having fallen far from the position of influence it had had in Anderson's day. By 1863 Miller was left the sole European representative of the Mission in Madras, with all the schools in the district on his hands and the English services and the catechists." Tremendous task as this was for a newcomer, it had its compensations.

" He was thus able," says Principal Meston,[1] " from the very outset of his career to shape his policy untrammelled by the views of men senior to himsef. It soon became manifest that he was born to lead, and it was perhaps well that circumstances thus early placed him where his peculiar gifts found abundant scope. Within three years a policy had been fixed by that great animating mind wherewith God so opportunely enriched our Mission. What that policy is has been made abundantly clear during the 45 years of Dr Miller's service for the Church in India. It is also writ large in the activity of every missionary society which concerns itself with the educated classes of India."

Miller, it is clear, was no ordinary man! By 1865 the school had recovered its position of influence. Four years later he was presenting candidates for University degrees, and 1874 he sent home to the Free Church Foreign Mission Committee a proposal, which had the backing of all the missionary societies on the spot, to the effect that the Free Church Institution in Madras should become the central Christian College for the whole of southern India. It was a daring, a completely novel, and a very far-reaching scheme that Miller propounded, and it is greatly to the credit of 1875 Free Church General Assembly that they had the wisdom and the courage to approve it, for to-day we see that, in the Providence of God, that was the first big step on the road leading to the great United Church of South India, of which Miller must always be regarded as one of the architects.

Opened officially on 1st January, 1877, the Madras Christian College never looked back.

" College and school," said Principal Lindsay, of Glasgow, reporting twelve years later on what he had seen in India,[1] " occupy a magnificent range of buildings forming three sides of a square. On the fourth side, separated by a street, is the boarding-house for Christian students, and behind it, also separated by a street, is the boarding-house for Brahmin students. The huge pile of buildings is occupied from floor to ceiling with class-rooms which, large as they are, seem overcrowded, so great is the throng of students and scholars. The size of the place is

1 " Our Church's Work In India : Missions Of The United Free Church of Scotland " (Oliphant, Anderson & Ferrier. 623 pp.).

21

impressive; the swarming of intellectual life is a sight that once seen cannot be easily forgotten; the affectionate regard which the students have for their professors is very manifest; the intimate personal acquaintance that the Principal seems to have of every student in the College and every pupil in the Upper School is marvellous; but what distinguishes the Christian College at Madras from other educational institutions of a similar kind visited was the atmosphere of spiritual life which seemed to pervade it. That was the unmistakeable thing which left the deepest impression upon us."

Under the inspiring leadership of this great man the Madras Christian College went from strength to strength, growing in numbers, in influence, in usefulness, and in range of interests and activities with the passing of the years. Above all, it maintained its spiritual character and increased rather than diminished in evangelistic effectiveness, although no direct attempt was made at what is so often called proselytism. It was by the spirit that infused the institution and permeated the common life, the spirit so manifestly incarnate in him who controlled its affairs and gave himself so ungrudgingly to all that concerned its interest and its highest welfare, that atheist, agnostic and Hindu—especially the latter, were led by hundreds to Christ.

"The Madras Christian College," said Dr J. N. Ogilvie, in his "An Indian Pilgrimage,"[1] " is the lifework of one of the greatest missionaries Scotland ever sent to India, William Miller. In the Legislative Council of the Madras Presidency twenty of the members are old Christian College students, so is one of the Indian Cabinet Ministers, and all the Under Secretaries of the Government . . . In November, 1921, when a debate took place in the Legislative Council on the proposal to introduce a ' Conscience Clause ' in all educational institutions aided by Government—which would have paralysed the College in its main religious aim—member after member rose, told out what he owed to the Christian College — and stated that to pass such a measure would be both a hurt and a shame to India. The proposal was thrown out by 61 votes to 13 — the best tribute to missionary education that has been given in India for many a day."

As the years went by honours of one kind and another were showered upon Principal Miller. He was given the D.D. of Edinburgh and the LL.D. degree by both Aberdeen and Madras; the C.I.E. was followed by the Kaiser-I-Hind Gold Medal, 1st Class; and on New Year's Day, 1901, a vast concourse of people of all classes, and from over the whole of southern India assembled in

1 J. N. Ogilvie—"An Indian Pilgrimage: Travel Notes Of A Visit To The Indian Fields Of The Church of Scotland" (1922. William Blackwood & Son Ltd. 240 pp.).

Madras for the unveiling of a bronze statue in the city to this noted son of Thurso, whose memory his native town has still fittingly to honour.

William Miller spent the later years of his life in Scotland, keeping touch to the end with the great institution for whose development he had done so much. Living in rooms in Edinburgh in winter, and at Burgo Park, Bridge of Allan, in the summer months, he sent out periodically to his " old boys " a letter of greeting and encouragement, of news and of inspiration, which he called " The Voice of Burgo Park." He died on 15th July, 1923, at the age of 85, certainly one of the most remarkable men the county of Caithness has produced.

" He was," said a colleague who knew him well and loved him deeply,[1] " the greatest man I have ever known. Possessed of an amazing memory and a remarkable love, he was a strict disciplinarian with a tender and active sympathy. He helped countless students in need, visited them in sickness, and built for them a house near his own in the hills, where for years he had relays of them staying during the vacation, sharing their walks and their pleasures with them.

" We did not always think him right, but he was always great—a man utterly fearless in the path of duty and a born leader. No man has left a deeper impression on the mind and heart of the India of the South. At the time of his retirement he was the most trusted and influential man of British race in South India. In India his name is still a household word, uttered with reverence and affection in countless homes."

In Dr James S. Dennis' famous book,[2] " Christian Missions and Social Progress," under the heading " Commemorative Monuments of Distinguished Scottish Missionaries," there are printed, together on the same page, pictures of the statue of David Livingstone in Edinburgh and of William Miller in Madras. David Livingstone from Blantyre, and William Miller from Thurso—it is fitting that they should stand side by side!

1 George Pittendreigh, D.D., in " The Missionary Record Of The United Free Church of Scotland " (September, 1923).
2 James S. Dennis—" Christian Missions And Social Progress : A Sociological Study Of Foreign Missions (Oliphant, Anderson & Ferrier. 3 Vols. 1897-99. 1629 pp.).

## CHAPTER VII

# THE MAN FROM HALKIRK

A VERY singular personality! Those were the words Principal Martin used, in paying tribute, in the United Free Church General Assembly of 1923, to his deceased colleague, the Very Rev. Principal James Iverach, D.D., of Aberdeen. In the Chair of the Assembly that year, as Moderator, sat David S. Cairns, Iverach's successor at the northern theological seminary.

"A man of large body," says Dr George M. Reith,[1] who knew Iverach well and appreciated him fully, " with a tall, massive, yet somewhat loosely-built frame, his dark hair and beard clustered about a head of the type that one associates with the ancient Greek philosophers. His voice could hardly be called clear; there was a reedy overtone in it, but it was always distinctly audible. His manner of speech was rather offhand; there was a ' take-it-or-leave-it ' air about it, but the matter was always weighty."

Such was James Iverach, born in the parish of Halkirk in 1839, brought up under John Munro, one of the Disruption worthies of the North; a brilliant student at Edinburgh, a successful minister alike in a mining village and an Aberdeen Church Extension charge, a theologian of distinction, a keen and able controversialist, whether by voice or pen, an able administrator, and a born raconteur—" the kind of man who likes to leave a room with a burst of laughter exploding behind him."

" One always felt," his admirer confesses,[1] " like a novice at the feet of a rabbi who had not taken, but been given, all knowledge for his province. One felt in his presence like an adoring but nervous worshipper of Olympian Zeus; and when his hand dived into his capacious coat pocket, as it often did in conversation, one almost feared that he was feeling for a thunderbolt wherewith to blast the feeble opinion of his interlocutor. For the keenness of his intellect—perhaps the richest, the most subtle, and the most versatile in the whole Church — had its counterpart in the sharpness of his tongue."

It was with the publication of his third book that James Iverach sprang into fame, and it was the impression made by that book that carried him from the pulpit of Ferryhill Free Church in the Granite City to the Chair of Apologetics in the nearby College at " Babbie Law's." The title was a striking one—" Is God Knowable? "—and in the mood of the hour it struck a responsive chord in many a heart. " It contains in brief

1 George M. Reith—" Reminiscences Of The United Free Church General Assembly " 1900-1929 (1933. Moray Press. 360 pp.).

compass," said Professor Selbie, writing long afterwards,[1] "more good things than may be found in many large volumes devoted to the same subject."

That was in 1887. As a student Iverach had achieved distinction in both Mathematics and Natural Philosophy. At home in every branch of Natural Science he "was thus admirably equipped for the difficult task of mediating between science and philosophy, and between both and religion." Ordained to a charge in the mining town of West Calder, he went after a short but successful ministry there, to launch the new Free Church cause in the growing suburb of Ferryhill, in Aberdeen. The commanding position of the new building gave it prominence from the start, and its graceful spire became one of the well-known landmarks of the city.

"As a preacher," says Alexander Gammie,[2] " he made his mark in the city. He came to be known as a man of exceptional gifts—a theologian and thinker of originality and power. While devoting himself to his studies, he was also diligent in the work of his pastorate, and the new cause prospered under his charge." A frequent contributor to the columns of the " Spectator," he wrote for the "Aberdeen Free Press," as it then was, a long series of brilliant and penetrating reviews of the leading theological, philosophical and scientific works of the day. In the Presbytery his voice was heard to effect, especially in the closing stages of the famous Robertson Smith case.

Opened in the year 1850, the Aberdeen College of the Free Church had never attained either the numerical strength or the popularity of its southern counterparts at Glasgow and Edinburgh. In 1887, when Iverach began his work, there were 33 students; in 1902, shortly before he became Principal, there were only 17. He himself had the extraordinary experience of being moved about from one Chair to another as vacancies on the College staff occurred. " During the thirty-three years of his professoriate," says his colleague, J. A. Selbie, " he had taught all the subjects embraced in the theological curriculum, with the single exception of Hebrew—surely a wonderful testimony to his all-round endowment."

Iverach himself was apt to resent the frequent attempts made to belittle the significance of the Aberdeen College, and to bring its career to a close as a financial embarrassment and a redundancy. It was in the General Assembly of 1905 that he let himself go. Transferred to the Chair of Dogmatics, his third appointment, and elected Principal in succession to Dr Salmond, he made, on accepting office, the kind of speech that was far from usual on such occasions. Characteristic in every way of the man,

1 Tribute in the " Missionary Record Of The U.F. Church."
2 Alexander Gammie—" The Churches Of Aberdeen : Historical And Descriptive "
   (1909. Aberdeen Daily Journal. 399 pp.).

the sting was in the tail of it (as Reith puts it[1]), "I might respectfully hint to my brethren," said the new Principal, as he looked
round the crowded, hushed, and somewhat anxious House, "that
they should speak a little less of the College, and pray for it a
good deal more."

All his Assembly appearances and interventions were notable,
but sometimes his words wounded, notably in the year of the
famous Dods-Bruce Heresy Case. " He assailed the leaders of
the heresy hunt with such vigour and such bitter sarcasm that
they quailed before him. All who heard the speech admitted
that it was severe, almost brutal, but it was both merited and
effective. The Assembly triumphantly vindicated the accused,
but the speech long rankled in the breasts of the discomfited,"
says the historian of the United Free Church Assembly.[1]

Moderator in 1913, he resigned his Chair seven years later,
retaining the Principalship, however, until his death. It was in
the Assembly of 1921 that he made his last, long-talked-of,
appearance, achieving perhaps the most completely characteristic
of all his triumphs as a debater.

Rev. James Barr, Home Mission Secretary, had been chosen
by the minority to lead the opposition to union with the Church
of Scotland. Mr Barr's speech was full of quotations " cited for
the most part from the stores of an extraordinarily retentive
memory." The honours of the day, however, were with the
Principal, who spoke for less than three minutes.

" He told the story of a northern farmer who was driving
his gig across a burn by a ford. The stream was in heavy spate,
the pony got ' laired,' and the farmer had considerable difficulty
in extricating it. Later in the year, when being driven to the
same ford, now a small trickle, the pony baulked, and the farmer
said, ' Toot, beastie, I doot yer memory is better than yer judgment.' Rarely did the Assembly hear an anecdote so much to the
point, and rarely did it laugh so uproariously."[1]

There was another side, however, to Iverach. In 1909, when
the United Free Church decided to accept the invitation which
had come to enter into negotiations for union with the Church of
Scotland, it was he who was chosen to lead the General Assembly
in prayer. In 1913, as Moderator, his opening address on " The
Heritage of the Scottish Church," with its emphasis on the
fundamental conception which had dominated its history—union
and communion with the Kinsman-Redeemer—made a profound
impression on all who heard it. Convener of the Business Committee of the House, he took a leading part in the negotiations
for Union. Deeply entrenched in a family life which yielded to

1 G. M. Reith—" Reminiscences Of The United Free Church General Assembly."

26

many " the memory of a beautiful spectacle of harmony and devotedness,"[1] he was greatly loved by his students.

" They revered his massive intellect,[2] they welcomed his readiness to share with them his unrivalled stores of information, they enjoyed his genial wit and humour, his ' table-talk ' when he presided at the Students' Dinner, and all the manifold exhibitions of his large-hearted humanity."

The Principal was in his 84th year when he died. All his life he had enjoyed remarkable health, and he passed away on an August Sunday morning after a brief illness, still a member and an elder in the Church, whose first minister he had been, at Ferryhill. His reputation as a preacher and a thinker, instead of diminishing, had grown with the years.

"A very singular personality," said Principal Martin at the succeeding General Assembly, he had rendered " a great and varied and memorable service."

## Chapter VIII

# THE FOUNDER OF THE BOYS' BRIGADE

O N the road out from Thurso to the harbour of Scrabster, and thence to the Orkney Islands, travellers leave the town at the end of Smith Terrace, a long row of modern houses commanding a magnificent view of the Pentland Firth. Just beyond is a much older white-washed house, standing well back from the road, on the sea wall of which the following inscription will be found carved on a finely polished slab of grey granite :—

PENNYLAND HOUSE
SIR WILLIAM ALEXANDER SMITH
FOUNDER OF THE BOYS' BRIGADE
WAS BORN IN THIS HOUSE ON
27th OCTOBER, 1854.

To the left of the inscription is the crest of the B.B., with its familiar anchor and Cross, and the well-known motto, " Sure and Stedfast." This year the whole world will be commemorating the Caithness man, who now lives in history as the pioneer of uniformed youth organisations, numbering as they do to-day so many millions of boys and girls.

The Smiths were a military family. William's father had served with the 7th Dragoons in the Kaffir War of 1849-50; his grandfather, the Adjutant of the 78th Highlanders, had fought with Wellington at Waterloo.

1 His wife was a Caithness woman—Margaret, daughter of D. Macdonald, Thurso.
2 J. A. Selbie—Tribute in the " United Free Church Missionary Record."

27

The third son in a family of four, young William Smith had seen many a shipwreck from the windows of his boyhood home, looking as it did straight across to the forbidding cliffs of Hoy, and standing so near to the dreaded Needle's E'e. When he was just old enough to remember, the shipwrecked crew of the brig, " Henry Polchard," had found shelter at Pennyland after their ordeal.

A born leader among the boys of the town, he is said to have formed a company of 20 lads and drilled them on the sands of Thurso Bay, as far back as 1865. Three years later his father died abroad, and William went to Glasgow to live with an uncle, and to begin his business career in that city, after finishing his education at the Western Institution.

A fellow schoolboy in Glasgow has recorded some of his early memories of the lad from Thurso.

" I was at once attracted," he says,[1] " by his manly bearing, his handsome countenance and form, his musical northern accent, and his warm and generous disposition, and we formed a friendship which became firm and lasting. My recollection is of Bill Smith's physical strength and gentleness, of the chastity and purity of his nature, of his dauntless courage and fine courtesy, and of his longing for a soldier's life."

Beginning his business career at 15, young Smith early parted company with his uncle, whose ways he found too stereotyped and old fashioned, and joining what became the firm of Smith, Finlay & Co., soon made his own way in the world of commerce.

Joining the Volunteer movement in 1873, W. A. Smith quickly rose to the rank of Sergeant and a year later he was commissioned in the 1st Lanarkshire Volunteers, with which he had connected himself. " Tall and erect, his fresh-coloured face always lit up with a pleasant smile, the men of his company worshipped him."

Coming under the influence of D. L. Moody, the American evangelist, he connected himself with College Free Church, then under the vigorous ministry of Dr George Reith, the father of Lord Reith, of B.B.C. fame. In the Young Men's Society of its North Woodside Mission his friends and intimates included James Moffatt, the future New Testament scholar and Bible translator, and the brothers, James and John Hill, who were to become his right hand men in the early days of the Brigade movement.

It was out of Smith's experience as a Sunday School teacher, trying to keep control of a class of unruly boys at the Mission, that the idea of the B.B. took shape. " Can't you make some use of your volunteer methods in the Sunday School? " his partner Finlay had asked, and the Boys' Brigade was the fruit of that happy suggestion. Boys, as he saw them, were " not a nuisance

1 F. P. Gibbon—" William A. Smith Of The Boys' Brigade (Collins. 173 pp.).

to be suppressed, but a force to be harnessed." Their high spirits, their energy, their fun could all be directed into the right channels. Given a title, a uniform and a badge, together with something of the fellowship, the team spirit, the discipline and the *esprit de corps* he had found in the Volunteers, and what might not be done with them?

A little doubtful at first about this very novel experiment, and dubious especially, as so many were to be later, about its semi-military character, the Mission authorities finally gave their consent, and with three officers and twenty-eight boys, the B.B. was launched on its great career on 4th October, 1883.

"The boys," Smith had told his committee,[1] "would be taught elementary drill, physical exercises, obedience to the word of command, punctuality and cleanliness. It would be something they could regard as distinctively their own, to which they could become attached, of which they would be so proud that they would be ashamed to do anything that might bring discredit upon it. Thus would be engendered that *esprit de corps* which public school boys acquire as a matter of course, but which was almost entirely lacking in elementary school boys. Organised games would follow, and he believed the outcome would be discipline and order in the Sunday School."

That 1st Glasgow Company still exists, and it still meets in the old premises in North Woodside Road, although the College Church itself has long since ceased to function as a congregation.

Smith came to the first meetings at which his great scheme was launched with every detail thought out—badge, aim, uniform and motto, and the passing years have seen amazingly few changes. The uniform may have altered slightly, the old pill-box cap being replaced by something more up-to-date, and the range and scope of activities has greatly widened, but the B.B. stands now for what it did then—"The advancement of Christ's Kingdom among Boys, and the Promotion of Habits of Reverence, Discipline and Self-Respect, and all that tends towards a true Christian manliness."

Smith's success was immediate, and his example was quickly copied. Companies soon sprang up all over Scotland. The Archbishops of the English and Irish Churches followed their Presbyterian brethren in giving the movement their benediction, men like Lord Roberts and Lord Kinnaird became patrons, and by 1895 there were 418 companies with 1300 officers and 17,000 boys. Thurso and Wick being numbered among them.

From the time of its formal inception as a movement in Smith's own house in Glasgow, on a January day in 1885, the "B.B." never looked back, and when its Jubilee was celebrated

1 William A. Smith Of The Boys' Brigade.

29

the Prince of Wales was able to tell the thousands of boys present that since its inception a million lads had enrolled in its ranks.

Within three years of the launching of the 1st Glasgow Company, it had spread to America and New Zealand; soon it was to go all over the world. Out of it came in the course of the years the Jewish Lads' Brigade, the Catholic Boys' Brigade, the Church Lads' Brigade and many other movements, those for girls not least among them. When in 1908, Baden-Powell launched his Boy Scouts, he was to pay generous tribute to the man who had first seen the possibilities of harnessing the energies of the growing boy in this way.

In 1908, the Semi-Jubilee year, honours were showered upon the founder, who had long since been compelled to give up business and devote his whole time to the work. Glasgow gave him a cheque for 1000 guineas and his portrait. " There is no person," said Lord Provost Sir William Bilsland, " whose portrait more deserves to adorn Glasgow's walls of fame." King Edward gave him a knighthood, and years later, addressing a great gathering of boys in Windsor Great Park, his grandson, King George VI, told his hearers that " meeting two of the greatest needs of the times, their founder had built on the twin pillars of religion and discipline." " He not only started a great movement," said His Majesty, " but one from which all our present widespread youth training was destined to spring."

" It would have been worth while founding the Boys' Brigade," said Henry Drummond, who adopted the movement so enthusiastically, and who did so much to further its spread across the Atlantic, " if only for the sake of the officers. It opens a new door for that vast aristocracy of young men of the more educated classes, who have hitherto swelled the ranks of the unemployed. This splendid enterprise has been initiated just in time to save hundreds of the best of them to their Church and country. The Officer will owe to his boys the calling out of sympathies which he scarcely knew existed, the exercise of talents which were slowly wasting, and the development of his whole character towards a nobler and stronger manhood."

Sir William Smith died just before the outbreak of the First World War, in which so many of his boys were to play so notable a part. The Memorial Services in London—at St Paul's Cathedral —and in Glasgow were memorable and moving occasions.

" When anyone asked me," said Lord Guthrie, speaking at the latter,[1] " how he could get an idea, accurate and expeditious, of what the Boys' Brigade stood for, I used to say ' Read our Motto, and then go and take a good look at Sir William Smith. You can get that impression about him if you look at his photograph. There he stands, as we can scarce yet realise we shall

1 William A. Smith Of The Boys' Brigade.

never see him again—virile, alert, masterful, yet so genial, so considerate, so tactful, so unaffected, so modest.' "

The celebrations designed to mark the centenary of the Founder have already begun, and in a striking tribute in a recent number of " Life and Work," the Church of Scotland magazine, the writer has this to say :—

" It is a remarkable tribute to the genius of the founder that the plan he evolved for the senior boys of that Glasgow Sunday School 70 years ago, is proving to-day just as attractive and suitable to the boys of many lands throughout the world as it did to the boys of those far-off Victorian days. The most sucessful B.B. Companies in this country are those that adhere most strictly to the principles and methods of the original Company . . . To-day thousands of men who are leading lives of Christian purpose and showing forth a Christian example in many walks of life, frankly acknowledge their debt to the founder of the B.B. . . . It has brought into the family of the Church boys who had never been in Sunday School or under any Christian influence until they joined it."

" In these times," continues the writer, who happens to be the Duke of Hamilton and Brandon, K.T., Lord High Commissioner of the Church of Scotland General Assembly, " when the infiuence of organised Christianity seems to have lost so much ground, we should be thankful that the B.B. has remained true to the Founder's idea, that this great movement for boys should be carried on under the ægis of the Churches, that the leaders should be chosen by the Church to which each company belongs, and that the training and teaching imparted to the boys should be in the Church's hands . . . I believe that the Boys' Brigade is destined under God to do greater service still in winning for Jesus Christ the young manhood of Scotland and of the other countries which our movement is serving to-day."

## CHAPTER IX

## HENDERSON OF LOVEDALE

HE was a Watten man, the youngest of a family of ten, brought up on a little farm in the parish, and it was a Watten woman he married. Called to be the successor of Dr James Stewart, of Lovedale, the greatest name in the missionary annals of Africa after Livingstone, men said later that he prepared himself for his lifework with a rare thoroughness, and that he gave himself to it with an abandon that broke even his strong Caithness fibre.

The parish of Watten lies near the centre of Caithness, traversed by the Georgemas and Wick section of Britain's most northerly railway. About a quarter of its surface is under cultivation, the rest being moorland or rough grazing country with almost no woodland at all. The Gunns, father and son, had been ministers there since 1805, first in the old Parish Church, and later, after the Disruption in the Free Church, and when James Henderson was born, at Dunn, on 31st October, 1867, Alexander Gunn, the son, had been exercising his powerful ministry in the district for fully thirty years. He was to continue for another twenty, and his life has been ably sketched by Alexander Auld, in his [1] "Ministers and Men of The Far North," a rich storehouse of good things for those interested in their country's past.

It was in Livingstonia, as the trusted colleague of Dr Robert Laws, the world famous pioneer of Nyasaland, that James Henderson served his apprenticeship in what used to be known as "The Dark Continent," but has since come to be called "The Continent of Opportunity." Going out in 1895, after adding short courses in medicine and education to his already full qualifications, Henderson gave ten years of outstanding service in pioneering work there in Central Africa. Fruitfully engaged in translation, as well as in exploration and administration, his chief contribution to the work of the Mission and to the development of the Colony, was made in the educational field. Head of the noted Overtoun Institution through its first critical decade, he was Chairman of the Commission which gave Nyasaland its second educational code and for years he acted as honorary educational adviser to the Government.

"At Overtoun," said Dr Donald Fraser long afterwards,[2] " he trained his selected lads who were to be the leading teachers and ministers of the Livingstonia Mission. As his experience grew he laid down the educational code on which it worked for years, and which became the accepted basis of all future revisions. Character training was the purpose of all his education, and so effective was this bit of work that the senior ministers and missionaries of to-day all carry the stamp of his personality on them. Amid his absorption in education he never lost his keen evangelistic purpose. Week by week he undertook journeys among the mountains that he might publish Christ in the scattered villages, and in the long vacation he led bands of students into the hinterland, opening new territory and setting down schools and teachers wherever he went. Through all these arduous and dangerous expeditions his tireless energy never seemed to know fatigue, and his sporting instincts led him to shooting adventures that

1 Alexander Auld—"Ministers And Men Of The Far North" (1891. 2nd Ed. John Menzies & Co. 300 pp.).
2 Memorial tribute in " Life and Work."

32

gave him an unrivalled reputation with his gun.   He married Miss Davidson, a friend of his boyhood."

About Henderson as a sportsman many stories were told. Let one of these suffice, revealing as it is of the man as well as of his skill with the gun.   He was hunting down a man-eating lion which had taken heavy toll of life in some of the villages. "At bay," says W. P. Livingstone, in his [1]" Laws of Livingstonia," " it turned and charged. It was a critical moment. Mr Henderson was kneeling. The lion leaped towards him, but at the third bound the cool eye and steady hand did their work and it fell over with a bullet in its forehead. The Doctor complimented Henderson on his splendid shot. ' It was a Higher Hand,' was the reply."

It was on 21st December, 1905, that Dr James Stewart, of Lovedale, died, and three months later Henderson was called to South Africa as his successor.   There was little doubt about the wisdom of the choice.   Lovedale was the largest and most famous native educational institution in Africa, and in James Henderson it found a leader and administrator of the front rank.

" He brought the very gifts necessary," said the " Christian Express of South Africa," " scholarly attainments, a keen sympathy with, and understanding of, native aspiration and endeavour; a full understanding of the difficulties confronting the missionaries of his time and a sure judgment of the relative importance of things passing and things fundamental in missionary endeavour."

Very early it became clear that there was one field he was going to make peculiarly his own—the economic condition of the Bantu people and the urgent need for improvement there.   The poverty which imperilled the very decencies of life and the utter degradation in which so many were compelled to live weighed on his spirit, and called forth not only his deepest sympathy but the service of his voice and pen and the dedication of all his great powers and influence.   " He is one of the few men," says Ray Phillips, in his famous book, " The Bantu Are Coming,"[2] " who have taken time and energy to look carefully into the native economic situation in this country."

Co-operation between Churches and Missionary Societies, and between both of these and Government, was another of the things for which Henderson strove.   A prominent figure in every gathering of the General Missionary Conference of South Africa, he was the moving spirit behind the formation, in 1925, of the Ciskeian Missionary Council, which was to mean so much to the Bantu

1 W. P. Livingstone—" Laws of Livingstonia " (N.D. Hodder & Stoughton Ltd. 385 pp.).

2 Ray E. Phillips—" The Bantu Are Coming : Phases of South Africa's Race Problem " (1930. S.C.M. Press Ltd.   238 pp.).

people. Cultivating the closest relations with his Anglican and Methodist colleagues, he carried through a notable series of surveys designed to ascertain accurately the spiritual, social and economic conditions in both urban and rural areas.

At Lovedale, Henderson wore himself out before his time. "In his Nyasaland years," says Dr Shepherd,[1] his successor, "his wonderful physique never seemed to know fatigue. But that he overtaxed his strength became evident, for he began to suffer from terrible headaches . . . He devoted himself unremittingly to the care of Lovedale, the furtherance of the South Africa Native College scheme (which was to result in the great enterprise at Fort Hare about which so much has been written in recent years, and where so many of the native leaders of modern South Africa and South Central Africa have been trained); Church Courts, General Missionary Conference, the work of Alice Town Council, whose sessions and committees he attended with amazing regularity and often far into the night, to the special concerns of " The South Africa Outlook," to which he contributed monthly, and to the religious, educational and economic advancement of the Bantu people. All through he carried the open, enquiring mind that ever distinguished him, the same desire to see mission service fitted in to larger plans, the same fresh spirit always ready for new enterprises, and the same love of spiritual religion that ever befriended any movement that made for lifting men and women nearer God. Unfortunately there was, too, the same spirit which insisted on carrying more burdens than he could well bear, and the same conscientious diligence which drove him into more hours of work in a day than a man can give without hurt to his body."

In 1923 Henderson had to get leave of absence from his work for a year. He went to the United States, studied negro educational work at the famous Tuskegee Institution and came back greatly refreshed for another spell of strenuous labour. In 1927 he broke down again and was off for several months. The end came in July, 1930. He was only 62.

" His name," says Dr Donald Fraser, " is indelibly written in the history of South Africa. He will be remembered not only for his brilliant talents but for the mark which a life wholly devoted to a single purpose and assiduously disciplined in the extension of the Kingdom and broad thinking can make on the people. He took up Stewart's scheme for a Training College for Africans and Fort Hare was the result. Every movement that made for the quickening of the religious life of the students and for the evangelistic energy of the native Church found a warm friend in the Principal.

[1] R. H. W. Shepherd—" Lovedale, South Africa : The Story Of A Century " (1940. Lovedale Press. 531 pp.).

"For years he had consistently overstrained his wonderful physique and spent himself without stint for his adopted land of Africa. The weary eyes of his latest photo too clearly portrayed the strain that for years had been upon him, and his breakdown two years ago had given warning that he was carrying burdens greater than he could bear. His passing was the quiet ending of a completed life. Some of his great enterprises had already been launched on successful voyages and greater plans for still new things had been made and were already under way. The week before he died I had written him two letters, one submitting names for his successor in the Principalship, the other intimating the offer of the first payment of money for a Bible School for Evangelists whose initial plans he had completed.

"Through thirty-five years of missionary service in Central and South Africa he had never grown stale or ceased to see new avenues opening up for better service for Christ. When we reckon up his service and the mark he left on Africa, he must be counted among the great missionaries of Africa."

"In every quarter of the country," says Dr Shepherd, in the centenary history of Lovedale,[1] "tribute was borne to his statesmanship, his fulness of knowledge, his far-reaching vision, his courtesy, his love of children, his fearless championship of Bantu interests, his deeply spiritual nature. On Sunday morning and Monday afternoon great throngs gathered under the oaks, and men told of what he had meant to them and the gift he had been to Lovedale and South Africa."

Preparations were made to have the funeral in the neighbouring town of Alice. On Sunday, however, a deputation of the students came to ask that their beloved Principal might be buried among them. They were willing to work all through the night, if need be, to make that possible. A site was therefore chosen, on Sandile's Kop, half-way up the hill, on the Fort Hare side. "From dawn on Monday," we read,[1] "students, apprentices and staff toiled to make the grave and a new motor-road, a 'Road of Loving Hearts' like that made for Stevenson in Samoa. An hour before the funeral was due all was ready." That afternoon two thousand people passed up the hill over the newly-made track to pay their tribute to this great-hearted son of Caithness.

1 R. H. W. Shepherd—"Lovedale, South Africa : The Story Of A Century " (1940. (1940. The Lovedale Press, C.P., S. Africa. 531 pp.).

## Chapter X

# THE CAITHNESS ORIGINAL

THERE stands on my shelves in its appropriate place, with its faded purple cover, the one volume I possess of the many that John Horne wrote—his " Caithness Originals." Faithfully limmed in those pages are the characters one has got to know so well—" Gollie," " Feber," " Fadlie," " Boustie," " Nellie Gundy," " Belle Royal," " Ca' Bonis," " Moonzie," " Creepin' Geordie," " Willie Wagtail," " Tailor Lintie," and " The King of Mount Syria."

I close the book and I think of the others which might so fittingly stand beside it—history, topography, poetry, essays, letters, sketches, critiques—all so instinct with the spirit of the county, and I realise as I had never done before that John Horne was himself " The Caithness Original," the living embodiment of many of the qualities and quaintnesses he so lovingly and graphically described!

" If I were asked to state in one work," said his friend John Mowat,[1] in a public tribute to this notable son of the North, " the secret of the attractiveness of John Horne, I would say individuality. It is graven on his strong, kind face. It bubbles over in his speech. It asserts itself in his written work. Most of us are bits of one another, unconscious as it may be, or studied, but nevertheless, copies. John Horne is himself — a graft of the Norland."

Born at Louisburgh in Wick—" the old grey town where life took up its song for me "—John Horne served his time in the case-room of the " Northern Ensign " newspaper, now defunct. Of his school days he has given us more than one sketch in his books, and of the spiritual experience through which he passed as a lad he has written with moving simplicity and power. It was with the little Baptist Church in the town that he associated himself, and later he was to write its history,[2] " formed about 1806— its first meeting place a loft in Kirk's Land, off High Street, behind the shop of Alexander Corner, draper."

" After I joined the Church at Wick as a young convert," he wrote years later to a friend, " a few of us took meetings at various places within reach. One fine Sunday we set off by the sands to give Mr Scott a hand in his evening service at Keiss.

1 " Public Appreciation Of Pastor John Horne, Ayr, &c." (July, 1932. "John o' Groats Journal." 22 pp.)
2 John Horne—" History Of Wick Baptist Church " (1894. " Northern Ensign." 16 pp.).

We arrived much too soon. The Sabbath School was about to ' skail.' We lay on roadside facing the sea. The sun blazed on it like the sea of glass in paradise. Everything was still; the scene was altogether idyllic. As we sat gazing in wonder and admiration at the ocean—so quiet, peaceful and immense—the children broke into their closing hymn

" I will sing you a song of that beautiful land, the far-away home of the soul,
Where the storms never beat on the glittering sand, while the years of eternity roll."

The youthful voices—the sea, sometimes so stormy and wicked—the calm shore of the hymn—these seized my imagination with a sudden enthralment of pathos and suggestion that has remained with me to this day."

" I have seen the sunrises in southern lands," he was to write elsewhere, " but the best of them were apathetic compared with the flare and pageantry of our northern sky on a summer morning. Nor have I ever been so thrilled anywhere, or by anything, as I have been by the langerous, slow-motion dayset on our modest fields, when everything was being bedded in cuddling shadows of homeliness and peace. My sympathies have been with lowly themes and with unpretentious places and people. Immensities easily tire me. I prefer a landscape where every hillock has a name and a memory. If anyone should say that this is mere sentiment, I can only answer that to me it is the truest realism."

The man who could write like that—who could speak of Scouthal " with its trees half-grown and bent and twisted, as if struggling to their feet against the northern wind," of " Dunnet Head, with its jagged crevices—studios, where wind and weather carve their fantastic subjects," and of " The Needle's E'e,— this imposing piece of Nature's freak architecture, cut out with careless art and impressive effect "—could not be confined for long to the caseroom of a small provincial paper, and soon John Horne was venturing on the journey South.

It was to Spurgeon's Pastors' College, in London, that he made his way, and on the Baptist ministry that his heart was set. " This was the straighest and quickest cut to his goal," says John Mowat,[1] " and he took it. We have visions of the forceful north-country youth arresting and attracting the student circle with the charm of his individuality. And it is not to be expected that the genuine worth of the Scottish lad would fail to attract the Principal. Spurgeon took a special interest in the Caithness boy and in his future career."

1 " Public Appreciation, &c." (op. cit.).

Winning a high place in his classes, John Horne left College to undertake the rebuilding of a congregation that was beginning life afresh after an interval of more than thirty years. Formed in 1837, the Baptist Church in Ayr had ceased to exist in 1850. Restarted in 1886, its meetings were being held in the Free Gardener's Hall, and over its first twenty members John Horne was settled as pastor in the autumn of that year. From the first the little cause prospered, a derelict theatre known as the Queen's Rooms being purchased the following year for £1,350.

" It was a bold venture for so young a Church," says the historian of the denomination,[1] " but at the pastor's second anniversary the members numbered 145." During the 5½ years of Mr Horne's ministry the church continued to prosper. Both by voice and pen he kept it before the public in town and country. He was also a vigorous advocate of temperance, nearly all the members being abstainers. In 1892 he left for Springburn, where he was invited by the Baptist Union to initiate a new cause."

In Ayr John Horne had started with a membership of 27; in Springburn he began with 17, the fruits of a mission begun by Rev. Edward Last, carried on by a variety of lay workers. Here in a crowded working class district in north-west Glasgow his earlier success was repeated, and again an early move had to be made to a larger building. The membership increased steadily until failing health compelled the minister to resign.

Four years later he was able to resume work, this time in Kirkintilloch. Neither there nor in the interval, was his pen allowed to remain idle.

" A man of striking individuality " says William Sunter, in " The History of Kirkintilloch," " he was also a preacher of great attractiveness — practical, impressive and human. Frank and outspoken, Mr Horne's views with respect to certain theological doctrines gave offence to the more orthodox in the town, and a controversy broke out that wounded the man's sensitive nature. Not too liberally gifted with physical health, Mr Horne, after a ministry of six years, resigned his pastorate in April, 1909. He will long be remembered in Kirkintilloch, where he left a fresher atmosphere in the religious life of the town than he found at his coming."

The remaining years of John Horne's life were to be given more fully to literature, and winning the fight with ill-health in a very wonderful way, he passed the alloted span in full possession of his powers, living to be honoured by his native town in a quite distinctive and altogether appropriate way.

1 Ed. George Yuille—" History Of The Baptists In Scotland " (1926. Baptist Union Publications 312 pp.).

It was on 20th July, 1932, that a large and representative company of Caithness people met in the boardroom of the Bignold Hospital for the dedication of a bed above which this inscription was placed—

" This bed has been named by natives of the county in honour of JOHN HORNE, Caithness Poet and Author, in appreciation of his influence in fostering love and loyalty to the Homeland— July, 1932."

" This form of recognition " said the " John O' Groat Journal," " was a happy thought on the part of those who decided upon it, and the London, Edinburgh and Glasgow Caithness Associations had reason to feel gratified at the measure of public response to their appeal. Nothing came from Mr Horne's hand—whether sketch, poem, story or article—that did not bear the marks of literary grace, culture, felicity of expression, delightful humour, and high powers of original thinking."

The gift of this bed, said Mr Horne himself, was entirely in line with his sympathies, and likewise, he might add, with his experience. He hoped no one in the company needed a bed as often as he had done.

" Since cradletime," he continued,[1] " I have been little more than a weakling, and the fight for a decent appearance of health has been continuous. Anything I may have accomplished has been done in brief flashes of health. You will understand, therefore, how much I appreciate such a testimonial. As long as the inscription attached to this bed is readable it will witness to the goodwill of the natives of Caithness to one whose only claim to their regard is that he shares with them the sentiment of a common affection for the soil from which we have all sprung."

Recounting some of the local enterprises he had carried through —the memorial stone at Altamarlach, the Calder statue by the riverside, the Caithness Soldiers' Tower at the North Head, the " Donald Horne " Room in the local library, and the tablet listing distinguished visitors to the town on the Rosebank wall, Mr Horne went on to speak of his literary work.

When he began to write no one else was writing about Caithness and he become a sort of symbol of the old home and the sentiments associated with it. He had no ambition to set himself up as a figure of distinction. He cast into prose or verse the haphazard questions that came to him unsought and sent them out to find or lose their way as the case might be. The loyalty of Caithness people did the rest—and that was why he was here that day. He never accepted himself as other than an influence making for love and attachment to the homeland. He wished that he might

1 " Public Appreciation of John Horne, &c." (op. cit.).

2 " Round The Old Home : Letters And Speeches by John Horne."

attain to a kind of incarnation of the spirit of his native county, " so that I might instil into others a reverence for the rustic mother who nursed us on her mossy lap."

That was John Horne's last visit to his native town. Within two years he had passed to his reward. It was shortly after his death that his daughter gave to the world, in the shape of some of his letters and lectures, what is one of the most prized volumes we have from his pen."[1]

" On my study wall at home," he writes in these pages, " is hung a map of Caithness. It is so placed that at sundown it catches the sun's last lingering smiles. Now and then I sit in the twilight and look at the photograph of that grey county that rises out of the sea. It is too light to turn on the gas and too dark to read. So I sometimes spend the trailing minutes of the day in reverie before that map—the last radiant touches tarrying on its familiar outline. And I like to think that when the Mirk comes over us at last, and its deepening shades close around us, memory will first become oblivious to far-off places and things and then draw home. The last spot to retain its light for us, the last district on the map of recollection to be illuminated by the flickering light of consciousness, the last impress of earth on our spirits ere they glide to Immortal Shores, will be the kindy image of our northern homeland, from whose mossy doorsteps we first saw the jovial sunlight and beheld the watching stars."

1 Ed. Janey Horne Robertson—" Round The Old Home : Letters And Speeches By John Horne " (1935. " John o' Groats Journal," Wick. 135 pp.).

# FOR FURTHER READING

The following are recommended—

## General

John Mowat—A Bibliography of The County of Caithness, with Notes (1940—Peter Reid & Co., Ltd., Wick—178 pp.).

D. Beaton—Ecclesiastical History of Caithness and Annals of Caithness Parishes (1909—William Rae, Wick—344 pp.).

John Macinnes—The Evangelical Movement in the Highlands of Scotland: 1688 to 1800 (1951—Aberdeen University Press—299 pp.).

Alexander Auld—Ministers and Men in the Far North (1891—2nd Ed.—John Menzies & Co.—300 pp.).

D. Beaton—Some Noted Ministers of the Northern Highlands (1929—Northern Counties Publishing Co., Inverness—285 pp.).

David Stephen—Gleanings in the North (N.D.—2nd Ed.—Alexander Rae, Wick—219 pp.).

---

Chapter 1—John Kennedy—The Apostle of The North: The Life and Labours of the Rev. John Macdonald, D.D., of Ferintosh (1932—New Ed.—Northern Counties Publishing Co., Inverness—343 pp.).

Chapter 2—James Hamilton—A Memoir of Lady Colquhoun (1845—4th Ed.—James Nisbet & Co.—312 pp.).
The Works of Lady Colquhoun of Luss (1852—James Nisbet & Co.—462 pp.).

Chapter 3—D. P. Thomson—Those Ministers of Galashiels (1946—J. McQueen & Son, Ltd., Galashiels—23 pp.).

Chapter 4—Archibald Auld—Memorials of Caithness Ministers: Memoirs and Sermons of Rev. W. Ross Taylor, D.D., Thurso, and Rev. Alexander Auld, Olrig: With brief Notices of Some of Their Co-Presbyters (1911—W. F. Henderson—392 pp.).
William W. Smith—Kelvinside Church, Botanic Gardens: 1859-1934 (1937—Blackie & Son—192 pp.).

Chapter 5—J. M. E. Ross—William Ross of Cowcaddens: A Memoir (1905—Hodder & Stoughton—328 pp.).

Chapter 6—Our Church's Work in India: Missions of The United Free Church of Scotland (Oliphant, Anderson & Ferrier—623 pp.).
William Miller—The Madras Christian College: A Short Account of its History and Influence (1906—Macniven & Wallace—24 pp.).

Chapter 7—Alexander Gammie—The Churches of Aberdeen: Historical and Descriptive (1909—Aberdeen Daily Journal—399 pp.).
George M. Reith—Reminiscences of The United Free Church General Assembly (1900-1929—Moray Press—360 pp.).

Chapter 8—F. P. Gibbon—William A. Smith of The Boys' Brigade (N. D.—Collins, Glasgow—173 pp.).

Chapter 9—Robert H. W. Shepherd—Lovedale, South Africa: The Story of a Century: 1841-1941 (1941—Lovedale Press, S. Africa—531 pp.).

Chapter 10—John Horne—History of Wick Baptist Church (1894—Northern Ensign, Wick—16 pp.).
Public Appreciation of Pastor John Horne, Ayr: His Literary and Other Works for Caithness—Warm Tributes to His Achievements; Mr Horne's Interesting Reply—(Reprinted from the John O' Groats Journal of July 22, 1932—22 pp.).
Ed. Janey Horne Robertson—Round the Old Home: Letters and Speeches by John Horne (1935—John O' Groats Journal, Wick—135 pp.).

## CONTENTS

**List of Books Recommended for Further Reading.**

**Price One Shilling.**

*Chronicle*, Inverness

# TALES OF THE FAR NORTH-WEST

## A Sutherlandshire Miscellany

*by*

## D. P. THOMSON

---

### PRICE ONE SHILLING

---

Obtainable at the Church of Scotland Bookrooms, through all bookshops, or direct from the Author—Rev. D. P. Thomson, Barnoak, Crieff, Perthshire.

# THE FAR NORTH-WEST !

THE county of Sutherland has many claims to distinction. One of the largest in Scotland, it is at once the most northerly and the most sparsely populated. With its 600 miles of sea lochs and 60 inches of rainfall on the west coast, it enjoys 21 hours of sunshine in June, but has a correspondingly dark winter. Its hundreds of fresh water lochs and innumerable rivers and streams make it an anglers' paradise. Its people have contributed far more than their share both to the armed forces of the Crown and to the pioneering and settling of the new lands beyond the seas. Its scenery is magnificent, with views that will live for long in the memory of those who have seen them.

" The tourist," says Black's Guide for 1863, " must not look for woodland beauties, but he will find himself recompensed by the severe grandeur of the majestic mountain forms, by the unbroken stillness of the large inlets of the sea, or of the fresh-water lakes, and the impressive altitude of its abrupt and rugged sea-worn cliffs . . . The inns in all parts of Sutherlandshire are in most cases excellent, clean, comfortable, and frequently provided with unexpected accessories of progress in the arts of life, and very reasonable accommodation for families and gentlemen."

That could not have been written fifty years earlier. " Sutherlandshire," says *The Abridged Statistical History* of 1853, " was the last district in Scotland which was subjected to the improvements of modern times. Till about the beginning of the present century it was a country lying in nearly the same condition as it must have exhibited centuries before, and in many respects shut off from the progress of that civilisation which had been so beneficially spread over the rest of Britain."

To this day, let us realise, the larger part of this great county of 1800 square miles has no railways and few bus routes, with but the most infrequent and inconvenient services. There are no seaports at which passenger vessels call, and there is no airport. To get from one valley to another by public transport may take anything from 12 hours to two days.

Small and widely scattered as the population of Sutherland is, it has shown in the past thirty years a sharper decline than that of any other mainland county, and only Banff has a smaller proportion of people in the 15-65 age group. There is only one burgh—the little Cathedral town of Dornoch—and only one community, Brora, with a population of over 1000. There are no inhabited islands today, although as recently as 1931 Roan, or Ellan-na-Roan, at the mouth of the Kyle of Tongue, supported more than 60 people.

*[Continued on page 3 of cover*

# CONTENTS

= × =

To

THE MINISTERS AND ELDERS

of

THE PRESBYTERY OF TONGUE

— so few in number —

on whose shoulders so heavy

a burden rests

# TALES OF THE FAR NORTH-WEST

------ ■■ ------

## CHAPTER I

## JOURNEY'S END

MAELRUBHA had travelled far. "There are few parts of the
North and West of Scotland," says Dr Frank Knight,‡ "that
have not some association with his name."

Born in the neighbourhood of Londonderry, on the 3rd of
January, 642, A.D., he was of royal blood on both sides; his father
a descendant of Niall of the Nine Hostages, a Scot; his mother of
Comgall of Bangor, a Pict. Few men could have been better quali-
fied by family connection and heritage to work for the cementing of
those two hostile races.

Educated at the famous monastic and missionary training centre
at Bangor in Northern Ireland, it was as a young man of 29 that
he set sail for Scotland with a full complement of disciples, following in the footsteps of his famous relative, Columba, who had pre-
ceeded him by little over a century.

The first two years were spent in exploration and investigation,
and the final settlement was made at Applecross, the one port of
call made by the modern passenger ship as she voyages from Kyle
of Lochalsh to Stornoway in Lewis.

Maelrubha had sailed up Loch Fyne from the Sound of Kil-
brannon, commemorating as it does an earlier missionary,
"Brendan, the Explorer." A church at the foot of Glen Barr, in
Kintyre, testifies to his presence there. Traversing Islay and
Knapdale in the course of his journeyings, he had reached Amulree
in Central Perthshire,. and both Fife and Angus have traces of him.
"Sailing still northward," says Dr Knight,‡ describing one of his
many voyages, "the saint at last reached Applecrossan in Ross-
shire, and in the midst of romantic and beautiful scenery he
recognised that he had at last discovered the site for which he had
been in search for so long a period. The fierce northern gales which
sweep the Minch scarcely reach its protected waters, and its
encircling rampart of rugged mountains to the east shut it off from
the invasions of fierce tribal enemies on the landward side. From
this remote and quiet spot Maelrubha evangelised with extraordinary

‡ G. A. Frank Knight—"Archæological Light On The Early Christianising of Scotland.

devotion and zeal. Increasingly his influence, and that of his missionaries, spread into the heart of the mainland and throughout the western islands. From 673, when he founded his monastery, till 722, when he died—a period of forty-nine years—Maelrubha was the great and revered father of the Pictish Church,[†] a saint beloved for his eminent piety, and for his noble and unselfish life."

There are many traces of the man and his work, both in Skye and in the Outer Isles. All over the north-west one will find these names—Maelrubha's Chair, Maelrubha's Well, Maelrubha's Seat, Maelrubha's Ferry, Maelrubha's Sanctuary, Maelrubha's Fair, Maelrubha's Village, Maelrubha's Copse. It is believed that he crossed the Black Isle to Forres, and re-established there a Church that had died out, kindling afresh the flame of faith and devotion among that people on the shores of the Moray Firth.

It was on his last missionary journey that he came to what were then the wilds of Sutherlandshire—northwards through the mountains to Strathcarron, from his home and base at Applecross, and then by Strath Oykell to Loch Shin. There, in what is now the Parish of Lairg, he is said to have built the first Christian Church the county knew. From Loch Shin he went on over the lonely moors and through the mountains, this intrepid missionary of the Cross until he came at last to Durness, to-day the most north-westerly village and parish in the mainland of Britain. It was here, on the shores of Balnakiel Bay, that he erected the first Christian building on a site that has ever since been a centre for religious worship. Here, outside the crumbling walls of a much later church, the bones of Rob Donn, the " Burns of the North," lie.

From Durness it is possible, thinks Dr A. B. Scott,[†] the historian of the Pictish Church, to trace the footprints of this great missionary pioneer as he journeyed on what was to be his last expedition of all. An ancient cell at the mouth of Loch Eriboll is said to recall his presence there, and on the rocky promontory at Farr he is said to have built a church. It was at Skail, nine miles up Strathnaver, long centuries afterwards to be the scene of the celebrated Sutherland Clearances, that this heroic missionary met his death by martyrdom, the first to suffer for the faith in the northern counties of Scotland.

" Against the interior wall of a Pictish Tower," says Dr Frank Knight,[‡] " is an ancient beehive cell, probably erected by the saint. At the edge of a wood below Skail, at a spot still pointed out by local tradition, Maelrubha, while preaching the Gospel, was set upon by Danish pirates, who had landed upon the coast, and had penetrated inland. Ferocious pagans as they were, hating the very name of

† A. B. Scott—" The Pictish Nation : Its People And Its Church "

‡ "Archæological Light On The Early Christianising Of Scotland."

Christ, and rejoicing in brutality towards all Christian bodies, they attacked him with swords, murdured him, and dragged his body into a thicket. His disciples reverently laid their master not far from the Teampull near which he was slain. A rough, cross-marked stone, single in type, on the banks of the clear-running Naver, marks the spot where, in the deep peace of the quiet strath, this heroic pioneer for Christ rests. The date of his martyrdom was 21st April, 722. It was 51 years since he had sailed from Ireland, and during all that long period he had been an untiring missionary of the Gospel —he seems never to have revisited his native land, but to have devoted his whole life to incessant evangelistic and church-planting effort.''

There is another tradition—to the effect that the body of their master was reverently carried back to Applecross by the disciples who had accompanied him on his journey, but the pilgrim who stands beside that rough-hewn block of grey granite at the bottom of the field which runs down to the Naver, in what is obviously a very ancient bcrial-place, will like to think that it is here, beneath the shade of these old trees, that the Apostle of The North-West sleeps till the day when the trumpet sounds.

## CHAPTER II

## THE DYER'S SON

HE was not the first minister of the Gospel in the North-West after the Reformation, but he was by far the most significant. There had been no one quite like him before; there has been no one quite like him since. He came to a district remote and savage, to a people steeped in ignorance and superstition, and he left the Parish of Durness a centre of light and power throughout the whole of the North, with the hymns and songs he had composed on the lips of all the people, and the truths they embodied enshrined in their hearts. On the shores of Balnakiel Bay to-day, looking across the Kyle to the Cape Wrath peninsula, you will see the ruins of the Church built for him by a grateful people, and in the Fernaig MS. you will find all that is left in print to perpetuate his memory.

Alexander Munro had a good start in life. His father, a dyer in Inverness, was the Laird of Kitwell, in Kiltearn, and his was a godly home. It was at the feet of Master Robert Bruce—'' The Voice of

Scotland " — that he found his Saviour and learned his Gospel. Bruce, of whom it was said that " no man since the days of the apostles spake with such power," had been exiled from the pulpit of St. Giles' in Edinburgh to Inverness by James VI in the year 1605, after having been imprisoned for some time in a deep rocky vault in the island of Inchgarvie in the Forth. The greatest of all Scottish preachers in the days preceding the Covenant, he found a ready response to his message in what was then " a small town made up of two intersecting streets, huddled under the shadow of the castle which dominated all the neighbourhood."

For four years Bruce was allowed to preach at Inverness every Sunday morning and every Wednesday, and to expound and take public prayers every other evening of the week. Little did the King realise what the consequences of his policy of mingled severity and leniency were to be for the people of the Highlands!

" The crowds that attended on Mr Bruce's ministry while there," says a historian of the Reay country,[†] " were immense. People came in great numbers from Nairnshire and Ross-shire, and even from Sutherlandshire. It was by no means uncommon for people from Golspie and the districts around to walk all the way to Inverness, and to consider their labour and fatigue abundantly repaid if only they got within hearing of Mr Bruce on the Sabbath."

The Earl and Countess of Sutherland were among those who mingled with the crowd, as was the dyer's son from Kitwell, and for him as for for them it was the turning point in life. Alexander Munro gave early and striking evidence of the change he had undergone, and, like Samuel of old, became the subject of direct divine revelations which determined the current of his life.

Deeply exercised in private prayer, " he thought he heard,[†] as it were, a voice urging him to devote himself to the Lord's service in the work of the ministry. On reflection, he attributed this impression to some vain imagination of his own heart, as he knew himself to be altogether unqualified, and thought himself unsuited for such an office. For a time he managed to drive the idea from his mind. But again, on two different occasions, the impression returned that he heard a voice in imploring tones urging him to devote himself to the ministry of the Gospel. On the last of these occasions he was led to understand that the sphere of his labours was to be Durness in the Reay country. Regarding all this as a call from the Lord, he could no longer decline. He entered the University of Aberdeen ; made very rapid progress in all his studies, and was ultimately licensed to preach the Gospel. Soon the way was opened for his coming to Durness, and he was ordained and inducted into the charge of that parish."

† J. S. Mackay in " Sutherland And The Reay Country."

At the time of Alexander Munro's settlement, the Parish of Durness extended from Tongue to Kylescu, and from Cape Wrath far into the heart of Sutherland, including what are now the parishes of Scourie and Kinlochbervie. There were no roads of any kind, and communications were slow, difficult and dangerous. The population was numbered—not as now in hundreds—but in thousands, and the people were steeped in ignorance and poverty. Possessed as he was of considerable poetic talent, the minister of Durness decided that the remedy for the situation confronting him was to be found in the cultivation of his muse. Versifying large portions of the Scripture in Gaelic, he composed a whole series of hymns descriptive of the great truths of the Gospel—Creation, The Fall, the Incarnation, The Work of Redemption, etc.

"These, says the chronicler,[†] he gave to the people, who sang them together at their winter evening gatherings and at their work during other seasons. He thus inaugurated a mode of instruction which was afterwards effectually followed up by others, notably by Mr John Mackay, tacksman of Taobhbeg, Mudale, at the head of Strathnaver. It was hearing the Mackay Fencibles recite Mackay of Mudale's hymns that first suggested to Dugald Buchanan the composition of his own very beautiful poems "—poems that have had a profounder influence on the life and thought of the 'Highlands than any other writings except the Bible itself.

A preacher of great power, Alexander Munro was used of God as the instrument of spiritual revival over a very wide area. The records of the Presbytery of Dingwall bear abundant testimony to this. All over the North, long after his death, as well as during his lifetime, his hymns were sung. "These paraphrases, popularly known as Munro's Verses (or as *Laoidhean Mhaighstir Alasdair* "— Mr Alexander's Hymns) were sung at private gathering for generations," says Dr Morrison.[*] "Some of them are still preserved."

"It would thus appear," says the historian of the Church in the Reay Country,[†] " that God was pleased to make use of human hymns in this instance, as He did those of Luther, for the diffusion of Gospel truths among a people who were uneducated and had not the written word; and through them gave instruction, guidance, comfort and encouragement to multitudes of His people."

Married to Janet Cumming, Alexander Munro was succeeded in the ministry at Durness by his son Hew. Another son, John, became minister of Alness in Ross-shire, " a man of great readiness and considerable learning " ; while his daughter, Christian, became the wife of a Chief of the Clan Mackay—Captain John of Achness, in Strathnaver.

* " Proceedings Of The Gaelic Society Of Inverness."
‡ J. S. Mackay in " Sutherland And The Reay Country "

## CHAPTER III

## STAINED WITH BLOOD

ON the shores of the River Hope, in the far north-west of Sutherlandshire, there lived in the days of Alexander Munro, Minister of Durness, a wild and lawless character, who rejoiced in the name of Donald Ic Mhorchaidh 'Ic Ian-mhor—Donald Macleod for short. Credited with no less than eighteen murders, this old villian had two sons, men of giant physique and with hearts as black as his own.

It happened on one occasion that Mr Munro was detained for some time on pastoral duty in the eastern district of his parish, being the guest of Sir Donald Mackay, afterwards the first Lord Reay, whose daughter his son and successor, Hew, was later to marry. When he left for home his host insisted that in view of the nature of the country through which he had to pass, and because of the wildness of the times, he should be accompanied by an armed attendant. It proved to be a wise precaution.

Coming to the banks of the Hope River, the minister deemed this a suitable opportunity to wrestle with the soul of Donald Mackay. The old rascal must be nearing the end of his earthly journey. It might be that before he came to the grave he could be brought to a sense of his sin, of his need of a Saviour, and of genuine repentance and faith. At least he could but try! So when he came to the old man's cottage he turned in at the door to tackle him. Donald, however, far from proving a subject of grace, took deadly offence at being spoken to in this way, and but for the presence of the armed man from Tongue the worthy minister of Durness might well have been his nineteenth victim!

Shortly afterwards the two sons, who had been absent at the time of this call, returned to their father's house. They were charged to follow the minister without delay, and not to show face again without the heart of the man who had so gravely insulted their aged father! They at once went in pursuit, but as they neared the object of their premeditated attack, they were challenged by the armed attendant, whose matchlock they were afraid to face.

" Fearing their father even more," we are told, " they killed a sheep and took with them its heart, which they presented to him instead of the minister's." The old man viewed it long and thoughtfully. " Ah well," he said, " I always thought the *Munroes* cowards, but never knew until now that they had the heart of a sheep."

In the ruined Church of Durness, Balnakiel Bay, built into the south wall, you will find the tomb of this unrepentant ruffian. The tradition is that after some deed of violence, perhaps more repulsive than those that had gone before, he was taunted and enraged by the prediction that his own carcase would be thrown into a pit, covered with sod, and trampled on by the meanest of God's creatures. It was to avoid such a fate that he offered to build this side of the church at his own expense if he were allowed to make a vault or recess in the wall for his coffin. The offer was accepted, and there to this day his dust lies.

> " Donald Mhic Mhorchaidh Hier lys lo
> Vas il to his friend, var to his fo
> True to his maister in veird and vo

| D | M | M | C |

1623.''

Who that master was we will leave the reader to decide !

CHAPTER IV

## REFUGEE FROM WARWICKSHIRE

IT is not known for certain either how Mr George Squair found his way to Sutherland or when he first appeared in what is now the Parish of Eddrachillis. One of the " outed ministers " of England, three hundred of whom were expelled from their churches in 1604 by James I of Great Britain, and nearly 2000 in 1662, after the restoration of Charles II, he was the spiritual successor in the North-West of Alexander Munro, the famous Minister of Durness, whose son was a man of a very different type.

Coming among this northern people, whose outlook and background were so different from his own, Mr Squair, says Alexander Macrae,[†] " set himself to learn the Gaelic language, which he so mastered that he was able to preach to the people in their native tongue. With no ecclesiastical status and no salary, he did the work of an evangelist in what was then a needy corner. He lived happily among the people as one of themselves."

Persecution, however, broke out on a wide scale throughout Scotland as the Covenanting struggle became more intense, and not even the wilds of Sutherlandshire proved immune. Mr Squair's whereabouts were discovered and the red coats were sent north to find him, to apprehend him, and to bring him south for trial.

[†] " Kinlochbervie "

"His followers," says Mr Mackay,* "were obliged to seek out all manner of hidden paths to wait upon him, and all manner of secret places wherein he might minister to them."

Hotly pursued on one occasion, he passed the hut of one of his faithful people, and came to a field in which a girl was busily weeding.

"What are you doing?" he asked her. "Weeding potatoes," she answered. "And have you, while so engaged," said the fugitive minister, " any thought about the interest of your soul?" "Yes," was the ready and perhaps unexpected reply, " while weeding the potatoes I am praying the Lord that He may weed the love of sin out of my heart."

"If that be so," said the minister, " you will try to conceal me from my persecutors, who are close behind, and in doing so tell the truth."

"Come quickly, then," said the girl, " and lie down in the deep furrow between the beds, and let me cover you with the weeds."

Scarcely was this accomplished and the girl started work again, when the pursuers appeared. They asked her roughly if she had seen Mr Squair pass that way just before. "Yes," she said, " he came the way you have come, and stood where you are standing. If you are active you may catch him soon."

The soldiers hurried on their way and were soon well out of sight. Their prey, they thought exultingly, was now within their grasp! Liberated from his hiding-place of weeds, the hunted minister broke into song:—

> " Ev'n as a bird out of the fowler's snare,
> Escapes away, so is our soul set free,"

he sang, and the delighted lass sang with him, taking care to supply him with what food she had by her before sending him off in the opposite direction as quickly as possible.

Long years afterwards, Mr Squair, who survived the persecution, married a native of the parish—it may, thinks the historian of Kinlochbervie, have been this very young woman. Their daughter married a Mr Munro, of the Parish of Rosskeen, and a son of that marriage became Rev. George Munro, the celebrated minister of Farr, whose generous hospitality has been immortalised by Rob Donn, the Durness poet, the " Burns of the North." On the back of the pulpit in the old Parish Church of Farr, says Mr Mackay,* will be found inscribed his name, the date of his induction, and that of his death.

Joined by three of his compatriots from the south, Mr Squair had eventually to fly the Reay country with them. Reaching Dun-

* In " Sutherland And The Reay Country "

robin, in eastern Sutherland, in safety, they were there hidden for many months in a cave in the Golspie Burn. Broken by mental and bodily suffering, Mr Squair was never able to return to Eddrachillis. In his old age he is said to have made his home with a son, who lived and died in Dornoch. Never formally inducted to a charge, he will live for many a day in the hearts of the people of the North as their Covenanting minister.

CHAPTER V

# A COVENANTING COMMUNION

WHEN the days of persecution began for the Covenanters, after the restoration of Charles II, Mr George Squair, the only Presbyterian minister left in the Reay country, was often on the run. Many were the hardships he underwent in these days, and many the narrow escapes from capture or death he experienced. Danger notwithstanding, he was, however, determined that the people committed to his charge should not be denied the greatly prized privilege of sitting down once more at the Lord's Table, even if the celebration had of necessity to be in some lonely and inaccessible spot.

There were, we learn, two places in the district at which congregations were accustomed to assemble for this purpose—" one in Eddrachillis proper, named *Larach nam Bord*, at Airidh nan Cruithneach, above Scourie ; the other on the march between Oldshoremore and Drumnaguy, in Oldshorebeg, at a spot between Captain Mackay's house and the rising ground to the north."

These places were not, however, considered safe under the circumstances, and so a more secluded spot was selected at the head of Loch Inchard, between the hamlet of Rhiconich and Lord Garbat. Information was then passed with the greatest secrecy to all whom it was thought might wish to be present.

On the appointed day about 100 people gathered, coming from the hamlets and clachans in the two adjoining peninsulas, and from the lonely scattered cottages on the hillsides.

" When they came to the place," we are told,* " they found themselves in the centre of a glade overgrown with birchwood, and sheltered by wild and beetling rocks. The pulpit desk was a birch tree, sawn off at a considerable height, and the tables were formed

* J. S. Mackay in " Sutherland And The Reay Country " (pp. 337-8).

with turf, covered with green smooth sod." The minister took for his text that day, the words spoken by Thomas, the apostle, after he was convinced that his Master had really risen—"My Lord and my God." The whole service, as may well be believed, was a memorable one.

"All there felt so much of the Lord's presence, and their bonds so loosened, and their fears so dispelled, that all, without a single exception, felt constrained to say with Thomas, 'My Lord and my God,' and without exception commemorated the dying love of their Redeemer."

Many years afterwards, during a time of great spiritual blessing, George Brodie, who had been settled in 1724 as the first Minister of the newly-formed Parish of Eddrachilis, asked one of his elders whether he had ever before experienced a time of greater blessing and power.

"Only once," said the old man, "at the memorable communion at Rhiconich, when Mr Squair preached with his Bible placed before him on the stump of a tree ; and when the five score present—of whom I am the last remaining one—sat down at the Lord's Table, exclaiming, 'My Lord and my God.' "

CHAPTER VI

# THE SABBATH BREAKERS

A COUSIN of General Mackay, the victor of Killiecrankie, Rev. John Mackay of Durness, was a man who would stand no nonsense. Noted for his piety, his learning and his physical prowess, he was graduate of both Edinburgh and Utrecht in Holland. A strict disciplinarian, he wielded his authority with complete impartiality, making no exception even in the case of the wife of his bosom.

From hamlet to hamlet he went, over the great area of the as yet undivided parish, collecting the people together in some suitable house in the district for their periodic catechising. One by one, first the families, and then the individuals comprising them, were required to give answer to the prescribed questions of the Shorter Catechism.

"These catechisings," says the historian, "were the principal means of the people being educated in the great and leading truths of their salvation ; the means also that afforded the best opportunity of educating their minds and consciences in the principles of morality, and in enforcing the application of these principles to their every day life and conduct.''

Catechising on one occasion, Mr Mackay found himself confronted by one of weak mind. There was no use wasting time on him, he was told—this poor creature without his natural faculties.

'' Call him,'' said the minister imperiously, '' he is one of God's creatures, and He is able to convey His own truth to his mind, however defective he may be.''

The lad was called. '' Have you a soul?'' asked the minister. '' No,'' was the unhesitating reply. '' Had you ever one?'' continued the questioner. '' Yes,'' said the poor lad.

'' And what has become of it?'' demanded the inquisitor. '' God knew that I was not able to keep it,'' was the surprising rejoinder, '' that I would only destroy it, so He has taken it into His own keeping.''

The examination of that poor lad proved to be the most memorable encounter of the day for all who were present, not least for the minister himself.

Now it happened that owing to negligence of some kind or another the water required for use in the manse on a certain Sabbath Day was not drawn on the Saturday as usual. The servant lass, with the knowledge and approval of her mistress, took the utensils to the spring on the morning of the Lord's Day and brought in the needed water. She did not go unobserved. Soon all the neighbours were speaking of it.

The minister did not hesitate ! Calling together his Kirk Session he laid the matter frankly before them, himself retiring from the meeting that they might come to an independent finding as to what discipline should be exercised. The finding was that the servant girl should stand in the presence of the congregation, at a diet of public worship, with her water pots, one on either side, thus acknowledging her offence, and submitting to being solemnly admonished from the pulpit by her minister and master. As for the minister's wife, she was to be admonished privately by her husband.

Mr Mackay was indigant ! Partiality of this kind could not for a moment be tolerated. So when the appointed day came, Mrs Mackay had to stand beside her servant girl.

'' Let us hope,'' says the chronicler of this so revealing incident, '' that the minister was charitable and in a tender mood when the admonition was given, and that he apportioned the guilt impartially !''

CHAPTER VII

## THE PLIGHT OF A PRESBYTER

" THAT admirable evangelical minister, Murdo Macdonald of
Durness,"† had many claims to distinction. An accomplished musician and " a most melodious and powerful
singer," he composed numerous Gaelic airs. The friend and
confidant of Robert Donn, the " Burns of the North," who became
one of his elders, he was made the subject of a beautiful Gaelic
elegy by the poet. Clerk to the Presbytery of Tongue for some
years, he took an active part in the controversy waged in the Synod
of Caithness and Sutherland over the curtailment of the number of
days to be observed at the dispensation of the Lord's Supper.

It is to his MS. Diary, in eight substantial octavo volumes, however, extending as it does to some 4000 pages of " very small but
legible writing," that future generations will turn with growing
interest and appreciation. Just enough of it has been given to the
public to whet our appetite for more.

It is from the *Diary* we learn of the books this lively minister
read in his far northern manse, within sight and sound of Cape
Wrath, and it is in the *Diary* that we get so many delightful glimpses
both of the mind and heart of the writer and of the life lived by a
busy and conscientious parish minister in those far-off days before
the advent of roads or wheels.

Gurnal's *Directory*, Hervey's *Meditations*, Bennet's *Christian
Oratory*, Boston's *Fourfold State*, Henry Scougall's *Life of God in
The Soul of Man*—one wonders how these well-worn favourites found
their way, along with so many other volumes, to the shelves of the
manse library at Durness.

No narrow-minded pedant was this gifted, conscientious and
spiritually vital pastor. Of Fielding's well-known novel, *The
History of A Foundling*, he had this to say after spending the greater
part of three days on it, that " it was calculated to form the manners
of those who despise instruction in a more serious form."

For himself, being very fond of poetry, and having translated
Pope's *Messiah* into Gaelic verse, he recited it to his parishioners in
the course of his pastoral visits or when they, in turn, after having
attended the Fellowship Meeting on the first Monday of the month,
adjourned from the church to the manse for fellowship and hospitality. In these informal after-meetings, we learn, pastor and people

† *Vide* John Macinnes—" The Evangelical Movement In The Highlands Of Scotland"

14

discussed together not only the news of the day but the political questions of the hour. And that, be it remembered, was in the first half of the eighteenth century!

Now it happened on one occasion that the worthy Minister of Durness found himself compelled, during very rough weather, to attend a meeting of the recently-constituted Presbytery of Tongue—called for the purpose of arranging for the transfer of the Minister of Eddrachillis to the parish of Tongue itself.

Riding westward through the winter storm, Mr Macdonald was overcome by fatigue before reaching the further side of Loch Eriboll. Convinced that he could travel no further, he reluctantly sent word ahead to that effect. This, however, did not suit the book of Lady Reay, a strong-minded woman, who, with her husband, the chief heritor in the district, was personally interested in the ministerial transfer proposed. She sent back word that she would despatch a boat for him, and " by her positive orders he must come over all impediments to the Presbytery seat " !

The minister was in a dilemma. The thought of rounding Whiten Head in a small open boat in his condition, and in such weather, was just not to be entertained! He sent the messenger back to stay the coming of the promised boat, and to renew his apology.

In the middle of the night Mr Macdonald was aroused from his uneasy slumbers with the intelligence that the boat had arrived, complete with feather bed and blankets. Moreover, the boatman had orders from her ladyship to take no refusal. They were to wrap the minister firmly in the blankets, place him as comfortably as possible in the feather bed, and with all reasonable expedition convey him forthwith to the Presbytery!

" However surprising and disconcerting this command," the good man records in his *Diary*, " finding the sea so very mild in the morning, I came off early, and before twelve o'clock we arrived at Tongue."

This, however, must be added, that the Minister of Eddrachillis, whose transference was thus effected, proved to be of a weak and sickly disposition, and was never able to labour efficiently in his new parish. Six years later he died. There were things that not even Lady Reay could accomplish!

## CHAPTER VIII

## A FRUITFUL REBUKE

IN the literature of the North-West there are many references to the Rev. William Mackenzie, the much-loved Minister of Tongue for the long period of sixty-seven years.

"He was," says Donald Sage,* "a lively, eloquent preacher of considerable talent and fervent piety, also of a fine personal appearance. His wife was a woman of considerable accomplishments, and a great talker. Her husband was also rather loquacious, and, when they were both present, whether at their own hospitable board or elsewhere, conversation was not allowed to flag. They not only engrossed the whole of it, but went full tilt against each other, for the purpose of talking one another down, especially when they both resolved to tell the same anecdote." Mrs Mackenzie, besides her other good qualities, was a poetess; her verses, which very much pleased her friends, were hung in black frames on the parlour wall. The good old man of Tongue could never be happy without, not only all his family, but even his nephews and grandchildren, each filling a place in his establishment."

It was in the year 1769 that William Mackenzie came to Tongue as successor to John Mackay, to whom reference has already been made.† He found the great body of the people "ignorant and rude, wild and godless in their habits. Especially did their drinking customs and their Sabbath conduct deeply affect him."

It was the custom in these days to have a short English service in the middle of the longer and more popular Gaelic one. The new minister of Tongue could not fail to note, with sorrow and with apprehension, that many of the Gaelic-speaking people who left at the commencement of the English service and returned at its close, came back much the worse of liquor. Impossible as it was for him to investigate in person, he decided to avail himself of the help of a visiting friend to find out what really went on during this interval of retirement.

The report he got was disconcerting in the extreme. His friend returned to say that he had been "witness to all manner of bargainings about cattle, and to the buying and selling and partaking of strong drink," as well as much else.

The minister resolved to take action. On the following Sunday, when the people were about to leave as usual at the close of the Gaelic service, he bade them resume their seats for a little, as he had some things he wished to say to them.

† *Vide* p. 10     * "Memorabilia Domestica"

"He then made known to them," says the historian,‡ "what he had for long observed, and that he was aware of their doings while the English service proceeded, he exposed the godlessness of their conduct, the danger to which they exposed themselves; and urged upon them the duty and nature of a true repentance, and of turning to God for forgiveness with such deep earnestness and tenderness that many of them were broken that day, and many cast themselves upon the pardoning mercy of God."

The reactions of a congregation to preaching of that kind are impossible to predict, and the long-term effects on a community are even more difficult to anticipate. How little could it have been foreseen what the intervention of the minister that day was going to mean in the life of the Parish of Tongue, and how far-reaching its issues were to be throughout the whole of the North-West.

"So deep was the impression made," says the historian,‡ "so great was the power of God in their midst, that it is said that no fewer than thirty souls dated their conversion from that exhortation; and that for long thereafter there were added to the Church now and again such as were the fruits of that revival. It was immediately after this period when so many were added to the Church that the 'men's meetings' both on Fridays of communions and other times became so popular, and so honoured in the building up of those who, by the ministry of the Gospel, were gathered into Christ."

Still preaching vigorously at the age of 93, the veteran minister of Tongue was able to say in the eventide of his life, "My heart is in my work; there is nothing on earth I care for but my work. I know that Christ sent me to the work; I know that He gave me success in the work, and I know that when I get to heaven, many a soul from the parish of Tongue will meet me and welcome me as the humble instrument of getting them to heaven."

Would that there were more ministries like that, not only in Sutherlandshire, but in every part of our land!

‡ J. S. Mackay in "Sutherland And The Reay Country"

CHAPTER IX

## WATER OF LIFE

IT was on the 25th of June, 1789, the year of the French Revolution, that Mr John Robertson, formerly schoolmaster at Langdale in Farr, and later at Achness, was ordained as missionary at Eriboll. Shortly afterwards it was resolved that the Sacrament of the Lord's Supper should for the first time be administered there.

That mid-summer season was oppressively hot, and the drought was excessive. Naturally dry and arid as the soil of Eriboll is, that year streams, ponds and even springs were dried up. Not a drop of drinkable water was there to be had within a great distance of *Camus-an-duin*—the bay of the fort—where the people were to assemble for worship.

The Friday of that Communion season was a day of scorching and exhaustive heat, but in spite of the weather and the drought, the people came — from Durness, from Kinlochbervie and from Eddrachillis in the west; from Altnaharra and Loch Hope side; from Melness and from Tongue; from Strathy and Farr, and from the heights of Strathnaver.

"The place of meeting," says the chronicler,[†] "was one of great beauty, and the surrounding scenery of great grandeur. In front was a beautiful bay; behind, and on each hand, the hills rose to a great height, and formed a kind of amphitheatre; their sides being clothed with natural birchwood. To the right of the ministers' tent there stood the ruins of an old fort."

Long though the services were, and exhausting the great heat of that summer's day, there was no moving away of the people, and faint and parched as they were with thirst, it was evident that presence of God was being felt among them.

After all the speakers had finished, a venerable man, eminent for piety, who had already made his distinctive and memorable contribution to the expositions of the day, was called on to pray. It was quite evident that he was deeply moved, and that the physical and spiritual needs of the people weighed equally upon his heart.

"Would the Lord, who had given them so richly that day of the water of life to quicken, refresh, and sustain their souls, now be pleased to send them supplies of earthly water, from the heavens above or earth below, to refresh and sustain their bodies, as it was the intention of the multitude, though fainting for lack of water, to continue with Him still for three days, until the solemnities of the Communion season were brought to a close."

† J. S. Mackay—"Sutherland And The Reay Country"

18

The old man concluded his prayer in an atmosphere tense with emotion. The closing psalm was sung, the benediction was pronounced, and the people, gathered from far and near, retired to enjoy such kindly hospitality as the district could afford, uniting again for prayer meetings that evening and the following morning in the hamlets round about.

" On Saturday," says the chronicler,[†] " when the people began to assemble for public worship, they observed, to their great amazement and deeper joy, a stream of water issuing out from behind the tent and among the stones of the gravelly or sandy beach. Whether the spring was opened and the water made to gush forth as from Horeb of old, or whether there before and only now discovered, it matters not; it was looked upon, and for long thereafter named among the pious as *Tobar freagradh urnuigh*—" the spring answer to prayer "; and it continues to this day to refresh and supply the wants of storm-beaten sailors, who often, by stress of weather, are driven to take shelter in the land-locked bay."

[†] " Sutherland And The Reay Country "

## CHAPTER X

## A DIFFERENCE OF OPINION

THERE came to the Mission at Eriboll in succession to Mr John Robertson, in the year 1800, Mr Neil M'Bride of Kilbride, later to achieve fame as a minister in Arran. Characterised rather by fervour than by culture, he did not by any means see eye to eye with the leading laymen of the district. It was with Major Mackay of Eriboll, a much loved and popular figure, that his most frequent disputes took place.

In the eyes of the godly but somewhat narrow-minded minister, the worthy Major was guilty of two grave misdemeanors. One was that he allowed his daughter to play the piano ; the other that on New Year's Eve he was in the habit of giving an entertainment and dance to all his dependents. He did this in order that he might have them under his eye at that time of year, and might keep them from more questionable places of amusement. Neither explanation nor excuse, however, would satisfy Mr M'Bride. He was quite convinced that the Major was setting a very bad example to the district, and, being so convinced, denounced him in person from the pulpit. Enough was said at the time to show where public sympathy lay, but the sequel was one that could hardly have been foreseen.

It happened that Mr M'Bride was about to celebrate one of the infrequent communions held at Kinlochbervie, and with that end in view had to journey east to Tongue in order to get the needed bread and wine for the Sacrament. On his return to Eriboll, which was his headquarters, the " elements " and the Communion plate were securely packed in creels that they might be carried west the following morning on horseback, slung from a *cruban*. Kinlochbervie being reached in good time, the minister's needs were first attended to, then began the preparations for the solemn feast for which he had come. What was the astonishment and dismay, the horror and disgust, of the minister and elder to discover on unpacking the creels that everything had been abstracted — bread, wine, communion plate, all were gone! In their place lay a mass of stones and sods.

Clearly, this must have been done the night before they left Eriboll, and it was at Eriboll that Major Mackay and his minions lived! Whoever was to blame, it seemed certain that some of that household were involved. The immediate question, however, was what was to happen now, with the long-looked for Sacrament season just at hand? Before the Saturday came, wine and flour were secured. Bread, it seemed, was out of the question, but with his own hands Mr M'Bride baked scones instead. The outward provision might have been of the most primitive kind, but they said long afterwards that it was a Communion to be remembered for the blessing received by all who partook.

Whatever Eriboll may have thought, the good people of Kinlochbervie were outraged at the dastardly trick which had been played on the minister. Nothing would serve to satisfy them but the getting up of a public subscription to buy him a new set of communion plate. It was to Robert Mackay, who was going south for examination with a view to being appointed a teacher in the district under the Society for Propagating Christian Knowledge, that they entrusted their commission. He bought the plate. He got Mr M'Bride's name duly inscribed on it, but he arrived back at Kinlochbervie to discover that the minister had left the Reay country for good in the interval, and that with his departure the ardour of the people had cooled and the necessary funds had not been raised.

Left with the communion plate on his hands, inscribed with the name of a man no longer in the north, Mr Mackay presented it to his friend, Rev. Mr Falconer, of Eddrachillis, who in turn passed it on to his successor.

After the Disruption of 1843, it came into the possession of the Free Church in Scourie, but where it is now the writer has been unable to discover.

## Chapter XI

# THE FINAL VERDICT

A SHUFFLING, swaggering, tough, grey-headed old carle! It was Donald Sage who called him that, "this thin, spare old man," the Rev. James Dingwall, Minister of the Parish of Farr, in Sutherland, who was ordained in the year 1780, and died on the eve of Waterloo. But the day came when he was to change his mind!

James Dingwall was a native of the Parish of Tarbat, in Easter Ross, and he belonged to an ancient family of landed proprietors. Of humble parentage himself, he had enjoyed a liberal education, first at the local parish school, then later at King's College, Aberdeen. On the day of his settlement at Farr, by the Presbytery of Tongue, he had told the fathers and brethren that if he were asked the usual question, "Did he use any means, directly or indirectly, to procure the living?" he would give no reply. Was it that they admired an honest man, or because some of them had guilty consciences themselves, that they resolved to waive the question and proceed with the induction?

All his life Mr Dingwall was known as "The *Moderate* Minister of Farr"—regarded by too many of his parishioners as "a mere stipendary and a purely secular character."

There came a night when he nearly lost his life on the way home from Golspie with his stipend, which he had gone there to draw. Lodging in Kildonon, he started the following morning at break of day for home. It was at the very height of a winter storm. In the portmanteau on which he rested as a pillow at night the minister carried his money. It was placed behind him on horseback when he set out on his perilous journey.

"After beating up the whole day against the storm which drifted in his teeth," says Donald Sage,[†] "and floundering through fens, quagmires and wreaths of snow, he was overtaken by night whilst wending his way through *Beallach-nan-Creach*. There he was seized with an inclination to sleep, and, accordingly, dismounting from his horse, he twisted the bridle round his arm, laid himself down on a wreath of snow, and slept. When he awoke he felt benumbed with the cold, but he walked his horse to Ravigall, and on his arrival narrated his hairbreadth escapes, also some extraordinary dreams he had had during his repose on the Beallach.

[†] "Memorabilia Domestica"

"Worthy Charles Gordon, his host,[†] proposed first of all that his feet should be bathed, which was accordingly done, but, unfortunately, it was with warm water instead of cold, the consequence of which was that the majority of Mr Dingwall's toes were thereby, to the day of his death, rendered *hors de combat.*" He lived most penuriously, and saved some money. His wife was like himself. They had two sons and a daughter.

The story does not end there. The experience on the Beallach would seem to have left its mark on soul, as well as body.

"It is refreshing to me," says Donald Sage,[†] "in looking back on the past, to be enabled, on highly respectable authority, here to record that Mr Dingwall gave decided evidence at the close of his life of having died the death of the righteous.

"To a few select Christian friends who visisted him during his last illness, and who remarked that he must now look to Christ alone for help, he replied, with much solemnity and fervour, ' I look to him now, not for help only—that were comparatively nothing—but that He would be pleased, as He only is able, to do all for me.'

"Indeed, the general tenour of his life, when viewed apart from the prejudices excited by the weakness of his intellect, and the extreme levity of his manner, would lead us to conclude that, notwithstanding his infirmities, he had ' the root of the matter ' in him. He was ever most assiduous in the discharge of his ministerial duties; he was conscientiously just in all his dealings, and his apparent levity, or rather rapidity, in the expression of his thoughts was more the result of the character of his mind than that of vitiated principle or habit. Mr Dingwall will, in all probability, on the great day or reckoning, be numbered among those who then shall verify the words of our Lord—' Many that are first shall be last, and *the last* shall be first.' "

## Chapter XII

## STRATHNAVER NO MORE!

IT is Donald Sage who tells the story,[†] and Donald Sage was there to see it happen. It was an experience he could never forget, a memory that not even time could efface.

Born in his father's manse at Kildonan in 1789, and licensed at Loch Carron, it was at Achness that Donald Sage began to preach.

"For the first half-year after my appointment to the Achness

† " Memorabilia Domestica "

Mission," he tells us,[†] " I remained at Kildonan, and went to both stations to preach almost every Sabbath. With Thomas of Breacachadh I lodged on the Saturday evening before my first Sabbath in Achness. He provided me with a horse, and accompanied me the next morning, after an early breakfast, to the place where the congregation met. The rural church, or meeting-house, as it was called at Achness, was at the time almost ruinous, and until it was repaired the people were obliged to meet in the open air. After addressing them both in Gaelic and English, I returned in the evening to Breacachadh . . . My incumbency at Achness lasted for three years.

"  . . .The Mission at Achness was, in regard to locality and surface, of very great extent . . . The whole population in the Strathnaver district lay apart from the missionary's house, being divided from it by the Naver, a river of such volume and breadth in the winter months as completely to preclude the attendance of the people at their wonted place of worship during that season. The population . . . lived in detached townships. These in Strathnaver were Moudale, Tobeg, Grumore, Grumbeg, Ceannacyle, Syre, Langdale, Skaill and Carnachadh—all possessed by small tenants, and lying on the north and west banks of the loch and river of Naver.

" The church consisted of a long low house, with a large wing stretching out from the north side of it. The walls were built of stone and clay, the roof covered with divot and straw, and the seats were forms set at random, without any regularity, on the damp floor. The house of the minister was erected at the foot of a steep brae, and in the middle of a fen . . . It contained four apartments, a kitchen in an outer wing, a parlour with a bed in the wall, a closet and a bedroom . . . The place of Achness itself, once densely populated, was in my time entirely depopulated, and the only one left was a miller, who lived at its northern extremity."

It is the thrilling, moving and horrifying story of this depopulation that the writer now goes on to tell.

" The period of my ministry," says Donald Sage, in a later chapter of his book,[†] " was fast drawing to its close  The reckless lordly proprietors had resolved upon the expulsion of their longstanding and much-attached tenantry from their widely extended estate, and the Sutherland Clearance of 1819 was not only the climax of their system of oppression for many years before, but the extinction of the last remnant of the ancient Highland peasantry in the north.

" As violent tempests sent out before them many a deep and sullen roar, so did the advancing storm give notice of its approach

† " Memorabilia Domestica "

23

by various single acts of oppression. I can yet recall to memory the deep and thrilling sensation which I experienced as I sat at the fireside in my rude, little parlour at Achness when the tidings of the meditated removal of my poor flock first reached me. A tenant from the middle of the Strath had been to Rhives, the residence of Mr Young, the commissioner, paying his rents. He was informed, and authorised to tell his neighbours, that the rent for the half-year, ending in May, 1819, would not be demanded, as it was determined to lay the districts of Strathnaver and upper Kildonan under sheep.

" This intelligence when first announced was indigantly discredited by the people . . . But the course of a few weeks soon undeceived them. Summonses of ejectment were issued and despatched all over the district. These must have amounted to upwards of a thousand, as the population of the Mission alone was 1600 souls, and many more than those of the Mission were ejected. The summonses were distributed with the utmost preciseness. They were handed in at every house and hovel alike, be the occupiers of them who or what they might—minister, catechist or elder, tenant or sub-tenant, out-servant or cottar—all were made to feel the irresponsible power of the proprietor.

". . . Having myself, in common with the rest of my people, received one of these notices, I resolved that, at the ensuing term of Martinmas, I would remove from Achness, and go once more permanently to reside under my father's roof, although I would at the same time continue the punctual discharge of my pastoral duties among the people till they also should be removed. I could not but regard the summoning of the minister as tantamount to the putting down of the ministration of the word and ordinances of religion in that part of the country. And, indeed, it is a fact that, although this desolate district is still occupied by shepherds, no provision has, since that time, been made for their spiritual wants.[†]

" The people received the legal warning to leave for ever the homes of their fathers with a sort of stupor, that apparent indifference which is often the external aspect of intense feeling. As they began, however, to awaken from the stunning effects of this first intimation, their feelings found vent, and I was much struck with the different ways in which they expressed their sentiments. The truly pious acknowledged the mighty hand of God in the matter. In their prayers and religious conferences not a solitary expression could be heard indicative of anger or vindictiveness, but in the sight of God they humbled themselves, and received the chastisement at His hand. Those, however, who were strangers to such exalted and enobling impressions of the Gospel breathed deep and muttered

† Since that was written a Church has been built at Altnaharra, which to-day constitutes a Parish.

curses on the heads of the persons who subjected them to such treatment. The more reckless portion of them fully realised the character of the impenitent in all ages, and indulged in the most culpable excesses, even while this divine punishment was still suspended over them. These last, however, were very few in number—not more than a dozen.

" To my poor and defenceless flock the dark hour of trial came at last in right earnest. It was in the month of April, and about the middle of it, that they were all—man, woman and child—from the heights of Farr to the mouth of the Naver on one day, to quit their tenements and go many of them knew not whither. For a few, some miserable patches of ground along the shores were doled out as lots, without aught in the shape of the poorest hut to shelter them. Upon these lots it was intended that they should build houses at their own expense, and cultivate the ground, at the same time occupying themselves as fishermen, although the great majority of them had never set foot in a boat in their lives. Thither, therefore, they were driven at a week's warning. As for the rest, most of them knew not whither to go, unless their neighbours on the shore provided them with a temporary shelter; for, on the day of their removal they would not be allowed to remain, even on the bleakest moor, and in the open air, for a distance of twenty miles around.

" On the Sabbath, a fortnight previous to the fated day, I preached my valedictory sermon in Achness, and the Sabbath thereafter at Achna-huiaghe. Both occasions were felt, by myself and by the people, from the oldest to the youngest, to be among the bitterest and most overwhelming experiences of our lives. In Strathnaver we assembled, for the last time, at the place of Langdale, where I had frequently preached before, on a beautiful green sward, overhung by Robert Gordon's antique, romantic little cottage, on an eminence close beside us. The still flowing waters of the Naver swept past us a few yards to the eastward. The Sabbath morning was unusually fine, and mountain, hill and dale, water and woodland, among which we had so long dwelt, and with which all our associations of " home " and " native land " were so fondly linked, appeared to unite their attractions to bid us farewell.

" My preparations for the pulpit had always cost me much anxiety, but in view of this sore scene of parting they caused me pain almost beyond endurance. I selected a text which had a pointed reference to the peculiarity of our circumstances, but my difficulty was how to restrain my feelings till I should illustrate and enforce the great truths which it involved with reference to eternity. The service began. The very aspect of the congregation was of itself a sermon, and a most impressive one. Old Achoul sat right opposite to me. As my eye fell upon his venerable countenance, bearing the impress of eighty-seven winters, I was deeply affected and could scarcely articulate the psalm. I preached and the people listened, but every sentence uttered and heard was in opposition to the tide of our natural feelings, which, setting in against us, mounted at every step of our progress higher and higher. At last all restraints were compelled to give way. The preacher ceased to speak, the people to listen. All lifted up their voices and wept, mingling their tears together. It was indeed the place of parting, and the hour. The greater number parted, never again to meet each other in the land of the living.

" The middle of the week brought on the day of the Strathnaver Clearance. It was a Tuseday. At an early hour that day Mr Sellar the factor, accompanied by the Fiscal, and escorted by a strong body of constables, sheriff-officers and others, commenced work at Grummore, the first inhabited township to the west of the Achness district. Their plan of operations was to clear the cottages of their inmates, giving them about half-an-hour to pack up and carry off their furniture, and then set the cottages on fire. To this plan they ruthlessly adhered, without the slighest regard to any obstance that might arise while carrying it into execution.

" At Grumbeg lived a soldier's widow. She had followed her husband in all his campaigns, marches and battles, in Sicily and in Spain . . . After his death she returned to Grumbeg, her place of nativity, and as she was utterly destitute of any means of support, she was affectionately received by her friends, who built her a small cottage, and gave her a cow and grass for it . . . After the cottages of Grummore were emptied of their inmates, and roofs and rafters had been lighted up into one red blaze, Mr Sellar and his iron-hearted attendants approached the residence of the soldier's widow . . . She asked that, as her neighbours were so occupied with their own furniture, hers might be allowed to rest until they should be free to remove it for her. This request was curtly refused . . . She was told with an oath that if she did not take her trumpery off within half an hour it would be burned . . . No sooner was her task accomplished than the torch was applied, the widow's hut, built of very combustible material, speedily ignited, and there rose up rapidly, first a dense cloud of smoke, and soon thereafter a bright red flame. The wind unfortunately blew in the direction of the furniture, and the flame, lighting upon it, speedily reduced it to ashes.

" In their progress down the Strath, Ceann-na-coille was the next township reached by the fire-raising evictors. An aged widow lived there, who by infirmity had been reduced to such a state of bodily weakness that she could neither walk nor lie in bed. She could only, night and day, sit in her chair; and having been for many years confined in that posture her limbs had become so stiff that any attempt to move her was attended with acute pain . . . In her house I have held diets of catechising and meetings for prayer, and been signally refreshed by her Christian converse. When the evicting party commenced their operations in her township the aged widow's house was among the very first that was to be consigned to the flames. Her family and neighbours represented the widow's strong claims on their compassion, and the imminent danger to her life of removing her to such a distance as the lower end of the Strath, at least ten miles off, without suitable means of conveyance. They implored that she might be allowed to remain for only two days till a conveyance could be provided for her. They were told that they should have thought on that before, and that she must be immediately removed by her friends, or else the constables would be ordered to do it. The good wife of Rhinisdale was therefore raised by her weeping family from her chair and laid on a blanket, the corners of which were held up by the four strongest youths in the place. All this she bore with meekness, and while the eyes of her attendants were streaming with tears, her pale and gentle countenance was suffused with a smile. The change of posture and the rapid motion of the bearers, however, awakened the most intense pain, and her cries never ceased till within a few miles of her destination, when she fell asleep. A burning fever supervened, of which she died a few months later.

"... I had occasion the week immediately ensuing to visit the manse of Tongue. On my way thither, I passed through the scene of the campaign of burning. The spectacle presented was hideous and ghastly! The banks of the lake and the river, formerly studded with cottages, now met the eye as a scene of desolation. Of all the houses, the thatched roofs were gone; but the walls, built of alternate layers of turf and stone, remained. The flames of the preceeding week still slumbered in their ruins, and sent up into the air spiral columns of smoke; whilst here a gable, and there a long side-wall, undermined by the fire burning within them, might be seen tumbling to the ground, from which a cloud of smoke, and then a dusky flame, slowly sprang up. The sooty rafters of the cottages, as they were being consumed, filled the air with a heavy and most offensive odour. In short, nothing could more vividly represent the horrors of grinding oppression, and the extent to which one man, dressed up in " a little brief authority," will exercise that power, without feeling or restraint, to the injury of his fellow-creatures."

## Chapter XIII

## LEAVING THE OLD MANSE

IT is Sir George Harvey's famous picture at which successive generations have gazed, asking to be told again what it was all about—that " Ten Years' Conflict " which ended in the Disruption of the Church of Scotland and the formation of the Free Church—the Church of Guthrie and Chalmers, of Candlish and Cunningham ; of John Macdonald of Ferintosh and John Kennedy of Dingwall and Gustavus Aird of Criech—the Church with which the overwhelming majority of the people of Sutherlandshire were to throw in their lot.    But it is from the pen of the Disruption minister of Durness that we get one of the most vivid descriptions of what actually happened to so many manse families when the day came to quit the familiar walls of their homes.

William Findlater came of a clerical race.    His grandfather and two granduncles had been ministers, as was their grandfather before them.    Educated at Aberdeen, the future minister of Durness had begun his career with that body which had done so much for Sutherlandshire—the Society for the Promotion of Christian Knowledge.    Even in his apprentice years as missionary at Eriboll, Kinlochbervie and Melness, it was said of him that " Mr Findlater is a minister every day of the week."

From Eriboll he had gone, in 1812, to Durness, that parish of so many famous ministries.    There he had produced the Gospel of St. Luke, with Gaelic and English in parallel columns, which he had used on Sunday evenings as a means of teaching his parishioners to read.

A man " whose piety, stores of information, cheerfulness, quiet playfulness and wit made him a general and delightful companion," he had married, in 1810, while missionary at Eriboll, Mary Thomson, the daughter of his predecessor in Durness.    When the Disruption of 1843 came there was little doubt as to which side he and his people would be found on ; with the Free Church of Scotland they threw in their lot practically to a man.

For a time minister and congregation were left in undisturbed possession of both Church and Manse.    The day came, however, when they had to go, and, when with the landed interests ranged solidly against them, no alternate accomodation was available—it had to be the inn for the minister and the open sky for the congregation, worshipping as they did on the seashore, in some cave or hollow, or on the bare hillside, as circumstances permitted.

" It was on a calm evening early in the month of July," wrote the old minister later, " that we took our final departure from the Manse. For several days the hurry and bustle always accompanying a removal, the packing up of furniture, distributing small tokens of remembrance, provisions and articles of dress among the poor, who came up from the neighbouring hamlets to bid farewell to my wife and children, occupied our time and occasionally suppressed the feelings which the varied recollections of home called up, a home which to us would be one no more. Here my beloved wife drew her first breath, as well as her eight children. Her last resort was the churchyard, where she stood over the graves of her sons, one a babe of a few weeks, the other a promising youth of twenty years of age, and over the grave of her venerable father, for forty-seven years the Minister of Durness. Some of the children were with a neighbouring family. After extinguishing the only fire, which was in the kitchen, putting the keys in the doors, leaving the rooms swept and emptied for the next incumbent, for a few minutes we retired, one to the study and the other to the closet. Few words were spoken and the outer door was locked.

" We called our son and the young children who had gone to take a last look of the garden and its house ; its walks had for some time been neglected, and the honeysuckle was spreading over them in sweet luxuriance ; a few roses were plucked, but they soon faded and their fragrance passed away ; not so the recollections of the scenes of their early days. The lake, the wild flowers on its banks, the fields and green knolls where the lambs skipped joyously, and the high hills in the distance—all this is vividly painted on their memories—' Scenes of their youth where every thought could please.'

" On the first rising ground which was to conceal the Manse from view, a momentary look was taken. Our hearts were full ; we were reminded that this was not our rest. The sunshine of my earthly joys had departed never to return.

" Upon our arrival at the inn, after a slight repast taken in silence, we united in offering up from heavy hearts the accustomed sacrifice of prayer and praise, committing ourselves to the guardian care of the God of Jacob. It was deemed expedient to divide our family ; our eldest son taking his two sisters and the servants to Thurso by boat, while I accompanied my wife, who all along manifested much courage, and the youngest children a day's journey by land, and then returned to the inn where I have since resided.

" Here in my old parish, I feel pleasure in proclaiming to a poor, yet patient people upon the hillside, or under a canvas tent, the glorious principles which have constrained so many of God's dear servants to come out and be separate, to deny themselves, take up their Cross and follow Christ, and to stand fast in the liberty whereby Christ has made them free." Dated 1844.

. . . . . . .

One is happy to be able to record that the following year, when the Duke of Sutherland, the principal landowner, relented and granted sites to the Free Church for churches and manses, William Findlater was permitted to enjoy the society of his wife and family once more, and there in the Parish of Durness, among an attached people, he continued to labour as long as health and strength permitted, returning at length to Tain, where he died in the 85th year of his age and the 57th of his ministry.

" After having lived so long within sound of the billows of Cape Wrath," says his biographer,[†] " he now lies in the same grave with his father and mother and his beloved Mary, in the quiet church-yard of Kiltearn, beside the calm ripple of the Cromarty Firth."

† E. J. Findlater in " Disruption Worthies Of The Highlands "

## Chapter XIV

## TRAGEDY AT TONGUE

IN the old kirkyard of Tongue, lying between the Church and Manse, hard by the northern sea, stands a striking granite obelisk to the three Mackenzies:

" Father, Son and Grandson
Ministers in Succession
For LXXVI Years In This Parish."

Of William Mackenzie, the grandfather, we have already written.[†] It is of the pathetic end of his son, Hugh, and his grand-son, William II, within a few weeks of one another that we have now to tell. In all the annals of Sutherland there are few more moving stories.

Born in his father's manse at Tongue in 1771, Hugh Mackenzie began his ministerial career as Chaplain to the Reay Fencibles, the

† p. 16

famous Sutherland Regiment, in Ireland at the close of the 18th century. While there he had urged on the military authorities that the Roman Catholic soldiers should not be compelled to attend his services. On this being granted they showed their gratitude to him by coming of their own accord.

In 1806 he was appointed Assistant and Succcessor to his father in Tongue, after having been for some time in the Parish of Dyke.

" Mr Hugh," says his biographer,[†] " had all the frankness and joyousness of a boy, and all the tender-heartedness of a woman; whilst a braver, manlier, more generous, or more courteous gentleman, I never met with. His piety was deep and ardent, and wonderfully childlike, whilst his humility was almost painful . . . He loved his people and his parish intensely. His liberality to the poor was literally unbounded. He was, I think, the most unselfish and forgiving man I ever knew. He was absolutely incapable of any revengeful feeling. He had a wonderful sympathy with the young in their joys and sorrows, in their difficulties and struggles, so that in any perplexity they more frankly consulted him than any friend of their own age . . . I never knew any minister so loved and admired by his people . . . We were all proud of him, and as we counted Ben Loyal nobler and more beautiful than any other mountain, so we counted ' Mr Hugh ' the lovliest and noblest of men."

" Mr Hugh Mackay Mackenzie, the only son of the Minister of Tongue," says Donald Sage, in his *Memorabilia*,[*] " was assistant to his father when I was at Achness. He laboured most assiduously in the pastoral office; but his health was at all times so very indifferent that his father, then near eighty years of age, seemed rather the assistant than his son. He married his cousin, Mrs Russel, a widow of great sense and prudence . . . The only fruit of the marriage was a son, who was named after his venerable grandfather, William."

It was in February, 1843, that the second William, then a young man of 27, became Assistant and Successor to his father. " William," says the writer we have already quoted,[*] " had a more robust and more trained intellect than his father, and was a very powerful preacher."

When the Disruption came, three months after William's induction, the Duke of Sutherland's representatives made it clear that not an inch of ground would be given within the bounds of the Presbytery on which to build either church or manse. That meant for both father and son removal from the home in which they had

[†] A. C. McGillivray in " Disruption Worthies Of The Highlands "

[*] "Memorabilia Domestica "

been born and brought up, and it was the aftermath of that removal which led to the double tragedy, a tragedy which brought Tongue so prominently to public notice.

Mrs Mackenzie and the daughter went to live in Thurso, forty miles away, the old man and his son moving into one end of the parish schoolmaster's house.

"The change from the comfortable manse to these confined lodgings," says Rev. A. G. M. M'Gillivray,[†] himself a native of the parish, "and the lack of his wife's society and loving attendance, told heavily upon his (the father's) health. He never openly complained of his discomforts; but in his private letters to me he said repeatedly that 'they were killing him,' Latterly he was attacked by bronchitis and his son by bilious fever."

It was during what proved to be their last illness that the famous Dr Thomas Guthrie, of Edinburgh, one of the best-known leaders of the Free Church, went to visit them, and to a hushed and crowded General Assembly he gave later an account of that moving experience.[‡]

"I fancy most of the members of this House are aware," said the great orator, "that I had the pain—the exquisite pain—and I must at the same time say, the very high privilege, of seeing that noble father and his no less noble son witnessing, under the most affecting circumstances, a good and blessed confession. I shall never forget to my dying day the scene I witnessed . . . in a humble cottage, to which that father and son had retired, parting with family rather than part with their flock. I never was so unmanned by any sight I ever saw, if I may call it being unmanned, for I am not ashamed of being affected by such a sight.

"I shall not venture to describe what I saw. I shall only say, in the words of Scripture, that they were lovely and pleasant in their lives, and in their death they were not divided. I rise to bear my humble testimony to the worth of these men. I should rather say, to the worth of these martyrs, for these great principles for which we abandoned our earthly all. They lay on their dying beds in peace. Never shall I forget the sight of that venerable old man, a man who would have adorned any church, a man who would have adorned any society. Never shall I forget seeing him in his mean cottage, nature exhausted; buried in the sleep he had not tasted the livelong night, his venerable locks streaming over the chair where he was sitting sleeping, for in the bed he could not sleep.

† In " Disruption Worthies Of The Highlands "
‡ "Annals Of The Disruption "

" I went up to him and intended to awake him, but thought it cruelty to do so. I passed him over and over again in the room, and still he slept on, and after seeing his son lying in an adjoining closet on a fever bed—a son that had never closed his eyes all the night long either, for his father's groans were like daggers in his heart— I left that house and the last words I heard that son say on this earth were—' Mr Guthrie, this is hard enough, but I thank God I do not lie here a renegade. My father's conscience and mine are at peace '. . . I believe that the memory of these two men will live fresh in the minds of the people of the parish of Tongue for generations yet to come."

It was shortly after that visit that the end came, first for the father and then for the son.

" His elders came to bid the old minister farewell," says Mr M'Gillivray,[†] " and he welcomed them with the same courtesy and overflowing kindness as of yore. A few hours before his death a woman whose child had been ill entered the room, and the dying man recognised her and whispered, ' Ask how the dear child is ? ' He afterwards enquired eagerly if William (his own son) could be brought into the room to bid him farewell, and learning that William was too ill for that the old man looked upwards, muttering with dying lips, ' Thy will be done,' and shortly thereafter without a struggle entered into his rest, on the 30th of June, 1845.

" His body was carried into the schoolhouse in order that his son might be removed from the confined bed closet where he lay, into the room which his father had occupied. William requested to see once more his father's face, and so the body was brought into the room. He silently kissed the cold lips, and from that time he ' took the measure of an unmade grave.' They had loved one another very greatly. William had been much agitated and distressed by his father's moaning heard in the adjoining closet, but the silence that now ensued was more trying to him. He lingered on for upwards of three weeks[*] . . . On the 28th of July he too entered into his rest."

On the base of that obelisk in the kirkyard of Tongue round which the names and dates of the three ministers are carved—grandfather, father and son—there is just one verse of Scripture inscribed.

" They that be wise shall shine as the brightness of the firmament, and they that turn many to righteousness as the stars for ever and ever "—Daniel C.XII VI3.

† " Disruption Worthies Of The Highlands "

* Four, to be exact

## CHAPTER XV

## A WOMAN IN A THOUSAND

E VERY book that deals with the life of the Church in the Far North has something to say about her, and that something is always to her credit.

" There were a few individuals," says Donald Sage in the *Memorabilia Domestica*, "of whom I have most pleasing recollections, but who resided beyond the limits of my mission. The most distinguished as a Christian was Mrs Mackay of Sheggira . . . Her maiden name was MacDairmid, and she was a native of Argyllshire. Her husband was a respectable man, a native of the Reay country, but much her inferior in many ways. She was naturally a superior woman, quick in apprehension and particularly ready in repartee . . . She was, above all things, however, distinguished for the vitality of her Christian character."

" She was one among a thousand," says Dr Kennedy of Dingwall,[†] " Her brilliant wit, her exhuberant spirits, her intense originality of thought and speech and manner, her great faith, and her fervent love, formed a combination but rarely found."

" Familiarly known throughout the North as *Bean a Chreudimh Mhoir*, she was so interesting a personality and such a distinguished Christian," says Rev. Alexander Macrae of Tongue,[*] " that after a century her memory is still fresh and fragrant."

Peggy MacDairmid was one of a family of eleven—two sons and nine daughters. The home of her childhood was in Argyllshire, and she was known there as a giddy girl, full of fun and with a way of doing things quite unlike anyone else. It was with her brother, Colin, that she came North to a farm at Glendhu in Assynt, and it was his sudden and tragic death that awakened her to a sense of eternal realities. Out deer-stalking, he ventured on the ice and was drowned on Loch Stack. The shock to his sister was very great, and it was shortly after this, under the preaching of John Kennedy, Sen., then missionary at Eriboll and Kinlochbervie, that she came to a knowledge of the truth.

Engaged before her brother's death to Donald Mackay, who had a farm at Borley in Durness, she began her married life at Sheggira, in the parish of Kinlochbervie. It was there her children were born and reared, and there that she had the joy of leading her husband into a like faith with her own. The preaching of the Gospel was

† " The Days Of The Fathers In Ross-shire "
* "Margaret MacDairmid " by Alex. Macrae of Tongue

meat and drink to her, and that was something he just could not understand. Her frequent absences from home to attend communions and other religious gatherings distressed him. Then one day, after a heated argument in which they had been engaged, she withdrew to the barn to pray. He followed, and awed by the passionate tones in which he heard her pleading for his conversion, it was not long before he himself found the life which is life indeed.

From Sheggira they were compelled to move, as a result of one of the many " clearances " by which the earlier part of the 19th century was disfigured in Sutherlandshire, and they went to live at Achinver, in Melness, with a married daughter, Minnie. It was here that the remainder of her life was spent, the Duchess of Sutherland eventually giving them a free liferent of both house and land.

" Hers," says her biographer,[*] " was a beautiful countenance. Her hair was dark brown, almost black, and wavy. She had brilliant black eyes. The pure white skin, the high broad forehead, and the oval contour of a bright and sunny face made her the centre of attraction in youthful circles . . . She owed little to art and nothing to artfulness. Her handiest mirror was often the surface of a pail of water."

Of Mrs Mackay of Melness, as she came to be known in later years, innumerable stories are told.

" The woman of great faith! " exclaimed a minister on being introduced to her for the first time. " No," was the swift rejoinder, " the woman of small faith in the great God."

" Passing through Bettyhill on a beautiful morning," we are told, " she was carrying her hat in her hand by its ribbon strings and twirling it round and round. ' What is your news this morning? ' she asked a man who was herding cows by the roadside. ' I have no news,' said he, looking stolidly and heavily at her. ' No news,' cried Peggy, ' Man, is it not good news that you, are still alive in the land of mercy! '

" ' Where do you come from? ' enquired a fellow passenger on a stage coach, on one occasion. ' From Cape Wrath,' said Peggy. ' And where are you going?' he continued. ' To the Cape of Good Hope,' was the quick reply, and that was the beginning of a conversation which soon got down to the deeper things. The gentleman has not prepared to admit that his heart was evil, as Peggy stoutly maintained. Passing round a corner the coach gave a sudden lurch, throwing off on to the road a box from the roof, which broke into pieces, releasing a number of chickens, to the great amusement of the passengers. ' Did you know what was inside that box? ' asked

* Alexander Macrae of Tongue

35

Peggy of her contact. ' No,' he had to admit. ' Neither can you know what is in your own heart till it is broken open to the Spirit of Truth,' was the swift and unexpected reply!''

Leaving a worthy minister's house at which she had called, she came with him to the gate, closed by some loose spars. While he was in the act of removing one of these Mrs Mackay bent down and darted through. '' Is that how you expect to enter the Kingdom?'' he asked. '' Yes,'' said she, '' and if you expect to enter it, you must bend your head also! ''

Children ran eagerly to her, dropping their play and gathering round to listen to whatever she might have to say. She did not scare them; she drew them.

At communions, whether in Ross-shire or in Sutherland, she was a well-known and much loved figure. '' In all these places,'' says Dr Kennedy,[†] '' her presence was like sunshine, any many a fainting spirit was cheered by her affectionate counsels. Her greatest enjoyment was to meet with anxious enquirers, and many such have cause to remember for ever the wisdom and tenderness of Mrs Mackay's advices.''

There was a certain Communion Sunday when the conversation round the fire in the evening took what she thought was a somewhat unworthy and worldly turn. She said nothing, but bent down under the table as if looking for something. Her host asked if she had lost anything. '' I thought we had all lost the Sabbath,'' was the reply, and the rebuke went home.

In the old days at Sheggira she used to walk barefooted through the moors to hear Mr Findlater of Durness. It was her custom to put on her boots when within sight of the church. On one occasion she found herself with only one. She knew who the culprit must be. ''You,'' she said, addressing the Adversary, ''you thought you would cheat me out of the service to-day, but I'll put my pride where my boots should be—under my feet,'' and so saying she walked in in her stocking soles, to find the missing boot as she wended her homeward way an hour or two later.

'' When she entered a worshipping congregation,'' says Eric Findlater, '' her very appearance would circulate a wave of joy over the faces of all—a circumstance that could not escape a stranger's notice, though he could not account for it.''

It was her hope that she might be permitted to spend her closing days in the Parish of Killearnan, sitting at the feet of John Kennedy of Redcastle, the man who, in his early days at Kinlochbervie, had been privileged to lead her to Christ, but that was not to be. When

---

† '' The Days Of The Fathers In Ross-shire ''

she lay in her last illness, the end of the road not far away, it happened that Mr Kennedy himself died, but they decided to keep the news from her.

Entering the sickroom, her husband sat down gloomily by the fire. " I know what ails you," said the sick woman at once, " you have heard of Mr Kennedy's death. I knew it before. He died on Sabbath evening," and mentioning a certain day not far distant, " before then I will join him in the Father's house." And so it came to pass, as did so much else that she predicted. It was on April 15th, 1841, that she passed to her rest, and after the Disruption her old friend, Rev. William Findlater of Durness, composed an elegy in her memory of forty-one double verses, in which " he portrayed her life and character in incisive language, and with real sympathy and insight."

> " Preachers and people seeing thee
> At worship on the Mount,
> Sang out with sweeter melody,
> Revived on thy account.
> The enchantment of thy presence,
> Re-echoed in their song,
> Revealed that of the wine of life
> Thou drankest deep and long."

CHAPTER XVI

## MEETINGS WITH " THE MEN "

" THE Men," says Dr Kennedy of Dingwall,[†] were so named not because they were not women, but because they were not ministers. It was necessary to distinguish between the ministers and the other speakers at a fellowship meeting, when notes of their addresses were given ; and the easiest way of doing so was by saying " one of the ministers," or " one of the men " said so and so. Hence the origin of this designation ; and speakers at religious meetings in the Highlands who are not ministers, are those to whom it is applied."

" It was immediately after the period when so many were added to the Church through the labours of Mr Munro of Farr and Mr Mackenzie of Tongue," says the chronicler of the religious history

† " The Days Of The Fathers In Ross-shire "

of Sutherland and The Reay Country,* that the "men's" meetings, both on Fridays of communions and at other times, became so popular, and so honoured in the building up of those who, by the ministry of the Gospel, were gathered into Christ.

"The parishes of the Reay country—especially Strathnaver—became noted at that time for the number and excellency of its outstanding men. Innumerable are the tales and anecdotes and sayings concerning them that discover their genius and piety, and the beauty of the spirit they cherished and manifested toward one another. At first, indeed, Mr Mackenzie and some others were jealous of the tendency of their meetings, but for a period of at least two generations—from 1780 until Disruption times—the ministrations of these godly men assisted largely both to maintain and extend the influence of the Gospel throughout the whole country."

"Who is that man who has just concluded that remarkable prayer towards the middle of the service?" asks Eric Findlater,‡ describing a Communion season in Durness,‡ at the other end of the Presbytery area. "His name is Andrew Ross. He is a native of Ross-shire, but has been residing in the parish of Tongue during the greater part of his long life. As you may perceive, his outward man is now failing; but the inward is growing day by day. The shock of corn is fully ripe, and may at any time be brought to the garner above. He is one of the most spiritually-minded men in the North. Did you not observe the extraordinary nearness of access which he had to God in that prayer which he has just offered up, and the peculiar expression he made use of in addressing the Almighty— 'Everlasting Love '—and as aften as the word escaped his lips the whole physical frame became agitated, his voice became choked, and his eye rained down tears: but they were not the tears of remorse but those of overpowering love. He is one whose spirit longs to be with Christ—which is far better—its very workings after emancipation will soon loose the pins of the frail tabernacle, and the soul of the man who stands before you will then find itself at rest and at home.

"George Campbell, a Gaelic schoolmaster, and a native of Sutherland, renews the discussion. He is a man of about sixty, dressed in a camlet coat, and with a head of long steel-grey hair, parted in the midst, and falling down in a mass behind. His features are well proportioned, and a quick intelligence courses over them as the aurora borealis does over his native sky. He is one of nature's orators, and so well toned in his voice, so harmonious his periods and so graceful his action, that it is like music to the ear."

* J. S. Mackay in "Sutherland And The Reay Country"
‡ "Annals Of The Disruption"

At Diaroacdcory, near Cnoç Stanc, we are told lived William Mackay, a real man of God. Coming to church at Tongue on a Sunday of drift and snow, over a distance of sixteen miles, where there was no road, he was asked by old Mr William Mackenzie, the minister, why he had ventured so far on so stormy a day.

There were three things, he said, that moved him to attend the House of God. The first was that the Lord had given him strength, and he considered it his duty to wait on Him in public worship. The second was that he came to add to the number in the congregation and thus encourage the minister when he knew that many would absent themselves. The third was this—he came so that if the Spirit of God should be moving in the church that day, He might might not find his pew empty. It is an example that might well be followed!

# FOR FURTHER READING

The following books are suggested for further reading:—

William Calder—County of Sutherland (N.D.—Highland News, Ltd., Inverness—80 pp.).

Census: 1951 Report on the Fifteenth Census of Scotland: County of Sutherland (1954—H.M. Stationary Office—31 pp.).

Adam Gunn and John Mackay—Sutherland And The Reay Country: History, Antiquities, Folklore, Topography, etc. (1897—John Mackay, Glasgow—399 pp.).

Angus Mackay—The Book of Mackay (1906—Norman Macleod, Edinburgh—449 pp.).

Charles St. John—A Tour in Sutherlandshire‡ (1884—David Douglas—2 Vols.—670 pp.).

John E. Edwards-Moss—A Season in Sutherland (1888—Macmillan & Co.—170 pp.).

Alexander Mackay—Sketches of Sutherland Characters (1889—James Gemmell, Edinburgh—352 pp.).

Alexander Mackenzie—The History of the Highland Clearances (N.D.—2nd Ed.—Alex. Maclaren & Sons, Glasgow—286 pp.).

Donald Sage—Memorabilia Domestica: or Parish Life in the North of Scotland (1899—2nd Ed.—William Rae, Wick—322 pp.).

G. A. Frank Knight—Archeological Light on the Early Christianising of Scotland (1933—James Clarke & Co., Ltd.—2 Vols.—880 pp.).

Archibald B. Scott—The Pictish Nation: Its People and Its Church (1917—T. N. Foulis—561 pp.).

John Mackay—The Church in the Highlands: The Progress of Evangelical Religion in Gaelic Scotland, 563-1843 A.D. (1914—Hodder & Stoughton—280 pp.).

John Macinnes—The Evangelical Movement in the Highlands of Scotland (1951—Aberdeen University Press—299 pp.).

J. B. Craven—A History of the Episcopal Church in the Diocese of Caithness* (1908—Wm. Peace & Son, Kirkwall—300 pp.).

Hew Scott—Fasti Ecclesiæ Scoticanæ: The Succession of Ministers in the Church of Scotland from the Reformation Vol. VII (1923—Oliver & Boyd—800 pp.).

Thomas Brown—Annals of the Disruption (1893—New Ed.—Macniven & Wallace, Edinburgh—841 pp.).

Alexander Auld—Ministers and Men in the Far North (1891—John Menzies & Co.—300 pp.).

Donald Munro—Records of Grace in Sutherland (1953—Free Church of Scotland Publications Committee, Edinburgh—254 pp.).

Alexander Macrae—Kinlochbervie: The Story and Traditions of a Remote Highland Parish and Its People (N.D.—The Highland Christian Literature Society, Tongue—82 pp.).

Alexander Macrae—Margaret MacDairmid: or Bean A Chreidimh Mhoir (1929—The Highland Christian Literature Society, Tongue—24 pp.).

‡ Only part of Vol. I deals with Sutherland                    * This included Sutherland

Nearly all the chief centres are on the east coast, up which, from Bonar Bridge to Helmsdale, the railway line from Inverness to Wick and Thurso runs.

The area with which this booklet deals—the Far North-West of the mainland of Britain—occupies more than half the country. This is one of the loneliest regions in Western Europe. Over vast tracts of country, as far as the eye can see, there is neither human being nor human habitation—often not even an animal to be observed Yet there is nothing in these islands to equal the scenery of this region.

" I dived," says H. V. Morton,[*] " into lanes as green and lush as any in Warwickshire, I came out to glimpses of sea, and nook and hill, of pine-covered slopes and slopes as bare as iron, of small rivers rushing over broad stony beds, of thin burns singing through leaves, and of slender white waterfalls leaping into the air from rocky ledges. And always, sooner or later, at the mouths of the lochs, I heard the thunder of waves dashing against the cliffs and saw the broad splendour of the open sea."

Like everything else both the message of the Gospel as carried by the early Celtic missionaries and the Protestant Reformation of Knox and Wishart and Melville, took longer to reach and penetrate this area than other parts of Scotland. To-day in Sutherlandshire Presbyterianism reigns supreme. There are no Baptists or Congregationalists — no Episcopalians or Methodists — and no Roman Catholics in the far North-West, at least none meeting as worshipping groups. Ninety per cent or more of the people belong to the Church of Scotland, although here, as elsewhere, church-going is not what it was.

The story of the Church in this region is a long and colourful one, full of the stuff of drama, and in these pages an attempt has been made to capture something of its interest, its fascination and its variety. To all who have helped in the collection of this material —and especially to Rev. Duncan Macmillan, Minister of the Parish of Altnaharra and Clerk of the Presbytery of Tongue, who was my guide, and Rev. John M. Watson and his wife, who were my host and hostess on the occasions of my only recent visits to North-West Sutherlandshire, and to my colleagues, Rev. William Shannon and Mr Alan Byers, of the Church of Scotland Home Board, who were my drivers—I wish to express my warmest thanks. Without their help and encouragement the compilation of this booklet and the preparations for the campaign with which it is associated would alike have been impossible.

D. P. THOMSON

Barnoak, Crieff, Perthshire
    30th July, 1955

[*] " In Scotland Again " (Methuen & Co., Ltd.)

# GEORGE WISHART:
## THE MAN WHO ROUSED SCOTLAND

"MASTER GEORGE WISHART"

# GEORGE WISHART:

## THE MAN WHO ROUSED SCOTLAND

*by*

## D. P. THOMSON, M.A.

This short sketch of the Life of George Wishart, the great Scottish Reformer, has been prepared at the request of the Wishart Quater-Centenary Committee.

The frontispiece is reproduced from the famous portrait in Edinburgh by kind permission of the Board of Trustees of the National Gallery of Scotland—and of the official photographers, Messrs T. & R. Annan & Son, Glasgow. Orchardson's picture of the Prison Communion is reproduced by kind permission of the authorities of St Andrews University.

..............................................

## PRICE ONE SHILLING

..............................................

CHURCH OF SCOTLAND PUBLICATIONS DEPARTMENT
121 George Street, Edinburgh

# GEORGE WISHART

## THE MAN WHO ROUSED SCOTLAND

### By D. P. THOMSON, M.A.

On the banks of the Luther Water in Kincardineshire, just below the foothills of the Grampians, lies the little village of Auchenblae. Its population is less than four hundred. High above it, looking down on the bridge that spans the river between, and commanding a fine view of the fertile Howe of Mearns to the south, stands the Parish Church of Fordoun, the mother kirk of the county. In the churchyard just below it is the old ruined chapel of St. Palladius, the "Apostle of the Mearns," long a popular place of pilgrimage.

Less than a stone's throw from the old chapel, and close to the outer railing of the churchyard, you will find a noble granite obelisk surmounted by a flaming urn. Round it is a spiral inscription, carved in bold white letters on the polished grey granite surface. It reads thus : " This monument is erected to the memory of one of Scotland's first and most illustrious martyrs, George Wishart of Pitarrow in this parish, and as a testimony of gratitude to the great Head of the Church for the work of the Reformation on behalf of which his servant suffered. He was born in 1513, and was burned at St Andrews 1st March, 1546. ' The righteous shall be in everlasting remembrance.' "

That is Scotland's simple and moving tribute to one of her greatest sons. " He was," says John Knox,[1] the friend and disciple who knew him so well, and who carried to its conclusion the work he began, " a man of such graces as before him were never heard within this Realm, yea, and are rare to be found yet in any man, notwithstanding the great light of God that since his days hath shined unto us."

Wishart's portrait hangs in the Scottish National Gallery in Edinburgh. His place in the history of his country and in the

[1] ' History of the Reformation in Scotland.'

1

story of her Church's great struggle for light is secure. A man of ripe scholarship and spiritual power, it was he who gave to his native land that Calvinistic theology by which its life and outlook have been so greatly shaped. Scotland's first great expository lecturer, he was the originator of field preaching in Great Britain. A champion of liberty and a friend of the poor, he was beloved of the people. A man of singularly magnanimous spirit, he made friends wherever he went. He died a martyr at the age of thirty-three, and he left behind him a reputation that the intervening centuries have only served to enhance.

## A WISHART OF PITARROW

Sprung from an old French family settled in the Mearns in the twelfth century, George Wishart was born at the mansion-house of Pitarrow in the year of Flodden Field. Scotland was then in a very unsettled state, so many of its natural leaders having fallen in battle. For some years bands of thieves roamed the land, and bitter feuds in Church and State divided the people into hostile factions.

Abroad, events were moving fast. In 1517, when Wishart was a boy of four, Martin Luther nailed his ninety-five theses to the door of the church in Wittenberg, thereby heralding the real beginning of the Reformation struggle. In Scotland the invention of printing speedily brought in at the ports thousands of smuggled copies of the New Testament, and these were distributed and read over wide tracts of country. In 1528 Patrick Hamilton, the first Scottish martyr of the Reformation, was to be burned at the stake at St Andrews.

George Wishart was a younger son of Sir James Wishart, Lord Justice Clerk of Scotland from 1513 to 1524, a man of ability and learning. For generations the family had been distinguished as statesmen, ecclesiastics, lawyers, and soldiers. William Wishart had been Chancellor of the realm in the reign of Alexander III. and Bishop successively of Glasgow and St Andrews. A generation or so later Robert Wishart had been one of the Governors of the Kingdom. In a charter of 1442 appears the name of Sir John Wishart, the first titled member of the family of whom there is any record.

George Wishart's mother—his father's second wife—was Elizabeth Learmont, a daughter of the Laird of Balcomie and Dairsie in Fife. She was closely related to many of those who early espoused the cause of the Reformation, and aided and sheltered the first Protestant preachers. There is no register extant recording the birth of her illustrious son, but a fine old picture of the martyr, long in the possession of a distant relative, bears the inscription, " M.D. XLIII. Aetat 30." This serves to fix the year.

The mansion-house of Pitarrow, so long the home of the Wishart family, stood about two miles south-west of Fordoun, near the banks of the Bervie Water. It was demolished in 1802, but parts of the old wall and garden are still visible, and many of the ancient stones, some of them bearing the initials of the family, will be found incorporated in the walls of the present farmhouse of Pitarrow. Over the main gate of the steading are the Wishart Arms carved in stone—a spread eagle, with the words " Fear God " on a scroll above it. Many years ago, when the old garden was being trenched, a plain gold marriage ring of great age was discovered. It bore this pithy couplet :—

In God most just
Is all my trust.

Such was Wishart's heritage.

# THE BACKGROUND OF HIS BOYHOOD

In a document of 1506 there is a reference to " our modern village of Auchenblay." Close to it at that time stood the historic town of Kincardine, from which the county takes its name. All trace of it has long since disappeared. It was in Kincardine Castle, a royal residence for nearly three hundred years from the tenth century, that John Baliol had signed away the crown of Scotland to Edward I. That was on 2nd July 1296. Tradition has it that Kenneth III. was murdered nearby in 994 A.D. A hundred years later, in a field in the farm of West Mondynes, in this same parish of Fordoun, Duncan II. met his death. The whole district is rich in traditions of the Scottish kings, and is full of prehistoric, Roman, and other remains. That was the kind of background that a boy of George Wishart's ancestry could hardly fail to appreciate, and in one of the old Roman forts he may well have played as a youngster.

3

"Doubtless," says one of his modern biographers,[1] " George Wishart received his education in the School held in the Mensal Church of Fordun, and frequently quenched his thirst at ' Paldy's Well ' on the Mount of Finella (one of the outspurs of the Grampians), and found a never-ceasing source of pure delight in the rapid rolling Luther that gladdens and brightens the quiet pastoral valley. From the school of Fordun George Wishart proceeded to King's College, Aberdeen, where a famous Angus man, Hector Boece, discharged the duties of Principal with remarkable distinction, and succeeded in inspiring the youth entrusted to his care with a fervent love for classical studies and liberal theological opinions." That, it must be admitted, is only conjecture, but King's College being the one school in Scotland where Greek was then taught, it is reasonable conjecture. There is no record of Wishart's name having been entered at the older University of St Andrews, where the 400th anniversary of his death has been so strikingly commemorated.

Did Wishart complete his studies on the Continent ? Of that we cannot say for certain. His friend and patron, John Erskine, son of the neighbouring Laird of Dun, who was four or five years older, did go abroad, and Wishart may well have accompanied him. The two families were on the friendliest terms and were related to each other by marriage. John had been at Aberdeen under Hector Boece, and was reputed to be equally at home with his sword and his books. A man of wide culture and generous disposition, popular at Court, and yet possessed of great moral courage, the fifth Laird of Dun was to become the friend of Knox as well as Wishart. He was the first man of substance to embrace the Reformation, and when the Presbyterian Church was constituted he became the " Superintendent of Angus and Mearns." Later, he was at least four times Moderator of the General Assembly.

## " THE SCHOOLMASTER OF MONTROSE "

The estate of Dun lies midway between the towns of Brechin and Montrose, and the Erskines exercised, in virtue of their wide territorial rights and great wealth, a considerable influence on the fortunes of the two burghs. When John Erskine returned from foreign travel he brought with him a distinguished

[1] J. Moffat Scott : ' The Martyrs of Angus and Mearns.'

French scholar, Pierre de Marsiliers, whom he introduced into the school at Montrose, of which he was for long the Provost, as its first teacher of Greek. That was in 1534, and shortly afterwards George Wishart, then twenty-one years of age, joined Marsiliers, first as pupil and later as assistant and colleague. One may judge of the impression he made there by the fact that to the end of his days the Reformer was known as "The Schoolmaster of Montrose."

It was no mean title! Montrose is a Royal Burgh. It had been a place of importance at least as far back as the tenth century. Mills and salt pans had been established there in the reign of Malcolm IV., and his successor, William the Lion, resided for something like twenty years in the town. In 1244 it was reckoned one of the chief places in the kingdom, and it was from the harbour of Montrose that James Douglas is said to have set sail for the Holy Land carrying the heart of King Robert the Bruce nearly a century later.

It was while he was teaching Greek to the children of the old seaport town that George Wishart first came under suspicion of heresy, and it was David Beaton, then Abbot of Arbroath and later Cardinal-Archbishop of St Andrews, who impeached him to Hepburn, Bishop of Brechin, the diocesan of Angus.

Beaton, in spite of his close family ties with the Wisharts, was to be the Reformer's lifelong and implacable enemy, bringing him in the end to the stake beneath the windows of his castle. The crime with which he now charged the son of the old Lord Justice Clerk was that of using the Greek New Testament as a medium of instruction in the classroom, thereby introducing heretical doctrine to the minds of his pupils. That was in 1538, and Wishart needed no reminder of the fate that might be in store for him. Four years earlier David Straiton, the son of a neighbouring Mearns laird, had been burned at Edinburgh, and in the interval the penalties against heretics had been made much more severe. Discretion at the moment seemed the better part of valour, and the young schoolmaster fled to England without waiting to be tried. Twenty-one years later Marsiliers was still teaching at Montrose, and among his pupils that winter was Andrew Melville, destined to be the leader of what might be called the second phase of the Reformation.

5

# ARRAIGNED FOR HERESY AT BRISTOL

When we next meet George Wishart he is fulfilling a completely new rôle. The schoolmaster has become the preacher, and the little classroom at Montrose has been exchanged for the pulpit of St. Nicholas, the mother church of Bristol, the great seaport city of South-Western England. Just how Wishart came to be there we have no means of knowing. He may well have sailed from Montrose, and exiled Scots in the south may have pressed him to join them in the comparative safety of that busy centre.

Bristol was then the principal city in the undivided diocese of Worcester, over which Hugh Latimer, the Reforming Bishop and future martyr, reigned as Bishop. Latimer was a Cambridge man, and while still a member of the University had been led into the light by Thomas Bilney—" Little Bilney," who suffered death by fire in the Lollard's Pit at Norwich on 19th August 1531, one of the earlier martyrs of the English Reformation. Latimer himself was a cautious man. Not yet had he broken with the teaching of the Roman Church, and it may not have been he who gave Wishart a Reader's licence enabling him to preach in the city churches without let or hindrance. It may have been Henry Holbech, who had been appointed Suffragan Bishop of Bristol just before Wishart went south, and who would be presiding over the affairs of the diocese during Latimer's absence in London.

The four years during which Latimer occupied the See of Worcester (1535-39) were among the most momentous in the history of the English Church and nation, and the months immediately preceding Wishart's advent in the south had seen the suppression of the monasteries, the authorisation of the first fully accredited version of the Bible in the English tongue, and the issue of the First Articles of the Reformed Church of England. Bristol itself was a place in which advanced opinions were freely propagated, and no town in England at that time had such a record for violent theological controversy.

It was in the spring of 1539 that Wishart first appeared in the pulpit of St. Nicholas in Bristol, and the eloquence that later affected John Knox so profoundly had two immediate results as far as his hearers there were concerned. It produced a deep impression on their minds and hearts, and it revived

6

in the most unhappy way the flames of religious discord that had blazed up so often in that city in the years directly preceding. Wishart himself was soon in trouble. The city was in such an uproar, Latimer's biographer tells us,[1] that the authorities were compelled to put him in prison until the charges of heresy which had been made against him could be formulated and investigated. The Scotsman had many devoted partisans, and the threats they addressed to the municipal authorities were, it must be admitted, couched in the coarsest possible language.

It is to that interesting old document, 'The Mayer's Calendar' of Bristol, a contemporary record of first-rate interest and importance, that we turn for an account of what transpired.[2] " 30 Henry VIII.," reads the entry, " That this year, the 15 May, a Scot named George Wysard, set furth his lectture in St. Nicholas Church of Bristowe, the most blasphemous heresy that ever was herd, openly declarying that Christ nother had not coulde merite for him, nor yet for us ; which heresy brought many of the commons of this town into a great error, and divers of them were persuaded by that herectical lecture to heresy. Whereupon the said stiff-necked Scot was accused, by Mr John Kerne, deane of the said diocese of Worcester and soon after he was sent to the most reverend father in God, the Archbishop of Canterbury, before whom and others, that is to signify, the Bishops of Bath, Norwich, and Chichester, with others as doctors ; and he before them was examined, convicted, and condemned in and upon the detestable heresy above mentioned ; whereupon, he was injoyned to bere a fagot in St. Nicholas church aforesaid, and the parish of the same, the 13 July, anno forementioned ; and in Christ church and parish thereof, the 20 July, abovesaid following ; which injunction was duly executed in aforesaid."

Of this incident there have been two interpretations current —the one that the words are to be taken at their face value, and that what Wishart denied was the mediatorial work of Christ, his own views of divine truth at this time being very imperfect. The other is that the sense of the passage has been altered by the careless but quite understandable omission of one word, and that what we should actually read is : " openly declarying that Christ's *mother* nother hath nor coulde merite for him ; nor yet for us." On that reading Wishart was con-

---

[1] R. Demaus—'Hugh Latimer.' A Biography.
[2] Lorimer—' The Scottish Reformation.'

demned for a bold affirmation of Protestant opinions ; and it was those opinions for which he was later to give his life, that he at this time recanted, abjectly and publicly.

This at least must be borne in mind in judging of the whole question—that 1539 was a critical year in England, in the course of which the whole religious situation was radically altered. On 28th February Henry VIII. had issued a proclamation charging all his loving subjects to observe and keep the ancient ceremonies. On 28th April Parliament had assembled, and a few days later Convocation had met at Westminster, both summoned by Henry, with a view to securing, by force if need be, unity in religious opinion. On the 28th of June the " Act for abolishing diversity of opinions " received the Royal Assent. Known as " The Bloody Statute " or " The Whip with Six Cords," it affirmed the long-disputed doctrines of transubstantiation, clerical celibacy, and auricular confession, provided for the maintenance of private masses and prescribed the severest penalties for heretics, speedily filling the jails, and sending many to the fires at Smithfield. That, then, was the atmosphere in which Wishart's offence and trial took place, and whatever may have been the nature of the error with which he was charged, he may be judged to have escaped very lightly at a time when Latimer himself was thrown into prison.

## IN EXILE ON THE CONTINENT

" The Bloody Statute " had the immediate effect of sending scores of Protestant Englishmen into exile on the Continent. With one such party, in all likelihood, as soon as he was free of the penalties imposed on him at Bristol, travelled the Scotsman, George Wishart; first to Germany, it would seem, and later to the Swiss Cantons.

Of the years Wishart spent across the water we have only the scantiest records, but some things we do know for certain. One is that it was not in Germany under Luther and Melancthon, but in Switzerland, where Bullinger had succeeded Zwingli in the principal Reformed Church at Zurich, and where Calvin and Farel had recently begun their great work in Geneva, that his deepest and most lasting impressions were received. And it was in the course of a conversation with a Jew, on a voyage down the Rhine, that two of the great lessons of his life were learned.

Henry Bullinger, son of a priest, and disciple and successor of Huldreich Zwingli, was in every way a remarkable man. He it was who, as leader of the Reformed Party among these hardy mountaineers of the Swiss Cantons, carried on a simultaneous struggle against Catholics, Zealots, and Lutherans. He it was who took the principal part in the drawing up, at Basle in 1536, of that great national creed of Switzerland, the First Helvetic Confession. And he it was who, more than any other Continental Protestant leader, stamped the impress of his personality and teaching on the Reformation in England through the medium of men like Hooper, Latimer, and Ridley. On Wishart his influence seems to have been decisive.

The Scotsman was captivated by the Helvetic Confession, with its insistence on the supremacy of the Word of God as the final source of authority and its own sole interpreter, and with its clear and closely reasoned doctrine of the Sacraments, at once lofty and evangelical. This great Protestant symbol he proceeded to translate into English, weaving it at the same time into the very texture of his own life and thought.

With the ecclesiastical organisation Bullinger had built up Wishart was equally fascinated. Its discipline and order wedded to simplicity appealed strongly to him, as it did in greater or less degree to the visitors who came to Zurich from every reformed country in Europe. When the Scotsman returned in due course to his native land he brought this with him as the model to be adopted in the organisation of those little evangelical communities which were to result from his eloquent preaching of the Word, and the Church in Scotland as we know it to-day owes much to Bullinger's influence, alike in its doctrine and its discipline. To say that is not to disparage in any way the work of Knox or the influence of Calvin, but these came later. It was under Wishart that the real foundations were laid.

Of his memorable encounter on the Rhine it is best that Wishart should himself tell the story. " I once chanced," he said long afterwards, " to meet with a Jew when I was sailing upon the waters of the Rhine. I inquired of him what was the cause of his pertinacie, that he did not believe that the true Messiah was come, considering that they had seen all the prophecies which were spoken of him to be fulfilled ; moreover, the prophecies taken away, and the sceptre of Judah ? By many other testimonies of the Scripture I vanquished him, and approved that Messiah was come — the same which they call Jesus of Nazareth. The Jew answered again unto me, ' When Messiah cometh, He shall restore all things, and He shall not abrogate the law which was given to our fathers, as ye do. For why ? We see the poor almost perish through hunger among you, yet you are not moved with pity towards them ; but among us Jews, though we be poor, there are no beggars found. Secondarily, it is forbidden by the law to faine any kind of imagery of things in heaven above, or in the earth beneath, or in the sea under the earth, but one God only to honour ; but your sanctuaries and churches are full of idols. Thirdly, a piece of bread baken upon the ashes ye adore and worship, and say that it is your god.' "

" These Jewish censures upon the practices of Christendom," says Lorimer, who recalls the story,[1] " appear to have made a deep impression upon Wishart. He never forgot them. He used to refer to them in his preaching, as a proof of the bad impression which was made upon the minds of unbelievers by the use of images in Christian worship, and by the Popish doctrine of the Real Presence ; and it is not improbable that words which he quoted so often as a lesson to others may have had some salutary impression, when he first heard them, upon himself. It is certain that Wishart became in his own person an eminent instance of that humane concern for the poor, with the want of which the Jew reproached the Christian world at large ; and no less so of that zeal against religious " imagery " and bread worship, of which the latter had set him so fervent an example."

## "MAISTER GEORGE OF BENNET'S COLLEDGE "

Wishart returned to England in the winter of 1541-42, and when we next meet him he is at Cambridge, a student and tutor of Corpus Christi College. It is to Emery Tylney, one of his Cambridge pupils, that we are indebted for a lifelike picture of the great Scottish Reformer, as he was at that time. " About the yeare of our Lord, a thousand, five hundreth, fortie and three, there was, in the universitie of Cambridge," says Tylney,[2] " one Maister George Wischart, commonly called Maister

[1] Peter Lorimer : ' The Scottish Reformation.'
[2] C. Rogers, ' Life of George Wishart.'

George of Bennet's Colledge, who was a man of tall stature, polde headed, and on the same a French cap of the best. Judged of melancholye complexion by his phsiognomie, blacke haired, long bearded, comely of personage, well spoken after his country of Scotland, courteous, lovely, glad to teach, desirous to learne, and was well trauelled, hauing on him for his habit or clothing, neuer but a mantell frise gowne to the shoes, a blacke Millian fustain dublet, and plaine blacke hosen, course new canuasse for his shirtes, and white falling bandes and cuffes at the handes. All the which apparell, he gaue to the poore, some weekly, some monethly, some quarterly as hee liked, sauing his French cappe, which hee kept the whole yeare of my beeing with him. Hee was a man modest, temperate, fearing God, hating couetousnesse, for his charitie had neuer ende, nighte, morne, nor daye, hee forbare one meale in three, one day in foure for the most part, except something to comfort nature. Hee lay hard upon a pouffe of straw, course new canuasse sheetes, which, when he change, he gaue away. He had commonly by his bedside a tubbe of water, in the which (his people being in bed, the candle put out, and all quiet) he eused to bathe himselfe, as I being very yong, being assured offen heard him, and in one light night discerned him ; hee loved me tenderly, and I him, for my age, as effectually."

That is a very charming picture that Tylney paints, and his conclusion is no less interesting :—

" If I should declare his love to mee and all men, his charitie to the poore, in giuing, relieuing, caring, helping, prouiding, yea infinitely studying how to do good unto all, and hurt to none, I should sooner want words than just cause to commend him.

All this I testifie with my whole heart and trueth of this godly man. Hee that made all, gouerneth all, and shall judge all, knoweth I speak the truthe, that the simple may be satisfied, the arrogant confounded, the hypocrite disclosed.

EMERY TYLNEY."

## RETURN TO SCOTLAND : IN RETREAT AT PITARROW

The time was coming, however, even while Emery Tylney was drawing that delightful picture of his tutor, for George Wishart to return to Scotland. It was an opportunity for which he had long been waiting.

King James V. of Scotland had died at Falkland Palace on 13th December 1542 at the age of thirty-one, leaving as his heir an infant girl of a few days old—the ill-fated Mary, Queen of Scots. Of the two strong men in the kingdom, the Earl of Arran, whose sympathies were with the Reformed cause, and Cardinal David Beaton, the powerful and unscrupulous Archbishop of St Andrews, the former was appointed Regent. Arran favoured an English alliance, while Beaton, of course, inclined to the French. And so it came about that in June 1543, Commissioners from Scotland journeyed south to London for the purpose of negotiating a marriage between Edward, Prince of Wales, the heir to the English throne, and the infant Mary of Scotland. It was the chance for which Wishart had been waiting, and when the party reached London he at once set off from Cambridge to join them. Included in their number was James Learmont of Balcomie, a near relation on his mother's side.

When Wishart got back to Scotland he had intended starting preaching right away, but the time was clearly not yet ripe for a venture so bold as that. For a period of a few months, therefore, he found a quiet retreat in his old home at Pitarrow, and there, on the walls of the great hall, he executed in his leisure hours a series of striking paintings in which he sought to give expression to what he felt. The paintings, which were in the brightest colours, were discovered under the wainscoting when the mansion-house was being demolished in 1802.

" One over the fireplace," says Dr Charles Rogers,[1] " represented the Pope on horseback, attended by a company of cardinals, uncovered. In front stood a white palfrey, richly caparisoned, held by a person in elegant apparel. Beyond was the Cathedral of St Peter, of which the doors were open, as if to receive the procession. Under the painting were these lines :—

*In Papam.*

Laus tua non tua fraus ; virtus non gloria rerum
Scandere te fecit hoc decus eximium.
Dat sua pauperibus gratis nec munera curat
Curia Papalis quod more percipimus.
*Hae carmina potius legenda cancros imitando.*"

Literally rendered, the inscription reads :—

" Thy merit, not thy craft ; thy worth, not thy ambition,

[1] ' Life of George Wishart.'

raised thee to this pitch of eminence. The Papal Curia, as we well know, gives freely to the poor, nor grudges its gifts."

But, as the writer informs us his verses are to be read by imitating a crab—that is, backwards—a very different meaning is derived, thus :—

"The Papal Curia, as we well know, grudges its gifts, nor bestows on the poor freely. To this pitch eminence thy ambition raised thee, not thy worth ; thy craft ; nor thy merit."

George Wishart, it is quite clear, was a versatile man !

# SCOTLAND'S FIRST EXPOSITORY LECTURER

During these months at Pitarrow, Wishart was waiting for his hour, and while waiting was preparing himself for what he knew must be a short and highly concentrated ministry. It was at Montrose in a hired house, " next unto the Church except one," that he began his work, and there, and under the friendly roof of John Erskine of Dun that he carried it on for some time. The effects were immediate and lasting. Old friends and former pupils flocked to hear him expound the Lord's Prayer, the Ten Commandments and the Apostles' Creed, and with them they brought others, first curious and a little critical, then profoundly impressed, and often in the end ready for any sacrifice. " In the accounts transmitted by contemporary writers," says Hetherington, the Church historian,[1] " we seem to trace the features of a character of surpassing loveliness, bearing a close resemblance in its chief lineaments to that of the beloved apostle John, so mild, gentle, patient, and unresisting, his lips touched with a live coal from off the altar, and his heart overflowing with holy love to God, and compassionate affection to mankind. The citizens of Montrose felt and owned the power of his heavenly eloquence."

" Montrose ever afterwards," says another writer,[2] " displayed a steady attachment to the cause of reform. The minds of the population had long been under training to welcome such a ministration as Wishart's. Montrose was one of the earliest towns in Scotland to receive importation of the English Testament. It was one of the first having teachers able to teach, and scholars willing to learn, the Greek Scriptures."

[1] W. M. Hetherington : ' History of the Church of Scotland.'
[2] Lorimer.

13

Andrew Melville, let it not be forgotten, was one of the pro-
ducts, direct or indirect, of this faithful sowing in the northern
burgh.

From Montrose Wishart made his way to the larger centre
of Dundee, some thirty miles to the south. Here, too, he found
a fruitful soil and a responsive people, and here more than
anywhere else he laid the foundations of his great reputation
as a preacher. Dundee had long been a great ecclesiastical
centre, one of the seven chief places of pilgrimage in Scotland.
Its historic old churches of St. Clement, St. Mary, St. Paul,
and St. Serf were as celebrated as they were wealthy. Its
great Franciscan Monastery had been founded by Devorgilla,
the mother of John Baliol, in 1260. Its famous cloister for
penitent women is commemorated still in the name " Magdalene
Green " given to the open space between the Tay and the west
end of the city.

In Dundee Wishart began lecturing chapter by chapter
through St. Paul's Epistle to the Romans. It was a method
of pulpit instruction which he had learned from Bullinger,
and which remained popular in Scotland until nearly our own
time.

The first popular outbreak against the abuses and corrup-
tions of the Roman Church took place in Dundee in the autumn
of 1543, the Black and Grey Friars' Monasteries being sacked
by the fury of the mob. It may have been this which led to
Wishart's being peremptorily ordered to desist from preaching,
an order which he was not slow to disobey. " My lords," he
said to the prelates, referring to this incident at his trial, " I
have read in the Acts of the Apostles that it is not lawful for
the threats and menaces of men to desist from the preaching
of the Evangel; therefore it is written, ' We shall rather obey
God than men.' "

" So long," says Lorimer,[1] " as Dundee herself, with her
Evangelical Constable, Sir John Scrymgeour, and her godly
magistrates and burghers, was willing to hear the words of
Eternal Life, Wishart was resolved not to desert his post at
the bidding of either regent, cardinal, or bishop. . . . Happily
for the cause of the Reformation, in the evil days upon which
it had again fallen, there was still one powerful living preacher
who stood forth to defend it in one of its chief strongholds,

[1] Peter Lorimer : ' The Scottish Reformation.'

and whose fervent appeals from the pulpit could do more to plead for it, and sustain the sinking hearts of its friends, than any letters, however excellent, from reformers in distant exile. George Wishart was still preaching on the Epistle to the Romans in the zealous burgh of Dundee, and multitudes were hanging on the lips of the greatest pulpit orator that Scotland had seen for centuries."

The time came, however, when Wishart was compelled to go. When in February 1544 the city was occupied for a space by the troops of Cardinal Beaton he was probably in hiding, but he was soon back preaching and teaching for several months more. Then Beaton proceeded to work on the fears of the magistrates, and, overcome by threats, it seemed that they were about to give way.

When Wishart was in the pulpit one day, surrounded by a great congregation, which included the Earl Marischal and several of the nobility, the church was entered by a man called Robert Mill, a renegade Protestant. Proceeding to the front of the pulpit, he charged the preacher, in the name of the Queen and the Governor, to depart from the town at once and trouble it no more. "Whereupon," says the chronicler,[1] "Wishart mused for a little space, with his eye bent upon the heavens, and then looking sorrowfully to the people, he said, 'God is my witness that I minded ever your comfort and not your trouble, which to me is more grievous than to yourselves. But sure I am, to reject the Word of God and drive away His messengers, is not the way to save you from trouble. When I am gone, God will send you messengers who will not be afraid either for horning or banishment. I have with the hazard of my life remained among you, preaching the word of salvation ; and now, since yourselves refuse me, I must leave my innocency to be declared by God. If it be long well with you, I am not led by the Spirit of truth ; and if trouble unexpected fall upon you, remember this is the cause, and turn to God by repentance, for He is merciful.'"

These words pronounced, we are told, he came down forthwith from the pulpit, and declining the pressing request of the Earl Marischal to accompany him to the northern parts of the kingdom, "with all possible expedition he passed to the westland."

[1] Peter Lorimer : 'The Scottish Reformation.'

# WISHART IN THE WEST COUNTRY

The district to which the Reformer now made his way had long been famous as the home of advanced theological opinion. Nearly a century before, the " Lollards of Kyle," as they were called, had figured prominently in Scottish religious history. The Earl of Glencairn, at whose invitation he went west, he had probably met in England. In the old Parish Church of Galston, and in the open air auditorium in front of Cessnock Castle, he preached regularly for the space of about four weeks, and in the towns of Ayr and Mauchline he had experiences that were quite unforgettable. It is John Knox himself who tells the story.[1]

" At Ayr," says Knox, " Gawin Dunbar, the Archbishop of Glasgow, by instigation of Cardinal Beaton, came with his gatherings to make resistance to Master George, and did first occupy the Kirk. The Earl of Glencairn repaired with his friends to the town with diligence, and so did divers Gentlemen of Kyle. When all were assembled conclusion was taken that they would have the Kirk. Thereto Master George utterly repugned, saying, ' Let him alone ! His sermon will not much hurt. Let us go to the Market Cross.' And so they did, where Master George made so notable a sermon, that the very enemies themselves were confounded. The Archbishop preached to his jackmen, and to some old bosses of the town."

At Mauchline things were slightly different. " The said Master George," Knox continues, " was required to come to the Kirk of Mauchline, as he did. But the Sheriff of Ayr caused man the Kirk for the preservation of a tabernacle that was there, beautiful to the eye. Some zealous of the parish among whom was Hugh Campbell of Kinyeancleuch, offended that they should be debarred their Parish Kirk, concluded by force to enter. But Master George withdrew Hugh Campbell, and said unto him : ' Brother, Christ Jesus is as potent upon the fields as in the kirk. He Himself oftener preached in the desert, at the seaside, and in other places judged profane, than He did in the Temple of Jerusalem. It is the Word of Peace that God sends by me. The blood of no man shall be shed this day for the preaching of it.' So, withdrawing the whole people, he came to a dyke in a muir edge, upon the south-west

' History of the Reformation in Scotland.'

16

side of Mauchline, upon which he ascended, the multitude standing and sitting about him. God gave the day pleasing and hot ; and he continued preaching more than three hours. In that sermon God wrought so wonderfully with him that one of the most wicked men in that county, Laurence Rankin, laird of Sheill, was converted. The tears ran from his eyes in such abundance, that all men wondered. His conversion was without hypocrisy ; for his life and conversation witnessed it in all times to come."

" This," says Lorimer,[1] " is the first time we hear of field preaching in the history of Scottish evangelism ; the stones of a dry dyke serving for pulpit, and the tufts of moss and moor-heather for benches and fald stool."

## AT DUNDEE IN THE PLAGUE YEAR

While Wishart was busy in the west, news reached him of the serious outbreak of plague in Dundee, following on famine. This was one of the " messengers of God not to be afraid for horning or for banishment " of which he had warned the people, and true to his promise, despite all the entreaties of his friends in the west, the Reformer hastened back to take his place alongside the stricken. " They are now in trouble," he told the good folk of Kyle, " and they need comfort. Perchance this hand of God will make them now to magnify and reverence that Word, which before, for the fear of men, they set light price."

" Coming to Dundee," says Knox in his history,[2] " the joy of the Faithful was exceeding great. Master George delayed no time, but gave signification that he would preach ; and, because the most part were either sick, or else were in company with those that were sick, he chose the head of the East Port of the town for his preaching-place ; and the whole sat or stood within, and the sick or suspected without the Port. The text on which his first sermon was made he took from the Hundred and Seventh Psalm : ' He sent His Word and healed them ' ; and therewith joined these words, ' It is neither herb nor plaster, O Lord, but Thy Word healeth all ! ' In which sermon he most comfortably did entreat of the dignity and utility of God's Word ; the punishment that comes for contempt of the same ;

[1] 'The Scottish Reformation.'
[2] 'History of the Reformation in Scotland.'

the promptitude of God's mercy to such as truly turn to Him ; yea, the great happiness of them whom God taketh from this misery, even in His own gentle visitation, which the malice of man can neither eke nor impair. By which sermon he so raised up the hearts of all that heard him, that they regarded not death, but judged them more happy that should depart, than such as should remain behind ; considering that they knew not if they should have such a comforter with them at all times."

But Wishart did more than preach—healing, comforting, and strengthening as his preaching must have been. " He spared not to visit them that lay in the very extremity," says Knox, " and comforted them as he could. And he caused minister all things that were necessary to those that might use meat or drink ; and in that point was the Town wondrous benevolent ; for the poor were no more neglected than were the rich." The lesson learned from the Jew that day on the Rhine had not been forgotten !

The significance of the spot at which Wishart took his stand, and where day by day he preached to listening hundreds, should not be overlooked. Just outside the city gate was the ancient Chapel of St Roque, the reputed helper of men in time of plague and pestilence. But St Roque had done nothing— his image and shrine had not availed. It was to the Cross men must learn to look, and to Him who had died thereon.

The East Port of Dundee is still standing, the only fragment of the old city wall to survive the ravages of time. There in the little-used " Cowgate " it is surmounted by a plaque recording with gratitude the Reformer's service to the city. Just a stone's throw away is the handsome Wishart Memorial Church. It was from that congregation that Mary Slessor went out to Calabar.

# TWO ATTEMPTS ON WISHART'S LIFE

It was during his ministry to the stricken in Dundee that the first of the attempts was made on Wishart's life, and again it is Knox who tells the story : [1] " While he (Wishart) was spending his life to comfort the afflicted, the Devil ceased not to stir up his own son, Cardinal Beaton. He corrupted by

[1] ' History of the Reformation in Scotland.'

money a desperate Priest named Sir John Wighton to slay Master George, who looked not to himself in all things so circumspectly as worldly men would have used. On a day when the sermon was ended, and the people departing, no man suspecting danger, and therefore not heeding Master George, the Priest stood waiting at the foot of the steps, his gown loose, and his drawn whinger in his hand under his gown. Master George, who was most sharp of eye and judgment, marked him, and as he came near he said, ' My friend, what would you do ? ' Therewith he clapped his hand upon the Priest's hand, wherein the whinger was, and took it from him. The Priest abashed, fell down at his feet, and openly confessed the verity. The noise rising and coming to the ears of the sick, they cried : ' Deliver the traitor to us, or else we will take him by force ' ; and they thrust at the gate. But Master George took him in his arms and said : ' Whosoever troubleth him shall trouble me. He hath hurt me in nothing, but he hath done great comfort both to you and to me, to wit, he hath let us understand what we may fear. In times to come, we will watch better.' ''

The second attempt on the Reformer's life was made in the course of what he knew now would be his farewell visit to Montrose and Dun. He went north to say " Goodbye " to those who had been among his most faithful friends, to exhort them to stand firm in the dark days he saw ahead, and to celebrate once more in their midst that Supper of the Lord which meant so much to him and them. He left for the north probably late in 1545, and when the plague had ceased in Dundee. " God," he told his friends there, " has almost put an end to the battle in Dundee. I find myself called to another." That other was a public disputation he was expected to engage in with the leading Romish theologians in Edinburgh in the near future. A Provincial Council was to assemble there in January 1546, and his friends in the west had prevailed on him to go, promising their support and assuring him of their presence.

It was while Wishart was " in retreat " near Montrose, quietly preparing himself for what he knew lay ahead, that a letter was put into his hands purporting to be from a dear friend, and asking him to come with all possible diligence, " for he was stricken with a sudden sickness." The messenger brought a horse for Wishart's use, and he mounted without delay and without misgiving. Riding along the road accompanied by a few friends, he suddenly stopped short and exclaimed, "I will not go ; I am forbidden of God ; I am sure there is treason ; let some of you go to yonder place," pointing as he spoke to a spot about a mile and a half from the town, "and tell me," he added, "what you find."

His friends, astonished, moved out to investigate, and at once discovered an ambush which had been laid for him, some sixty armed men, with jacks and spears, lying in wait to dispatch him. It was Beaton again who had planned this dastardly business. "I know," said Wishart, as he turned his horse's head backwards, "that I shall finish my life in that bloodthirsty man's hands, but it will not be after this manner." His death was to take place in circumstances which would at once be honourable to him and more useful to the cause he represented.

# A "GETHSEMANE" AT INVERGOWRIE

The time had now come for Wishart to leave for Edinburgh, and on the way west to Perth he lay for a night at Invergowrie, a little village just outside of Dundee. His host was James Watson, "a faithful brother," and others of the same persuasion were spending the night beneath that hospitable roof. Wishart was seen to pass from his room into the garden shortly before sunrise. He was followed by two friends, William Spadin and John Watson, who told the story afterwards of what they saw and heard that morning.

"When Wishart," they said, "had gone up and down in an alley for a reasonable space, with many sobs and deep groans, he sunk down upon his knees, and sitting thereon his groans increased, and from his knees he fell upon his face, and then they heard weeping, and an indigest sound, as it were of prayer, in the which he continued near an hour, and after began to be quiet and so he arose and came in to his bed. Then began they to demand, as though they had been ignorant, where he had been ; but that night he would answer nothing. Upon the morrow they urged him again. 'Maister George,' said they, 'be plain with us, for we heard your groans ; yea, we heard your bitter mourning, and saw you both upon your knees and upon your face.' With dejected visage he said, 'I had rather you had been in your beds, and it had been more profitable to you, for I was scarce weill occupied.' When they pressed him to let them know some comfort, he said, ' I will tell you. I am assured my travail is near an end, and therefore call to God with me, that now I shrink not when the battle waxes hot.' " [1]

" These words," says Lorimer,[2] " revealed the nature of the struggle through which he had passed. But he had left all his weakness at God's feet ; he had risen from the earth with renovated strength, like a giant refreshed with wine. ' God,' concluded Wishart to his two friends, ' shall send you comfort after me. This realm shall be illuminated with the light of Christ's Evangel, as clearly as ever was any realm since the days of the apostles. The house of God shall be builded in it ; yea, it shall not lack the very copestone. Neither shall this be long delayed. There shall not many suffer after me, till that the glory of God shall evidently appear, and shall once for all triumph in despite of Satan. But alas ! if the people shall afterwards be unthankful, then fearful and terrible shall the plagues be that follow after it.' " And with these words," says Knox,[3] who had it from the men concerned, " he marched forwards on his journey towards St. Johnston, and so to Fife, and then to Leith."

## CHRISTMASTIDE IN EAST LOTHIAN

When Wishart got to Leith he found that his friends from the west had not arrived, and as the days went by it became evident that for some unexplained reason they were not coming. Entirely without protection and in the near vicinity of powerful and unscrupulous enemies, the Reformer lay hidden for a while, the prey to deep dejection. " What differ I from a dead man," he asked himself, " except that I eat and drink ? To this time God has used my labours to the instruction of others and unto the disclosing of darkness ; but now I lurk as a man that were ashamed and durst not show himself."

Such a state of things could not continue. It was not in Wishart's nature to lie idle in the presence of so great a need, whatever the danger or the cost might be, and so he prevailed on his friends in the vicinity that he might be allowed to resume his ministry. On the second Sunday of December he preached

---

[1] ' History of the Reformation in Scotland.'
[2] ' The Scottish Reformation.'
[3] ' History of the Reformation in Scotland.'

at Leith on the Parable of the Sower. Knox was present that day and heard him, and it was the beginning of a short but singularly pregnant friendship. A tutor in the family of Hugh Douglas of Longniddry, and in priest's orders, he had been till then an obscure and unknown man. Now he was to emerge suddenly into the limelight, acting for a brief time as Wishart's guard and the bearer of his great two-handed sword, and then after the interval of a few weeks' seclusion to emerge as his successor, carrying eventually to completion the work begun by the pioneers and martyrs.

Just how charged with destiny that first encounter was it is difficult to overestimate. "Though Knox was now turned forty," says Dr W. G. Blaikie,[1] "their meeting was like that of David and Jonathan. The soul of Knox was knit with the soul of Wishart, and he loved him as his own soul. Though his study of Augustine and other Fathers had already taught Knox much of the doctrines of grace, it seems to have been through Wishart's preaching that the spark came that kindled his knowledge into a living flame."

In the congregation at Leith on that December Sunday, in addition to John Knox there were three East Lothian lairds who now constituted themselves Wishart's protectors, and who invited him to their houses in turn, affording both shelter and hospitality and the opportunities he sought for preaching. These were Alexander Crichton of Brunstone, Hugh Douglas of Longniddry, and John Cockburn of Ormiston, and a word must be said about each.

Of the three, Crichton had the most unsatisfactory record. Once the confidential friend of Beaton, he had finally quarrelled with the Cardinal, and had been sent on various diplomatic missions by his great rival, Arran. His adherence to the Reformed cause is thought to have been occasioned more by hostility to Beaton than by any deep spiritual conviction. Knox's employer and patron, Hugh Douglas, was a man of principle, who had early espoused the Protestant cause. Cockburn, who was the hereditary Constable of Haddington, became later Knox's attached and devoted friend. For the favour he now extended to Wishart he was later to suffer both forfeiture and banishment.

[1] 'The Preachers of Scotland: Sixth to Nineteenth Century.' (Blaikie is in error; he was only thirty.)

On the Sunday after his appearance at Leith, George Wishart preached in the Parish Church of Inveresk, near Musselburgh. As he went to the pulpit he espied two friars talking to the people as they entered the church. " Come in," he cried, " and you shall hear the Word of Truth, which, according as you receive it, will prove to you a savour of life or of death." At the close of the afternoon service that day Sir George Douglas, brother of the Earl of Angus, who had been in the congregation, bore public testimony to the impression that had been made upon him. " I know," he said, " that my Lord Governor and the Cardinal will hear that I have been present at these services. I shall made no denial, and I will fearlessly defend the preacher and uphold his doctrines."

The Governor and the Cardinal were now in Edinburgh, only a few miles away, and it was thought better that Wishart should be conducted for safety to Ormiston and Longniddry. The magnificent old yew tree under which he preached in Cockburn's estate on at least two occasions is still standing, and even then it must have been a veteran. The mansion-house of Longniddry was in the parish of Gladsmuir, and from there on two successive Sundays Wishart went to preach in the old church at Tranent. Then, on 14th January, he made his way to Haddington, whose magnificent old Abbey of St Mary's—the " Lamp of Lothian "—was by far the most important church in the district. Here, he might well expect, he would get his largest congregations.

Wishart was doomed to disappointment. On the first day the attendance was reasonably good, but on the second morning there were less than a hundred present. Just before the service a messenger arrived with a letter for the preacher. It was from Lords Cassilis and Glencairn to say that they would be unable to meet him in Edinburgh. The effect of that communication on Wishart was very great, and the subsequent scene is graphically described by Knox.[1]

" The said Maister George," writes his more famous successor, " paced up and down behind the high altar more than half an hour. His very countenance and visage declared the grief and alteration of his mind. At last he passed to the pulpit, but the auditure was small. He should have begun to have entreated the Second Table of the law ; but thereof in that sermon he spake very little, but began on this manner, ' O Lord, how long

[1] ' History of the Reformation in Scotland.'

shall it be that Thy Holy Word shall be despised, and men shall not regard their own salvation ? I have heard of thee, Haddington, that in thee would have been at a vain Clerk Play two or three thousand people ; and now, to hear the Messenger of the Eternal God, of all the town or parish cannot be numbered a hundred persons ! Sore and fearful shall the plagues be that shall ensue upon this thy contempt ! With fire and sword shalt thou be plagued. Yea, thou Haddington, strangers shall possess thee, and you, the present inhabitants, shall either in bondage serve your enemies, or else ye shall be chased from your habitations ; and that because ye have not known, nor will not know, the time of God's merciful visitation.' "

" In such vehemency and threatening continued that servant of God near an hour and a half, in which he declared all the plagues that ensued, as plainly as after our eyes saw them performed. In the end he said : ' I have forgotten myself, and the matter that I should have entreated ; but let these my last words as concerning public preaching remain in your minds till God send you new comfort.' Thereafter he made a short paraphrase upon the Second Table, with an exhortation to Patience, to the Fear of God, and to the Works of Mercy ; and so put end, as it were making his last testament. The issue declared that the Spirit of Truth and of True Judgment were both in his heart and mouth ; for that same night was he apprehended before midnight, in the House of Ormiston, by the Earl of Bothwell made for money butcher to the Cardinal."

# "ANE IS SUFFICIENT FOR A SACRIFICE"

It was arranged that after this last preaching at Haddington Wishart should go on to sleep at Ormiston House, the residence of his friend, John Cockburn. Before setting out he took affectionate farewell of Hugh Douglas of Longniddry and of John Knox. The latter begged to be allowed to accompany him, but the plea was in vain. " Nay, return to your bairnes " (his pupils), " and God bless you," said Wishart. " Ane is sufficient for a sacrifice." Knox, he realised, had a work to do for Scotland long after he himself was gone.

Wishart was accompanied on foot to Ormiston, on a frosty January day, by Cockburn and Crichton of Brunstone, with whom there was also John Sandilands, the younger, of Calder House in Midlothian. "After supper," says Knox,[1] who would have it from some of those present, "he held a comfortable purpose of the death of God's chosen children, and merrily said, 'Methinks that I desire earnestly to sleep'; and 'Will we sing a Psalm?' So he appointed the fifty-first Psalm, which began thus in Scottish metre :—

> Have mercy on me now, good Lord,
> After Thy great mercie,
> My sinful life does me remord,
> Which sore has grived Thee.

Which being ended," continues Knox, "he passed to his chamber, and, sooner than his common diet was, passed to bed with these words, 'God grant quiet rest.'

"Before midnight the place was beset about, so that none could escape to make advertisement. At the first word, Master George said, 'Open the gates. The Blessed Will of my God be done.' The Earl Bothwell called for the Laird and said, 'It was but vain to make him to hold his house; for the Governor and the Cardinal with all their power were coming'—indeed, the Cardinal was at Elphinstone Tower, not a mile distant—'but if he would deliver the man to him, he would promise upon his honour that it should pass the power of the Cardinal to do him any harm or scaith.' At this promise, made in the presence of God, and hands struck by both the parties for observation of the promise, Master George was delivered to the hands of the Earl of Bothwell."

The promise was not kept—perhaps Bothwell never meant to keep it. Wishart was lodged that night in Elphinstone Tower, which is still standing, and where Royalty is frequently entertained. Next day he was taken to Edinburgh Castle, then to Bothwell's seat at Hailes, and finally to the Sea Tower of St. Andrews Castle, where for the space of about a month he lay awaiting trial. As for the others—Crichton managed to escape that night, but Cockburn and Sandilands were taken, and they too were sent to Edinburgh Castle. Sandilands was later liberated; Cockburn escaped by scaling the Castle wall. Wishart was not so fortunate; he was only to be liberated by death.

---

[1] 'History of the Reformation in Scotland.'

# IN "PILATE'S HALL" AT ST. ANDREWS

Cardinal David Beaton was anxious that there should be as little delay as possible in the disposing of his victim. Some show of a trial there must be, but the issue would not be in doubt. To the plea of the Regent Arran " that he should do well not to precipitate the man's trial, but to delay it until his coming, for as to himself, he would not consent to his death before the cause were truly examined," he refused to give any heed, in spite of the fact that Arran had added these words of warning, " If the Cardinal should do otherwise, he should make protestation, that his blood would be required at his hands."

Certain steps, however, had to be taken that the death of the martyr might not seem to be merely an act of private vengeance. " The Archbishop of Glasgow," says Knox,[1] " was the first to whom the Cardinal wrote, signifying what was done, and earnestly craving that he would assist with his presence and counsel how such an enemy to their Estate might be suppressed." Between Gavin Dunbar and Beaton there had been no love lost, but in their attitude to heretics the two were as one man. " Thereto," continues Knox, " was not the other slow, but kept time appointed, sat next to the Cardinal, voted and subscribed first in the rank, and lay over the East Blockhouse with the Cardinal till the Martyr of God was consumed by fire."

The trial was fixed for the last day of February 1546, the anniversary of Patrick Hamilton's burning just eighteen years before. With Beaton and Dunbar were joined bishops, abbots, and other leading ecclesiastics from every part of Scotland. It was a colourful procession that made its way through the streets of St. Andrews to the Cathedral on the morning of that fateful day. Nothing was spared in the way of wealth and pomp to impress the multitude. As for the prisoner, he was brought from the Sea Tower by the Captain of the Castle himself at the head of one hundred armed men.

The proceedings began with a sermon preached by John Winram, Dean of the Cathedral and Sub-Prior of the Abbey. " A churchman of considerable rank and known ability," says

[1] ' History of the Reformation in Scotland.'

Rogers,[1] "Winram was suspected of tolerating the new opinions." It may have been that Beaton had hoped to trap him, or at least to put him in a most compromising position. What actually happened was something he had never bargained for. Winram took as his theme the Parable of the Sower, and, doing so, went out of his way not to attack heresy but to stress the New Testament ideal of the ministry and the necessary qualifications it lays down for a bishop. As for heresy—the test for that was Holy Scripture ! Such preaching cannot have been to Cardinal Beaton's liking, and the wonder is that the preacher was not placed in the dock beside the prisoner.

Immediately Winram concluded, Wishart was taken up to the vacant pulpit and the reading of the "Articles of Accusation" began. These were eighteen in number, the principal among them referring to his having preached after being prohibited, having denied that there were seven Sacraments, having alleged that every layman was a priest, having questioned both the existence of purgatory and the lawfulness of prayer to the saints, and having rejected auricular confession on the one hand and clerical celibacy on the other.

Opposite to Wishart, on a platform erected for the purpose, stood his principal accuser, John Lauder, Archdeacon of Teviotdale, who, not content with vulgar and scurrilous abuse, foaming at the mouth with rage as he proceeded with the indictment, spat in the prisoner's face, crying out, "Runagate, traitor, thief !" All this Wishart received in the spirit of utmost calmness, and with a forbearance, courtesy, and firmness that would have impressed any ordinarily constituted tribunal. For everything he said in reply he gave not only reasons but full scripture proof. All, however, availed him nothing, and so, as a final resort, he appealed to the Regent. "I refuse not my lord Cardinal," said the prisoner, "but I desire the Word of God to be my judge, and the temporal estate with some of your lordships to be mine auditors, because I am here my lord governor's prisoner." Like Paul of old, he had "appealed to Cæsar," but, unlike Paul, his plea had no avail. The bishops returned a unanimous verdict of "Guilty," and having commanded the laity to leave the Court, the Cardinal sentenced him to be burnt to ashes the next day in front of the Castle where for the past month he had lain a prisoner.

Charles Rogers : 'Life of George Wishart.'

When Wishart heard his sentence he immediately fell on his knees in prayer. " Gracious and everlasting God," he cried, " how long wilt Thou permit Thy servants to suffer through infatuation and ignorance ? We know that the righteous must suffer persecution in this life, which passeth as does a shadow, yet we would entreat Thee, Merciful Father, that Thou wouldest defend Thy people whom Thou hast chosen, and give them grace to endure, and continue in Thy Holy Word." His prayer being ended, he was led back to prison. There he was visited by two friars from the nearby monastery, who offered to act as his confessors. To them he answered, " I will make no confession unto you. Go fetch me yonder man that preached this day, and I will make my confession unto him." Winram was accordingly brought, but of what passed between them Knox himself had to admit that he had no knowledge. This we can say—that John Winram early identified himself with the cause for which Wishart died, that he was one of those who helped to draw up the Confession of Faith of 1560, and that when the Presbyterian Church was formally constituted he became one of its first Superintendents. For how much of that, one wonders, was the condemned man's influence responsible ?

## WISHART'S PRISON COMMUNION

Early on the morning of the day on which Wishart was to die John Winram came to see the prisoner again. The interview was too much for him, and he was overcome with grief. Recovering himself he asked Wishart if he would wish to receive Communion. " Yea, gladly," was the immediate answer, " if I might have it as Christ instituted it." The bishops, however, were not willing that he should have it in any form whatever. A condemned heretic, there would be for him no " benefit of kirk." Having brought back this answer, and the two having promised to pray for each other, the subprior bade his new-found friend farewell.

A little later, we are told, came the Captain of the Castle with some friends to ask if Wishart would breakfast with them. " Very willingly," he replied, " and more gladly than ever heretofore, and because I perceive that ye are good men and godly, and that this shall be my last meal on earth. But I exhort you that ye would give me audience with silence for a little time." They accordingly withdrew. After a short interval Wishart joined them at the table. " I beseech you," he said as he took his place with them, " in the name of God, and for the love ye bear to our Saviour, Jesus Christ, to be silent a little while, till I have made a short exhortation, and blessed this bread, and so bid you farewell." He then spoke for about half an hour on the institution of the Supper, and the death of Christ, and, having blessed the elements, partook of them with them. " As for myself," he concluded, " there is a more bitter potion prepared for me, only because I have preached the true doctrine of Christ ; but pray for me that I may take it patiently as from His Hand." Then he retired to his cell that the last precious moments of preparation might be spent alone with God.

(It is worth noting that Orchardson's striking picture of that prison Communion at the Governor's breakfast table has come just recently into the possession of St. Andrews University.)

## THAT FATEFUL FIRST OF MARCH

A few minutes later there came to his cell those who had been appointed to take him to the place of execution. Divesting him of his usual attire, they clothed him with a loose garment of black linen and then fastened bags of gunpowder to various parts of his body. That done, they led him to a room near the Castle gate, there to wait till the preparations outside were completed.

Meanwhile Beaton was perfecting his own arrangements. It was essential that any attempt at a rescue should be frustrated, and so all the guns of the Castle were trained on the scene of the martyrdom. These and other necessary precautions having been taken, the two archbishops took their places at the window that they might see justice done. Then " they bound Master George's hands behind his back, and led him forth with their soldiers from the Castle, to the place of their cruel and wicked execution." [1]

As Wishart came out of the Castle gate certain beggars met him asking alms. " I want my hands," said the martyr, " wherewith I was wont to give you alms, but the Merciful God of His benignity and abundant grace, that feedeth all men, vouchsafe to give you necessaries, both unto your bodies and souls." And as he came forth into the open, bearing his

[1] Knox.

29

head high, men noted that there was a chain of iron about his middle and a rope about his neck.

"When he came to the fire," says Knox,[1] "he sat down upon his knees, and rose up again, and thrice he said these words, ' O Thou Saviour of the world, have mercy upon me ! Father of heaven, I commend my spirit into Thy holy hands.' Then he turned to the people and said, 'I beseech you, Christian Brethren and Sisters, be not offended at the Word of God, for the affliction and torments which ye see prepared for me. But I exhort you, love the Word of God and suffer patiently. . . . I suffer this day by men, not sorrowfully, but with a glad heart and mind. . . . Ye shall not see me change my colour ! This grim fire I fear not ; and so I pray you to do, if any persecution come unto you for the Word's sake.' " Then he prayed for his accusers, as so many of the martyrs from Stephen's time had done, and turning round, he found the executioner on his knees almost in tears before him. " ' Sir, I pray you,' cried the unhappy man, ' forgive me, for I am not guilty of your death.' ' Come hither to me,' said Wishart, and when he had come he kissed him on the cheek and said, ' Lo ; here is a token that I forgive thee. My heart, do thine office.' "

The signal for the final act of this grim drama was the sounding of a trumpet. Wishart was tied to the stake and the fire was kindled about him, exploding the gunpowder but not putting an end to his sufferings. The Captain of the Castle, we are told, seeing that he was still alive, drew near to the pyre, and bade him be of good courage, while the onlookers groaned aloud with mingled sympathy and fury. As for Wishart, he made answer to the Captain in words that were long to be remembered, " This fire torments my body, but no way abates my spirit." Shortly after that his sufferings ended, and in a silence that was hot with anger, alive with questioning, and grim with foreboding, the populace made their way home.

"It was impossible," says Lorimer,[2] "for the people to behold unmoved so cruel an execution. It was remembered also that the governor had refused his concurrence—that the sanction of the civil authority had been withheld, and the fate of Wishart was pronounced unjust and illegal. That many of

[1] ' History of the Reformation in Scotland.'
[2] ' The Scottish Reformation.'

his opinions were such as the Church deemed heretical could not be denied ; but men had now begun to appeal to the Word of God as the test of truth ; and to be subjected to such inhuman torments for the declaration of its precepts was esteemed monstrous. The courage, meekness, and patience with which the martyr had borne his sufferings produced a deep effect ; and the invariable results of persecution were soon discernible in a spirit of increasing investigation, a revulsion from the tyranny of power, and a steady progress towards the truth."

## A GREAT HISTORIAN SUMS UP

If the life of Wishart had been spared, it has been asked often, and he had taken the place Knox later occupied as leader of the Reformation, what difference would it have meant to Scotland ? A gentler type of religion we might certainly have had, but would Wishart have been able, as his disciple so manifestly was, to grapple with the difficulties and problems of the situation so soon to emerge ? " Wishart was to Knox," says a discerning biographer,[1] " as Stephen had been to Paul. In both cases the martyr's mantle fell on one of broader shoulders and robuster build. The shocking death of the earlier witnesses turned out rather for the furtherance of the Gospel." Elijah's mantle, to change the metaphor, fell on Elisha, and " the effects of Wishart's teaching survive to the present day.[2] It was he who first moulded the Reformed theology of Scotland upon the Helvetic, as distinguished from the Saxon type ; and it was he who first taught the Church of Scotland to reduce her ordinances and Sacraments with rigorous fidelity to the standard of Christ's institutions. Wishart, in fact, died a martyr to the true doctrine of the Sacraments. When we compare his Articles with those of Patrick Hamilton, we become aware of the interesting fact that, while Hamilton gave up his life for those truths which were revived in the teaching of Luther and Melancthon, and which they held in common with all the Continental and British Reformers, Wishart gave up his, not only for these truths but also for those principles which gave a distinctive character to the Reform which Zwingli began in Zurich and Calvin perfected in Geneva."

[1] ' Charles Rogers : ' Life of George Wishart.'
[2] Lorimer.

31

Just what Wishart's life and death achieved, and what his place in consequence is in the life and history of Scotland, has been summed up admirably by one of our greatest Church historians.

" In 1546," says Principal T. M. Lindsay,[1] the acknowledged authority on the Reformation struggle in Europe, " George Wishart was seized, condemned, and burned for heresy at St Andrews. His martyrdom marked the beginning of the popular movement in Scotland in favour of Reformation. He had preached a pure Gospel fearlessly in many parts of the country. His gentle fearlessness, his blameless life, his eloquence, and the Gospel he preached had all produced a deep impression on the people of Scotland. Before the burning of Wishart there are no traces of any widespread sympathy with the Reformed opinions ; but after his martyrdom the general feeling in Scotland underwent a great, sudden, and almost inexplicable change. One of these silent revolutions which the most careless historian cannot help seeing, and which the most profound cannot hope adequately to account for, took place in Scotland. Wishart's birth dates the new birth of the Scottish Church and of the Scottish nation."

Than that there could be nothing truer—nothing finer.

[1] ' Religious Life in Scotland from the Reformation to the Present Day.'

The Ruined Chapel of St Palladius, Fordoun

Wishart's Prison Communion, by Orchardson

# GEORGE WISHART:
## THE MAN WHO ROUSED SCOTLAND

"MASTER GEORGE WISHART"

# ON THE SLOPES
# OF THE SIDLAWS

KING SEAT
FROM PITKINDIE.

*(By kind permission of Messrs Valentine and Sons, Dundee.)*

## *by* D. P. Thomson, M.A.

PRICE: ONE SHILLING

# ON THE SLOPES OF THE SIDLAWS

THE range of hills known as the Sidlaws stretches across the eastern half of Scotland, approximately from Perth to Forfar. Separated at the one end from the Ochils by the valleys of the Tay and the Earn, it is broken up at the other by foothills sloping down into Strathmore in the parishes of Glamis and Inverarity.

The area on which these heights look down is traversed throughout by the River Tay and its tributaries, of which the Ericht and the Isla are the most important,[1] the one coming down Glen Shee from the Grampians, and the other flowing through Glen Isla to the wide fertile plain beyond. Further up Strathmore lies the country of the North and South Esks.

Ranging as it does from the important commercial and industrial seaport city of Dundee to tiny hamlets tucked into the folds of the hills, and from important and historic towns like Forfar and Blairgowrie to purely rural parishes, destitute of even a village, this is primarily an agricultural region, and to-day its economy is of greater importance to the country as a whole than it has ever been before.

The scenery of the Sidlaws themselves is much finer and more diversified than the casual traveller would imagine or the current guide books would suggest. There may be no great heights to be climbed and no sublime grandeur to be contemplated, no famous battlefields to be found, and no royal palaces to be visited, but few regions of the same size have more to offer in romantic history, in contrasting natural beauty, and in scenic panoramas like those which unfold as one crosses from north to south by almost any of the secondary roads which traverse the parishes of Abernyte Kinnaird and Kilspindie, or from south to north on either of the main roads running from Dundee to Coupar Angus and Newtyle.

In the Sidlaws every variety of interest is catered for. There are fine old churches like those of Kettins and Fowlis Easter, with mediaeval paintings unmatched anywhere in Britain. There are historic castles almost every few miles, like those of Kinnaird, Fingask and Evelick, to name but three within a very short distance of one another. There are scenes like that in which the tragedy of *Macbeth* is set, where imagination can readily supply the details, and glens and dells and beauty spots, on a miniature scale though it be, round almost every other corner, on the good roads with which the region is honeycombed.

Here I have not attempted to cover anything like the whole field. Nothing whatever is said, for example, of three of the Sidlaw parishes — Eassie and Nevay to the east, Lundie and Fowlis in the centre, and Kinnaird further to the west, although these have their own peculiar charm and their own distinctive interest. What I have done is to try to recapture something of the rich and varied contribution which this lovely area has made to the life, work and thought of the Church of Christ in Scotland through the centuries. That contribution has been a rich one for a district whose population can never have numbered more than a few thousands.

In the Bibliography which is given I have had to content myself, for reasons of space, with books which will be found to bear specially on the tales told here. There are other and larger works, like those of Jervise and Warden, to which I have had occasion to refer frequently. To these, at some later date, I hope to have the opportunity of introducing the reader.

D. P. THOMSON.

Barnoak,
   Crieff, Perthshire.
    *24th January, 1953.*

---

1 And on the other side of the Earn.

## CHAPTER I

# The Laird of Nether Durdie

THE road which leads up from the Carse of Gowrie to the Sidlaw parishes of Kilspindie and Kinnaird passes just below Nether Durdie, for long a small private estate. Beyond are the hamlets of Kilspindie and Rait; while tucked into a fold of the hills behind is the magnificent pile of Fingask Castle, with its extraordinary collection of statuary dotted over the far-spreading gardens, depicting well-known scenes and characters in the works of Scott and Burns. The story of the family whose stronghold this was for so long has been finely told by Robert Chambers in his *Thrieplands of Fingask*.

It was in the year 1600 that Nether Durdie came into possession of young Peter Hay, eldest son of the house of Ross, and a cadet of the famous family of which the Earl of Errol was the head, nearly all of them still Roman Catholics.

James VI was on the throne of Scotland, John Knox had been dead for nearly thirty years, and the Union of the Crowns was only three years distant. Roman Catholicism was now proscribed, but Jesuit emissaries were everywhere active, with more than one Hay in their ranks.

Religion was a living issue in these days, and a man of independent mind and means, Peter Hay was determined to find things out for himself.

"As Plato and other philosophers had travelled over the world to acquire natural knowledge, he thought it both ignominious and dangerous for him if he should not pain himself to understand the truth of God's worship." And so he set out on a pilgrimage which was to take him first to Paris, and then to "the famous city of Rome, the chiefest theatre for the knowledge of things."[1]

Paris gave him his fill of what he had so missed in Scotland — he had attended as many as twenty masses in a single week, he wrote home to tell his kinsman, Lord Errol. In Rome, however, he was not so fortunate. True, the Pope was kind and courteous, and some of the Cardinals impressed him most favourably, but what he saw of cloistral life and plenary indulgences, of pretended miracles and flaunting vice, both staggered and shook him greatly. It was a very dis-

1 Balaam's Asse.

illusioned young man who made his way back to Paris, this time to sit at the feet of Isaac Casaubon, the King's librarian and great Protestant scholar from Geneva.

From Casaubon he went to London, where James was now installed in Hampton Court Palace — " The Most High and Mighty Prince James, By The Grace of God, King of Great Britain, France and Ireland, Defender of the Faith, etc." as the dedication of the Authorised Version of the Bible describes him.

James, by " his rare and singular wit " helped to establish Peter Hay still further in his new beliefs, and the process of conversion was completed some time after his return to Scotland.

" I went," he tells us,[1] " to dwell in Dundee, for the space of two whole years, where I did most diligently hear that excellent preacher, Master David Lyndsay, and his fellow labourer in the church of that city, in whose worth, I think, doth consist no small part of the happiness thereof."

Combining the study of theology with sermon tasting, he finally " got a sure hold of the thread of God's Word, which is our only guide through this mystical pilgrimage of human follies, of which thread Christ hath left the one end here with us on earth in His Word, and hath tied the other upon the gate of heaven, which He did first open."

His quest for light and certainty at last completed, Peter Hay returned to Nether Durdie, there to compose the book by which his name will long be remembered—

*A Vision of Balaam's Asse, wherein Hee did perfectly see the present estate of the Church of Rome. Written by Peter Hay, Gentleman of North Britaine, for the Reformation of his countrymen. Specially of that true Noble and sincere Lord Francis, Earle of Errol, Lord Hay, and Great Constable of Scotland.*

Dedicated to the Archbishop of Canterbury, and prefaced by an Address to the King, it is a curious and interesting book, running to some 300 quarto pages. Beginning with " The cause of my voluntary recantation of Popery," it proceeds to " a clear discovery of the tyranny of Rome, mounted in our time to her Meridian or Altitude, and of the treacherous trade and doctrines of the Jesuits."

Most interesting of all, perhaps, is Peter Hay's explanation of how he came to choose his title. He had been accused of going abroad, like Saul of old, to bring home his father's asses. So be it ! There were only two beasts mentioned in Scripture

1 Balaam's Asse.

as possessing the faculty of speech. Rather than " the worst of beasts, the serpent, which opened its mouth to suborn impiety and rebellion against God," he would be " the best and most simple, the most excellent for natural goodness," the ass which opened its mouth to reproach sin in the prophet !

*Balaam's Asse* was not Peter Hay's sole literary production. Years later, after he had left the Braes of the Carse for the estate of Naughton, in Balmerino, Fife, he published another— *An Advertisement to The Subjects of Scotland,* which created a much greater sensation. There was dynamite in this book ! It attacked the temporal lords who had acquired Church lands since the Reformation, boldly championing the cause of the poor tenants, " who by this change are brought to as pitiful a slavery as the Israelites under Pharaoh."

One portion, entitled *Reformation of the Barre and of Advocates, how necessary,* called forth *An Apology For Advocates,* in verse, by David Primrose, and in the controversy which broke out even before the publication of the *Advertisement* the Court itself was involved.

" You shall desyre Mr. Peitter Hay of Naughton," wrote King Charles I to his representative in Scotland, under date 12th July, 1626, " to deliver his booke to be perused by the Archbishop of St. Andrews and yourself, and when ye have reformed such things as you think fitting, causse put the same to the presse and publish it."

To the end of his days Peter Hay remained a convinced Episcopalian. Coming back through England from his pilgrimage to Rome he had been greatly impressed by hearing the *Te Deum* "gravely and reverently sung" in the Cathedral Churches of England. " How others are affected, I know not," he wrote,[1] " but for myself, methinks the very celestial temple of God is brought down among us, or we in these bodies wrapt up among the seraphims, and bearing parts in the quire of heavenly soldiers."

That was in 1617, when Episcopacy was on the eve of one of its greatest triumphs in Scotland. Long after the days of the Covenanters it kept its hold along the Braes of the Carse and in the foothills of the Sidlaws.

Just beyond Nether Durdie lies the hamlet of Kilspindie, whose Castle figures in Blind Harry's narrative as the place where William Wallace, the Scottish patriot, found refuge with his mother as a boy, and from which he went to school shortly afterwards in Dundee. The minister of Kilspindie

[1] Balaam's Asse.

at the time of the Restoration of Charles II in 1660 was "Mr.
Harie " Guthrie, settled there four years previously, appointed
permanent Moderator of the Presbytery of Perth and promoted
three years afterwards to the Bishopric of Dunkeld.

It was in Kilspindie Manse that Guthrie wrote his memoirs—
*An Impartial Relaition of the Affairs of Scotland,* he styled it, and
although it is far from being that it lives to-day because of a
certain vividness in the narrative.

It was in Kilspindie Manse also that a minister of much
later late, Rev. J. M. Strachan, edited, first the poems of
Charles Spence, the stone-mason, and later the short-lived
*Carse of Gowrie Gazette, The Voices of Yesterday,* and most colour-
ful of all, *Legends and Traditions of The Western Sidlaws,* that
collection of weird tales of the district which includes The
White Lady of Fingask, The Headless Spinner of Rait, The
Veiled Woman, and The Green Serpent of Kilspindie Castle.
And it was there in the Manse that the brothers Henry and
Arthur Wotherspoon were born, whose influence on the
worship of the Scottish Church has been so vital in the present
century.

Up on the hillside between Kilspindie and Rait stands
Annat Cottage, built by Dr. Moody Stuart, the originator
and outstanding figure of the famous evangelical group to
which Robert Murray M'Cheyne and the Bonars belonged.

"The first of the band," says Dr. Adam Philip,[1] " he out-
lived its most venerable members, and was not the least
remarkable.  He travelled widely and was equally beloved
by high and low.  The Jewish Mission owes more to him than
almost to any other.—At Kuttenburg, in Bohemia, a tablet
describes him as ' truest friend of our country and our
Church.'  Few have left behind them more memorable
sayings ; none exerted a deeper influence on the ministry."

To one of Dr. Moody Stuart's sons it was given to make
a quite distinctive contribution to the religious literature
of Scotland.  *Sabbath Nichts at Pitcoonans,* says Dr. Philip,
" has a local sparkle in its very title, and *Sandy Scott's Bible
Class* and *The Better Country* have the breeziness of the Braes.
Notably fresh, full of suggestion and surprises, with fine patches
of colour, quaint, reverent, sure in touch, and marked by
insight, they are an attempt to put the stories of the Gospel
and the central truths of revelation in the language of the
people."  There could be no greater or timelier service to
the Church of Christ in Scotland than that !

1 The Evangel in Gowrie.

## CHAPTER II

# Beneath Dunsinane Hill

IT was on 20th September, 1838, that young Andrew Bonar was ordained as Assistant and Successor to the old minister of Collace—the parish whose bounds embrace both Dunsinane Hill and Dunsinane House—and it was as the dawn of a new day for that whole area of Perthshire.

"When you came among us," said the tribute paid to him at his Jubilee, "Collace, as regards spiritual life, was comparatively a desert. When you left it was like a watered garden, 'a field that the Lord had blessed.' The effects of your faithful testimony remain to this day, both in living souls and in the social and religious habits of the people."

Born in Edinburgh in 1810, the son of a well-known solicitor, Andrew Bonar was the youngest of seven boys, three of whom became distinguished ministers of the Church, his brother Horace being one of the two greatest hymn writers Scotland has produced. Dux medallist at the High School, it was at the University that he became a member of that gifted and devoted circle which included Robert Murray M'Cheyne, whose biographer he was to become, his own brother Horace, and Andrew Somerville, the great evangelist. Like Wesley at Oxford these young men gave nearly all their spare time to prayer and Bible study, and to work among the poorest and neediest of the city.

It was through the influence of James Nairne, Laird of Dunsinane, that Andrew Bonar came to Collace, a purely rural parish which crosses the main north road from Perth to Aberdeen between Balbeggie and Burrelton, and sweeps right over the high Sidlaws into the rich valleys behind.

The first Protestant minister of Collace was Rev. James Anderson, whose famous poem, *The Winter Night,* published in 1589, was dedicated to "The Richt Godlie, worshippful, and vigilante Pastor in Christ's Kyrke, John Erskine of Dun, especial Planter and Builder of Christis' Kirke within the bounds of Anguse, Mearnes, Stormont, and Gowrie."

"Simple in thought and evangelical in spirit," says Dr. Adam Philip,[1] "it was well fitted to lodge the truth in wistful minds." Andrew Bonar thought so much of it that he had it reprinted more than once.

[1] The Evangel in Gowrie.

Less than a year after his settlement the young minister was called to go off on a great adventure. Meeting him on the road one morning a farmer in the parish hailed him thus in the broadest Doric, " You'll be gaun to Pairth the daay, Mister Bonar ? " " No ! " was the startlingly unexpected reply, " I'm going to Jerusalem." It was no idle word. Along with his friend Robert Murray M'Cheyne, of St. Peter's, Dundee, and two older ministers, Dr. Black of Aberdeen and Dr. Keith of St. Cyrus, the young minister of Collace had been chosen by the General Assembly of his Church to go on a " Mission of Inquiry among the Jews in Europe and the Near East." That was one of the turning points in his life, and it left a deep mark on his future ministry.

Early in April, 1839, the four ministers set out on their long journey, the first from the Church of Scotland ever to visit the Holy Land, and it was November when they got back again, after unforgettable experiences both in Palestine and in Europe.

With him the young minister of Collace brought home not only a sheaf of memories and a stack of notes, but souvenirs of his visit that can be seen to this day in the parish. On either side of one of the west windows of the house now known as Bonarwood grow the vine and the fig tree he brought from the Holy Land, while on the stone-work itself are carved two of his favourite texts in Hebrew.

A stone from Mt. Sinai, an olive leaf from Gethsemane, a piece of desert Shittim wood, and a shell from the shores of the Lake of Galilee, were among the illustrations he used to make the scenes and incidents of the Bible live for his people, as they had come to do for him in the East in the course of that memorable tour. While he was in the Holy Land Mr. Nairne of Dunsinane had three of his pastoral letters printed, and a charming picture has come down to us of the old precentor sitting on a grassy knoll in the village reading them aloud to the people on the Sabbath evenings.

M'Cheyne and Bonar came back to Scotland to find both their churches in the midst of a great spiritual movement, William Chalmers Burns, later to go out as a missionary to China, being its instrument. For many a long day they were to rejoice in the fruits of that work. Later when they came to prepare, at the request of the Jewish Committee of their Church, the *Narrative Of A Mission of Inquiry To The Jews,* of which Bonar's proved to be the major share, they exchanged manses for a few weeks, that they might have fewer interruptions. That book had a great sale, and it still lives as one of the most vivid records of travel in the Holy Land that has been penned. The interest in work among the Jews it awakened in the Church of Scotland has been maintained almost to this day.

A year after its publication M'Cheyne's short course was run. Long afterwards Andrew Bonar's servant would tell of his last visit to Collace — the last of many such, for the two men were inseperables. " They stayed at the kirk that nicht till eleven," she would recall,[1] " The folk couldna gi'e ower listenin' and Mr. M'Cheyne couldna' gi'e ower speakin."

Andrew Bonar kept a diary for over sixty years,[2] and the entries that follow speak more eloquently than any comment.

*Saturday, March 25th, 1843.* This afternoon about five o'clock, a message has just come to tell me of Robert M'Cheyne's death. Never, never yet in my life have I felt anything like this.

*Sunday, 26th.* O, what a night was Saturday ! In coming to the town about nine, the people had met in the Church, and wished me to come up.—During prayer the cries and lamentations of the people resounded through the Church as if their hearts were bursting.

*Saturday, April 1st.* Came up again from Dundee yesterday. Such a scene as was the funeral day upon Thursday ! Crowds of people upon all sides.

*Saturday, 30th September*—Beginning to write *Robert M'Cheyne's Memoir.*

*December 23rd*—Finished my *Memoir of Robert M'Cheyne* yesterday morning.

*Monday, 4th March, 1844.* The *Memoir of Robert M'Cheyne* is just about to appear. O that it may be blessed !

*Friday, March 27th, 1846.* Received a letter to-day telling me of the blessed effects of *Robert M'Cheyne's Memoir* on one in London.—Many tokens have I received of the Lord's blessing on that book."

There lies in front of me as I write a copy of the [3]Centenary Edition of *The Memoirs and Remains of Robert Murray M'Cheyne, Minister of St. Peter's, Dundee.* " I am constantly hearing of the great good that book has been the means of doing," writes Dr. Alexander Whyte, in a preface to it, dated 28th April, 1913.

---

1 Reminiscences of Andrew A. Bonar, D.D.    2 Andrew A. Bonar, D.D.: Diary and Letters.    3 Oliphant, Anderson and Ferrier.

That was not by any means the last edition. It is still being reprinted, and has long since passed the million mark, being among the world's best sellers. No ministerial biography in the long history of the Christian Church has had so great a circulation, or has exercised so deep an influence on the lives of men everywhere. If Collace be remembered for nothing else it will live as the place where this book was written. " Its history " says the author's daughter, Marjory, " would itself fill a volume."

Robert Murray M'Cheyne died on the very eve of what came to be known as the Disruption. When the Free Church of Scotland emerged, in May, 1843, Andrew Bonar became, as his friend would have done had he lived, one of its honoured ministers, a new church being built for him in the hamlet of Kinrossie. For thirteen years more he continued in Collace, passing then to Glasgow to take over a church extension charge. In 1874 Edinburgh gave him his D.D., and four years later he became Moderator of the General Assembly of the Free Church of Scotland.

Dr. Bonar lived to be a very old man, but he never forgot Collace and he often returned to the scenes of his former labours. Here are two characteristic entries in his Diary[1]:—

*Wednesday, 18th February, 1866.* What thoughts of the past as I stood on Dunsinane Hill and then came down among the people, and at last stood where I used to pitch my tent.

*Saturday, 20th July, 1872.* At Collace last Sabbath—I had a strange mixture of feeling. In the manse, and going out into the adjoining wood, my heart was full of old memories.— I reviewed my singular privileges in former days, when I had the presence, prayers, fellowship, and loving help of such men as M'Cheyne, Burns, Milne, as well as the heavenly atmosphere of the " times of refreshing."

" Among the thatched cottages of Kinrossie, with its pretty village green and antique market cross," says his own biographer,[2] in a book which has long since made its way to the four corners of the world, "stands the Free Church of Collace. (It is now the village hall.) Not far distant, on the edge of Dunsinane Wood, is the manse (now Bonarwood). The path from the manse through the wood became a spot hallowed by prayer and communion with God." And that, as his Diary shows, was the secret of Andrew Bonar's ministry.

1 Andrew A. Bonar, D.D.: Diary and Letters.
2 Reminisences of Andrew A. Bonar, D.D.

## Chapter III

# The Lad From Pitkindie

UP in the Sidlaws, between Dunsinane and Longforgan, on which it looks down from the Braes of the Carse, lies the sequestered parish of Abernyte, only a few miles from the busy city of Dundee in which many of its people work. Here in the churchyard, not far from the entrance gate, stands a plain slab of sandstone bearing one of the most remarkable inscriptions to be found anywhere in Scotland, an inscription that has perhaps no parallel as the record of a good man's life in all its outlines.

" Rev. William Ross," it reads, " eldest son of Robert Ross and Grace Weir, Agent of the London Missionary Society in South Africa. He began his career a farm servant. At the age of 21 he became a joiner ; at 30 he entered college and after full study was at 38 ordained a minister and appointed to Foreign Service. Ere long with the same tools as he had executed the finest of the woodwork in the Parish Church of Errol he erected at Taung a temple to the Living God, which he afterwards filled with worshippers. He laboured unceasingly for 23 years in the vast desert amongst abounding perils and died at Likatbong 30th July, 1865, at the age of 61 deeply lamented by the Bechuanas, the L.M. Society and by the friends of missions. He left 731 church members, 83 enquirers after salvation, 376 scholars and 11 native teachers.

> Not unto me, O God, not unto me
> But unto Thy name give glory."

That is a story that will bear telling in somewhat greater detail !

William Ross was born in the Parish of Errol in the month of August, 1802, a son of the soil, his father a capable man, his mother a good woman, the teaching of church and school being well supported by his home training. While he was still a child the family moved to Fife, but the sojourn there was a short one. Recrossing the Tay his father settled as a grieve on a farm in the Parish of Abernyte and it was there, in the heart of the Sidlaws, that young William grew up. "Nothing," says his biographer,[1] "delighted him more than

1 Quoted by Adam Philip—The Evangel in Gowrie.

to help his father, and there was nothing he touched in which he did not excel."

His parents belonged to the Secession Church, and the branch with which they had identified themselves was known as the " Burgher," being the smaller but more forward-looking of the two sections into which the followers of the Erskines had divided. The church at which the family worshipped was that of Pitrodie, a few miles along the foothills, in the Parish of Kilspindie.

For thirteen years, the people had been without a pastor. It was with the coming of William Proudfoot, when young Ross was eleven years old, that the little Burgher Kirk entered on the one great chapter of its history.

William Ross was approaching the most impressionable age of life when Proudfoot began his ministry, and it was not surprising that the preaching at Pitrodie moved the young lad greatly. It was when working in the field one day that he became quite overpowered at the thought of the love of Christ to him. " I came to the Saviour at 16." he wrote more than forty years afterwards from Africa,[1] "and I do not remember of ever since having doubted my interest in His atoning blood, and I am now, through God's infinite mercy, 60 years of age."

Young Ross's education had been of the scantiest, and the family resources were limited, but in spite of that he made up his mind to be a minister. Learning a trade would make it easier for him to pay his way, and so, at the age of 21, he left the plough and became apprentice to a joiner in Perth. Long afterwards in Africa he was to turn to good account both his knowledge of farm work and of carpentry. It was with great delight he used to tell, in his closing years, of how he had built the church at Taung entirely with the tools he had learned to use in Errol.

A lover of nature, a diligent student in his leisure hours, an active Sunday School teacher, and a faithful attender at the weekly prayer meeting at Pitrodie or in Perth, his thoughts were now beginning to turn to missionary work overseas. His first step was to become a teacher, and one of his friends has described how he came one day to the door of the little parish school in which he taught and offered to help all day in return for being coached in Latin and Greek at night. Later, with a friend and fellow student, he was

1 The Evangel in Gowrie.

to open an " Academy " in Inverness and to teach there for some years.

" We managed," says Ross,[1] " to defray expenses—I think our yearly income of £70 each was creditable.  With that and the £100 I had stored in the bank from my hard-won savings previously, and a small bursary I had received during my third year in St. Andrews, I have not come on my kind parents for my training, but have been able, I am thankful to say, to pay all myself."

Ross was 30 when he entered St. Andrews University, going from there at the close of his Arts course to the Divinity Hall of what was now the United Secession Church, where, under men like John Brown and Robert Balmer, he had five more years of preparation for his lifework.  A further year in Arts followed at London, and then, in 1840, he presented himself for licence as a probationer of his Church.

Robert Moffat, the famous pioneer missionary of South Africa, was at home on furlough then, and William Ross went to hear him.  Thrilled by the tale he had to tell, and deeply moved by the appeal he made, the Abernyte man offered his services as a missionary for Africa.  It was a chilling reception he met with, however, when he got back to Perthshire.  The family were not pleased !  They felt he was throwing his life away, and they professed to be more than doubtful if he were capable of learning Sechuana at 38.   But Ross was adamant, his mind was made up, and he knew well what he could do.  At the request of old Mr. Wilson the Parish Minister, he preached in the Parish Kirk of Abernyte on one of the Sundays before he left home.  It was a great assembly that gathered that day to hear " The Ploughboy of Pitkindie."

It was on the evening of 20th Nov., 1840, that two young men were solemnly ordained and set apart for service in South Africa under the auspices of the London Missionary Society, in the historic Albion Chapel, Finsbury, London. One of them was William Ross and the other was David Livingstone, destined to become more widely known and honoured, perhaps, than any Scotsman who has ever lived. Three weeks later they sailed together from Gravesend in the good ship *George* for Cape Town and Algoa Bay, carrying with them for Robert Moffat, who was to become Livingstone's father-in-law, 500 Sechwana New Testaments.

They landed at Simon's Bay, on 15th March, 1841, and made straight for Cape Town, 28 miles distant.  There in the home of Dr. John Philip, the Kirkcaldy man who superintended the work of the L.M.S. in South Africa, they were to spend their first weeks in Africa.

The two young men went up country together to Kuruman, where Moffat was, arriving on 31st July, 1841, and there they parted, never to meet again. Four and a half months later Ross was able to report that he could now speak Sechwana, and later he was appointed by the L.M.S. as Chairman of a Committee to revise the Sechwana Bible. So much for the fears of those who thought he would never learn the language !

Settling at Taung, 100 miles north of Kuruman, he had first to face the erection of a church. " The few lessons in drawing he had got at Collace School," says his biographer,[1] " enabled him to sketch what he had conceived. His skill as a carpenter helped him in his measurements and building. His knowledge of mechanics gave him skill with all sorts of tools." And so, with little aid from anyone, apart from a few women who helped with the carrying, and with Ross himself as " architect, quarryman, mason, sawyer, wright, glazier, thatcher, smith," in an amazingly short time the building was completed, the next thing being to fill it.

At the first Communion there sat down seven who had been naked savages when he came, and through all the years that followed he carried on a work among Chief Mahura's people that grew steadily in size, in usefulness, and in power, moving with them when they trekked to new territory, and beginning all over again the labour of building another church and manse.

At home in Scotland he was not forgotten. One congregation sent him a bell for his church, another undertook the support of a native teacher. Friends in many places contributed boxes for his work, and Lord Kinnaird supported him gladly with gifts both of seeds and of money.

William Ross never returned home. He had given his life to Africa, and in Africa he stayed. " The more we saw of him " wrote Mary Moffat in an early letter home, "the better we liked him. A hard-working, plodding man, itinerating seemed to be his forte."

He died on 31st July, 1863, worn out by ceaseless toil. William Ross was not a Livingstone, but he was of the stuff of which great missionaries and faithful workers in every field are made. Abernyte will do well to remember him.

1 Quoted in The Evangel in Gowrie.

## CHAPTER IV

# In the Taxwood Succession

"IT was not in the Highlands," says Dr. Ross Macduff,[1] introducing the district to the world, in one of the last of his many books, " it was not in the Lowlands that the Parish of Taxwood was situated. A sort of hybrid it was, with both features combined. There was no village either, in the larger sense of that word, but rather a hamlet, striking and picturesque for no other reason than on account of its simplicity. Except in two instances slated roofs were not to be seen to mar the unity of the thatched cottages, which clustered on either side of a winding road.—The distant view, only here and there obtained by glimpses, was terminated by a background of hills neither conspicuous in size nor artistic in outline, while the intervening portion was agreeably studded with bits of arable ground, tidy homesteads, trimly cut hedgerows, and, here and there, groups of old trees."

" For rural simplicity and artless loveliness," says a later writer describing Kettins, which is the real name of the village and parish, " it cannot be surpassed, the neatly kept cottages with their pretty flower gardens adding to Nature's beauty. The village green in the centre forms the field of many an innocent amusement ; the Church looks out from its belt of trees, and the manse nestling close below, with its peaceful shelter of yew trees, all embosomed in a magnificent wood.

" Serene, sequestered and supremely sweet,
For dreamy poet's habitation meet :
In tender beauty, peacefulness and ease,
With soft-murmuring stream and whispering trees :
Fair Kettins, Nature hath bestowed on thee
Such gifts as only for her favourite be ! "

Thus sings Henry Dryere, who knew and loved this district so well.

It was to this quiet spot, just on the eve of the Disruption, that John Ross Macduff came to begin his long and distinguished ministry in the Church of Scotland.

" In the course of the year 1842," he tells us, in his *Reminiscences*,[2] " I was licensed as a Probationer by the

---

1 The Parish of Taxwood and Some of its Older Memories (1883).
2 The Author of "Morning and Night Watches:" Reminiscences of a Long Life; edited by his Daughter (1896.)            13

Presbytery of Perth, and preached my first sermon in the Parish Church of Coupar Angus.—One summer day a year and a half before, I was stretched on a wooded bank overlooking the Forth, in company with two College friends and aspirants to the ministry. Our conversation, as is not uncommon in youth, turned on the possibilities of the future, and the idea suggested itself of naming any particular parish in Scotland for which each of us would have an individual and distinct preference.—I was not long in announcing my own."

" This day-dream " he goes on to say, " in the good providence of God turned out to be singularly prophetic. Eye and heart wandered to enchanted ground well-known to me, for it was within walking distance of my grandfather's home, Balgersho. By a happy combination of circumstances this happy haunt of memory became my own, and towards the end of the year I was presented by the Crown to the rural parish of Kettins in Forfarshire."

" To the charm of outer nature " says the veteran looking back across the years, "was added, in a remarkable degree, an important element, and one not always found conjoined with the other—that of the villagers themselves. I think I see now the old men in their homespun, and the old women in their tartan shawls and " subachs," seated, some on the score of deafness, on the pulpit stairs—I can vouch for the bulk being most interested and attentive hearers. The aged cottagers delighted and surprised me often during the week with their intelligent resume of the Sunday's sermon, not at all abashed to point out, in their own respectful way, any departure from the old Boston theology."[1]

The ministry which began so happily, and with such very real promise, might well have continued indefinitely but for the sudden and tragic death of the young wife of the manse. Left alone with his poignant memories at the age of 28, Macduff found the idea of a change growing on him, and when a call came to the Parish of St. Madoes, just across the hills, in the Carse of Gowrie, he was tempted to accept it. Often in later years his thoughts were to go back to Kettins, and in the months immediately following his departure there were moments not a few when he regretted the step he had taken. " Nice in their way," the parishioners of St. Madoes had not " the same primitive interest as those on the other side of the Sidlaws."[1]

One thing, however, he could and would do—that was to send a little souvenir in the shape of a printed message to the head of every family in his old parish. It would be something by which they could recall their young minister in the years to come.

" I thought it might be well," he tells us,[1] " to cast it in the shape of a few words for daily reading. That was the origin of *The Faithful Promiser,* the speedy and almost immediate sale of which, extending to hundreds of thousands, almost frightened me. That little volume seemed at once to point to what I afterwards called my special *niche* in the temple.—I obeyed the call. *The Morning and Night Watches,* the circulation of which may at this time be reckoned at half a million, was the first to follow."

" If " said Professor Charteris, long afterwards, " I were cast on a desert island with only one book in addition to my Bible, I should wish it to be the volume containing *The Faithful Promiser* and *The Morning and Night Watches.*" Coming from the founder of the Woman's Guild and Life and Work Committee Convener of the Church, who did so much to shape its policy in the latter half of the 19th century, there could be no higher tribute.

Dr. Macduff's later career was a very distinguished one, but the man himself counted for more than any of his achievements. " Of all men living or dead," said Dr. George Matheson, the blind poet preacher,[2] " he is the one who has influenced me most powerfully. He gave me my first sense of literary beauty, my first impression of oratory, my first idea of sanctity, my first real conviction of the beauty of Christianity. The tones of his voice are even now unconsciously reproduced in my own. I have retained more of his pulpit influence than that of any other teacher."

It was John Tulloch who succeeded Macduff in the Parish of Taxwood " a locality always dear to him," says Mrs. Oliphant, his biographer,[3] "in which he had family connections, and to which throughout his life, his thoughts went back tenderly."

Coming from a busy and exacting city parish in Dundee it gave this future leader of the Church of Scotland, " peaceful leisure in which to carry out many plans which were impossible amid all the interruptions of a minister's life in town. It extended his circle of friends, it widened his horizon.—The rural Church, the quiet country folk, the silence of the fields,

1 Reminicences.          2 Dr. Macmillan—The Life of George Matheson, D.D.
          3 Mrs Oliphant—Memoir of Principal Tulloch.

the homely pleasant house—were all delightful to the young pair, who found their manse a kind of paradise after the noise and tumult of Dundee."[1]

Tulloch was a shrewd observer, and his estimate of his parishioners was somewhat different to that of his predecessor. " There is a great deal of religiousness about some of the old bodies of cottagers," he wrote to his friend Smith. " I must know more of them before I can exactly say whether it amounts to religion. I doubt not, however, there are good humble souls among them." Four years later his verdict was more decisive. " I cannot say I find real religion and morality at all more prevalent in the country than in the town," he tells the same correspondent, " even in such a quiet and completely rural parish as this. Theological ideas are more current, but there seems a sad want of religious apprehension, above all of self-denying Christian practice. Life and doctrine band very loosely together, and this seems to me the black stain on all our Scottish Christianity."

Tulloch, like his predecessor, was a writer, but unlike him it was in Kettins itself that he began to employ his pen to some purpose, winning a prize essay that brought a substantial increase to the small stipend and making his name by articles in many of the leading journals. It was all a preparation for the part he was later to play—as Principal of St. Mary's College, St. Andrews, as Moderator of the General Assembly, and as the acknowledged leader of his Church in a difficult age.

In everything his young wife was his eager and intelligent helpmeet, and Mrs. Oliphant[1] paints a delightful picture of life in the manse at Taxwood, where the literary succession was being so well maintained.—" The evening scene near the fireside in the little study, when the children were asleep, and the young mother free to take her share of the work, copying in her more legible handwriting the sheets which in their original form would have daunted the most courageous examiner—her ear ever alert to a murmur from the little cribs above."

" He was still under thirty, she was twenty six—a pair formed for all the enjoyments of life, young in heart as well as in age, fond of all simple pleasures. One wonders if any circumstances of ease, or wealth, or gaiety, or all that makes up what in other spheres is called life, could have embodied a greater happiness or afforded a more beautiful spectacle than these laborious nights and days."

1 Mrs Oliphant—Memoir of Principal Tulloch.

## CHAPTER V

# A Child of Sir Walter's

ON the outskirts of Newtyle, not far from Kinpurnie Castle, stands the building known to-day as the Bannatyne Home of Rest.

" This House of Bannatyne " reads the memorial plaque outside, " founded 1560, was in 1892 acquired by Ex-Provost Alexander Hay Moncur and Mrs. Moncur and by them generously devoted and lastingly set apart and endowed as a Women's Home of Rest."

Let the visitor ask to be shown round and he will eventually be conducted to a small room in the tower, now used as a cupboard, where one of the most famous literary undertakings in the history of this country was carried out, in the grim year of the plague in the latter half of the seventeenth century.

" Few turrets of time-worn towers," says[1] Dr. William Marshall, in his *Historic Scenes In Forfarshire*,[1] "have been so honoured. Hundreds of them have been polluted with blood, and made famous by crime ; while the turret of Bannatyne House is only tarnished by unexampled poetical and literary devotion."

It is Sir Walter Scott himself who tells the story, in one of the many famous books issued by the Bannatyne Club of which he was the founder, and in whose pioneer work he took such an interest and a pride.

Born in Edinburgh on 22nd February, 1545 — the year of the Battle of Ancrum Moor, when Mary, Queen of Scots was three years old — George Bannatyne was the son of an Edinburgh lawyer, the seventh of his twenty-three children, his father being the proprietor of what was then known as Kirktown of Newtyle, a small estate at the foot of the Sidlaws.

When George was 27 his father presented him with a tenement in Leith and he set up in business for himself. Five years later he was made a Merchant and Guild Burgess of Edinburgh, and very quickly he acquired a considerable fortune. Meanwhile his eldest brother, now a Lord of the Court of Session, had succeeded to the Sidlaw property, taking Lord Newtyle as his title.

It was when the plague broke out in Edinburgh that George retired to his brother's house at Newtyle, there to carry out the great design with which its name will always be linked.

"In this dreadful period," says Sir Walter,[1] "when hundreds, finding themselves surrounded by danger and death, renounced all care save selfish concern for their safety, George Bannatyne had the courageous energy to form and execute the plan of saving the literature of a whole nation, and undisturbed by the universal mourning for the dead, and general fears for the living, to devote himself to the task of collecting and recording the triumphs of human genius ; thus amid the wreck of all that was material, employing himself by preserving the lays by which immortality is at once given to others and obtained by the writer himself."

The task he set himself was a colossal one. "The very labour of procuring originals," says Sir Walter, "must have been attended by trouble and risk at a time when all the usual intercourse of life was suspended. "He had to contend with old and mutilated copies, many of them well-nigh indecipherable, while the vast mass of material he accumulated had to be carefully examined and classified, and then laboriously copied out by hand" in a book which was to run to 800 pages.

"Ane most godlie mirrie and lustie Rapsodie maide be sundrie learned Scots poets and written by George Bannatyne in the tyme of his youth," was the way in which he himself described his work, and in six lines of poetry he has given us the system of classification and arrangement he adopted.

The book was to be divided into five sections :—

"The first conceirnes Godis gloir and our salvatioun ;
The next are morale, greve and als besyd it ;
Ground on gude counsale the third, I will not hyd it,
Or blytt and galid maid for our concollatioun ;
The ferd of luve and thair richt reformatioun ;
The fyift of tailis and stories weill disydit."

Of the poems here collected, including much of the best of Henryson, Dunbar, Sir David Lyndsay and Alexander Scott, which would otherwise have perished, Sir Walter has this to say[1]— "The insight they afford respecting the manners of Scotland at that early period is as valuable to the historian and antiquary as the poetical merit renders them to readers of taste and judgment. — It serves to show," he concludes, "how much the patience and energy of one individual, directed

---

by taste and good sense, was able to achieve for the preservation of the poetry of a nation within the limited space of three months."

Now in the Advocates' Library in Edinburgh, the MS. was printed in full by the Glasgow Hunterian Club many years ago for the benefit of its members. It remains to-day the most valuable source book we have for the period with which it deals.

It was in 1823 that Sir Walter Scott took the initiative in founding the Bannatyne Club, the object being to carry on, on a wider scale, the work which had been begun in Newtyle 250 years before. The aim of the Club was to be the printing of rare works illustrative of Scottish history, topography, poetry and miscellaneous literature, bound in a uniform and handsome manner, either at the general expense or at that of individual members. He himself became its first President, David Laing of the Signet Library was long its indefatigable Secretary, and among those most intimately associated with the venture were men like Lords Cockburn and Rutherford, Archibald Constable, the publisher, Francis Jeffrey, the Earl of Aberdeen, the Marquis' of Lothian, and the Dukes of Buccleuch, Hamilton and Gordon.

Originally intended to consist of 31 members, paying an annual subscription of five guineas each, the Bannatyne Club had to be enlarged to 100, so great was the pressure of eminent men in every walk of life anxious to join it. The Club printed in all 116 works, some of them as valuable as they are rare, and its annual dinner was one of the social events of the Edinburgh season, enlivened as it was by the presence of the leading wits of the capital and of the most eminent literary men in the Scotland of that day.

In the last edition of his poems will be found the Club song composed by Sir Walter, to be sung at its first annual dinner, by James Bannatyne, a namesake and descendant of the original George.

> " Assist me, ye friends of old books and old wine,
> To sing in the praises of sage Bannatyne,
> Who left such a treasure of old Scottish lore,
> As enables each age to print one volume more,
> One volume more, my friends, one volume more,
> We'll ransack old Banny for one volume more."

The first two publications of the Club were the *Lives of The Bishops of Dunkeld,* and among the volumes it made available for scholars everywhere, and ultimately for the general public, through the medium of the libraries, were *James Melvill's Diary, Alexander Hume's Hymns and Sacred Songs; The Letters and Journals of Robert Baillie* (the Covenanter); *The Collected Works of John Knox; Spottiswood's History of The Church of Scotland,* in three volumes; *Acts and Proceedings of the General Assemblies of the Kirk of Scotland from the Year MDLX;* and *Adamnan's Life of St. Columba.*

That was as it should have been, for the motive that had animated George Bannatyne was a high one, and the lines with which he had finished his great task at Newtyle were these :—

> " Here endes this buik, writt in tyme of pest,
> Quhen we frae labor was compeled to rest,
> Swa till conclude, God grant us all gude end,
> And aftir death eternall lyfe us sende."

Not only the Bannatyne Club, but the many others it sired or inspired — like the Maitland, the Spalding, and the Abbotsford — have enriched our common heritage in the history and literature of Scotland. They have helped us to understand better the part our Church has played and may yet play, in the life of the nation, and have made us aware in a new way of what is fundamental and abiding in the great traditions of our people.

To-day Bannatyne House carries on the work for which its purchasers designed it in 1892. A jute manufacturer himself, it was the wish of Ex-Lord Provost Moncur and his wife that this historic building, so beautifully situated at the foot of the Sidlaws, might, under its new constitution,[1] " enable working women employed in Dundee and the district to obtain, at moderate rates, the benefits of quiet rest, wholesome nourishment, bracing air, and cheerful surroundings," and so " recruit the health and strength necessary to enable them to follow their usual occupation."

That hope has been abundantly fulfilled, and when the Home celebrated its Jubilee, on 21st July, 1942, there was a great gathering of friends and well-wishers from a very wide area, a memorial tree being planted in the grounds by Miss Methven of Baldowrie, to commemorate the occasion.

1 Constitution of the Bannatyne Home of Rest, Newtyle.

CHAPTER VI.

# Eighteenth Century Auchterhouse

IT is to the pen of W. Mason Inglis,[1] a later minister of the parish, that we owe a graphic description of eigthteenth-century Auchterhouse, and of the part played by the Church in the life of that rural community.

When the century opened William of Orange had been on the throne of Great Britain for eleven years, Presbyterianism had been restored for a decade as the national form of religion north of the Tweed, and the ill-fated Darien Expedition had just taken place. Succeeding her father in 1702, Queen Anne was to see the Parliaments of England and Scotland united, as the kingdoms themselves had been a hundred years before, and was to rejoice in the series of brilliant victories gained by her arms on land and sea during what has come to be known as " The War of the Spanish Succession."

James VII, the last of the Stuart Kings, had died in exile, but within a year of the accession of George I thousands of Scots-men were to lay down their lives in an attempt to put his son, " The Old Pretender " on the throne, and Auchterhouse, as much as any place, was to feel the impact of that 1715 Rebellion.

The population of the parish was then about 600; the people lived for the most part in rude clay biggin's, roughly compact of boulders, paving slabs, divots, and coarse timber, and the highways were bridle paths and drove roads, traversible on foot or by ponies. There was no minister in Auchterhouse, and no Kirk Session ; the Church itself was in a dilapidated state, and the parish in a deplorable condition. Wages were miserable, and life on the tiny allotments and farms was a constant wearing struggle, with grim poverty, and even famine, never very far away. From 1693 to the beginning of the century, Dundee and the whole district round it had suffered from what was known as " The seven years' dearth."

The first steps to appoint a minister for Auchterhouse were taken by the United Presbyteries of Dundee, Meigle and Forfar, and the man of their choice, Patrick Johnstone, was one whom they themselves had licensed six months before the new century began. It was " Att Auchterhouse, 29th

December, 1702," that the ordination took place, and on the following Sunday the new minister preached and lectured for the first time, the collection amounting to 12s. 4d. Scots, or just over 1s. sterling. It was not always to be as much as that !

The church of that day had no pews, no flooring but the soil, with perhaps a thin covering of rushes or heather, no lighting except from small windows partially fitted with glass, and no heating of any kind whatever. Its interior was damp, cold and uninviting, and beneath its earthen floor all who could afford it were in the habit of burying their dead. Funerals required the presence of the beadle as well as the minister, and from the hire of the " mort cloth " which covered the coffin the Kirk Session derived a considerable revenue, an income for which it depended for the replenishmen of its Poor Fund.

There was no Session when Rev. Patrick Johnstone was inducted, and one of his first tasks was to secure elders. Without these the work of the parish could not be carried on at all, for elders then " were entrusted with the entire affairs of the parish. They formed the local authority, and not much was done without their counsel. They were the administrators of church discipline, the local board of supervision, the local magistrates and police, and the parish school board."

Discipline was, of course, a very important part of the elder's duties, and for the offenders with whom they had to deal—for failure to observe the Sabbath, for breaches of the moral law, for drunkenness, brawling, swearing and other unseemly behaviour, the services of the beadle were in constant requisition. It was he who kept the " jougs," or clasped padlocked collars ready for use, and had by him " a strong pair of branks, with a good tongue for silencing parish gossips, flyters, and local pests, and a linen sheet in which to array penitents ! There was also a tar brush in the background, which had a great reputation as a deterrent in this part of Angus," and when delinquents took their stand on " The Pillar," in front of the minister and the congregation at the Sunday service, to be made the subject of the " Wee Sermon," a scathing indictment they would not readily forget, " the beddal was in close proximity, kept his eye steadily on the offender, and had his staff ready for any symptoms of outbreak, levity, or misconduct."

It was the elders who were responsible for the collections, taken up, of course, in the old-fashioned ladles. After locking

up the collections in the strong box which they kept, for
which each elder had a key—and which required two keys
for its opening—they were required to sally out and make a
house-to-house visitation of the parish between services to
make sure that no one missed the afternoon diet of worship,
and to clear out the taverns in which not a few of the congregation might be enjoying, at too great leisure, their " cakes,
cheese and twopenny ale."

As the minister's right-hand men, they were required to
see that family worship was maintained in every home, and
that all heads of households who could read had supplied
themselves at least with copies of the Larger and Shorter
Catechisms and of the Westminster Confession of Faith.

It was the elders who supervised the school and paid the
schoolmaster, ill-remunerated as he was, his schoolroom in
his house " a miserable hovel of divots, with nothing but an
earthen floor, the fire maintained by the scholars bringing
peats for the purpose. If there were no peats forthcoming
there was no fire."

" The Session," we read, under date Jan. 5, 1708, " took
into their serious consideration the case and present circumstanc
of Mr. John Pitcairn, their schoolmaster, who is much dis-
couraged by the long distressed case of his family and the
smallness of his sellarie in the place, being only £24 Scots
(£2 Stg) and Four Pound (6s. 8d.) Clerk fie, payed wholly
by the Session, and a week on the ploughs of the parish, and
nothing paid by the heritors." The Schoolmaster's salary
was unanimously raised to £3 yearly !

It was upon the elders that the care of the poor and the
needy devolved, and just what this meant can best be shown
by one or two typical extracts from the Kirk Session records—

" There was given to Christian Biddie, a poor child, to
buy her shoues, 10d. Mistress Robertson, a minister's relict,
received from the Church box, 10d. To a dumb supplicat, 6d.
To two distressed families who lost all by the wreck going to
Virginia, 1s. 6d. Given to James Graham, an honest man
distressed and his family in Burntisland, upon ample certificat,
1s. 6d. To Robert Fraser, under gravel, 6d. To two broken
maimed seamen, 6d. To James Johnston, old, decrepit, and
troubled with the gravell, 1s. To two merchants shipwrackt,
6d. To James Brown, idiotish, in Kirriemuir, 6d. To two
gentlewomen, distressed, come from Ireland, 1s. ;  to ane

Campbell, under a sad epileptic, upon testificat, 1s., to James Jameson, a blind and honest man, 1s."

Sometimes the sum is larger—the need being greater and the case regarded as more deserving, such as these—" Given by the unanimous consent of the Session to James Christie, in Kirktoun, having a poor, small family, to help him buy a cow, 5s." " Given to Jean Watson, to bear her charges to the Infirmary at Edinburgh, 12s." " To George Watson, for board and instruction in music for his blind son, now attending a musician in Dundee, £4. To the Presbyetry bursar, 6s. 8d."

These, after all, were but doles, and there were cases that only a special collection would meet. And so we read—

" Nov. 27, 1709—That day Her Majesty's Proclamation was read and intimat anent a contribution to relieve the people in the Canongate of Edinburgh, who had their houses demolished and their effects consumed by an accidental fire— Collect, 5s.

Aug. 1, 1718—This day an Address was made by the distressed Protestants of Lithuania in Poland, and ane Act of Assembly appointing a voluntary contribution for their relief was intimat from the pulpit.

Sabbath, 15th March, 1719—The Minister intimat from the pulpit a voluntary contribution to be collected next Sabbath at the church door as ane help " to George Webster, to pay Mr. Smith of Perth for cutting his son of the stone gravel."

The collection was £1 Stg., and a recommendation was made to the Ministers of Lundie, Liff and Benvie, Longforgan, Inchture, Kinnaird and Abernyte to contribute for him in their several parishes. It was in this way that the folk in the Carse and the Sidlaws sought to help one another in a day when charitable provisions were so few, resources so scanty, and needs so many and so varied.

Collections there were during these years for objects so diverse as the erection of a place of worship at Kintail in Strathnaver; the Society for Propagating Christian Knowledge Through The Highlands and Islands; the distressed Protestants of Copenhagen, who had lost their homes in a great fire; the redemption of a slave in Algiers; the building of a bridge at Glenesk; and innumerable other objects, so widely did the interests of the good folks of Auchterhouse range, and so willing were they to help those in need despite the abounding poverty and distress around their own door. And in the giving, as always, they gained.

CHAPTER VII

# The Case of Mr. John Glas

APART from the case of Mr. John Glas, it has been said the Parish of Tealing has no history. The verdict may be disputed, but it was certainly Mr. Glas who put Tealing on the map, both for Scotland as a whole and for many beyond its borders.

Tealing lies on the southern slopes of the Sidlaws, just below the water-shed. Looking down on Dundee, its parish church is less than seven miles from the city. To this quiet spot there came as minister, in the year 1719, a young man who was destined to make history, and who was to give his name to a religious denomination as distinctive as any Scotland has known.

Born at Auchtermuchty, in Fife, on 5th October, 1695, John Glas belonged to a Perthshire family with a record in the ministry stretching back to the Reformation. Brought up at Kinclaven, in Perthshire, to which his father had been translated in 1700, he was educated first at the village school and then at the Grammar School in Perth. Graduating from St. Andrews University on 6th May, 1713, he passed to Edinburgh for the study of theology and philosophy, and in due course was licensed by the Presbytery of Dunkeld, within whose bounds Kinclaven then lay.

Right from the beginning of his ministry it was evident that he was a man who would take nothing for granted. Seven years before his settlement the Covenants had been solemnly renewed in the presence of a vast assemblage at Auchensaugh in the uplands of Lanarkshire. Here in his own parish of Tealing there was a " Cameronian " element determined to make things very uncomfortable for any young minister departing in any way from the strictest traditions of " the fathers." It was the constant pinpricking of these same " Cameronians " or extreme Covenanters that sent John Glas back to his New Testament, determined to probe this question to the roots.

The conclusions to which he came were startling. He could find no warrant at all for the commonly accepted identification of Church and State. That was something which belonged

25

essentially to the Jewish dispensation of the Old Testament, where to be a member of the one was necessarily to be a member of the other. Now it was entirely different ! The Church which Christ had founded was a purely spiritual fellowship. It had no connection whatever with the Kingdoms of this world. Nor had a magistrate any right to punish men for heresy. The only reformation for which the New Testament gave sanction was one carried out by spiritual, and not by political or physical, weapons.

For John Glas to believe a thing was to preach it, and soon the countryside was resounding with the dangerous heresies of the young minister of Tealing. It was his own father who told him that he was at once " an Independent and an Ishmaelite, whose hand would be against every man, and every man's hand against him." And it was his father-in-law who pointed out that he would find this a very unpopular doctrine, and that the kind of communion at which he aimed was a thing wholly unattainable. To this John Glas's answer was that " If he should get but a dozen shepherds at the foot of Seidla-hill to consort with in the love of the truth, he would be happy."

It was to be very much more than a dozen, however ! Opposition he met with, of the most bitter and virulent kind from many in his own congregation, but people began coming to him from all the surrounding districts, drawn partly by the power of his preaching and partly by the attractiveness to them of the doctrines he set forth, and it was on 12th July, 1725, that he took the decisive step of forming them into a fellowship. From that time onwards he was virtually minister of two congregations, the people of the parish over whom he had been set at his ordination, and this miscellaneous group he had now gathered round him, and in the leadership of which he was associated with Rev. Francis Archibald, Minister of Guthrie, in whose parish a similar ferment was at work.

The group at Tealing numbered about 100, and beginning with a monthly celebration of the Lord's Supper, instead of the very occasional observance then common, they went on to introduce, one after another, what they and their leader came to believe were not only valid but binding New Testament practices. These in time were to include the refusal to partake of things strangled, or of blood, the greeting of one another with a holy kiss, the washing of one another's feet, and the institution of a weekly " Love Feast," supplementary to the Lord's Supper. "The Kail Kirk," wits were later to christen the followers of John Glas, because of this practice !

It soon became obvious that, first the Presbytery of Dundee, and later the Synod of Angus and Mearns, would have to take action with regard to what was happening at Tealing. The case dragged on for three years, partly because of unwillingness to act harshly towards a young man held in as high respect as Mr. Glas was, and partly because of the difficulty of obtaining witnesses. Eventually, however, sentences of suspension and deposition were successively passed, and Mr. Glas, who had occupied for so long a completely anomalous position, found himself no longer a minister of the Church of Scotland.

For a time he continued in Tealing, and there are extant in Glasgow Communion Cups which bear the inscription — " This belongs to the Congregational Church at Tealing." Dundee, however, was obviously a better centre, and it was to the city that Mr. Glas and his growing family removed. The church his followers built there is still standing, and above the entry at No. 4 King Street the passer-by may note the words " Glasite Church " carved clearly. A furniture store to-day, the old building behind boasts an immense mural painting depicting the founder of the new denomination saying farewell to his manse in the Sidlaws. That, be it noted, was commissioned by the new proprietor after the Glasite Church itself had ceased to be.

From Dundee the new body spread rapidly. Adopting the principle of a dual ministry, with no distinction observed between preaching and ruling elder, it laid hands on men as various as a glover and a banker, ordaining them to its highest office without any course of training other than that which the whole fellowship enjoyed. Perth, Edinburgh and Dunkeld were occupied very early in the movement ; and Paisley, Leith, Arbroath, Montrose, Aberdeen, Leslie, Cupar and Galashiels were among the places to follow. In London and Liverpool, in Nottingham and Swansea, and in many other centres south of the Border the Glasite Church took root, and in the person of Robert Sandeman, Glas's son-in-law, and by far the most outstanding of its younger leaders, it passed over later to the United States, where in the course of years even greater extremes of doctrine were to develop.

John Glas lived to be an old man, and although his followers never numbered more than a thousand or two at the most, they included in their ranks not a few of wealth and culture. Michael Faraday, the great scientist, was for long an elder of the Church in London, and ministers of at least four denominations resigned their charges to throw in their lot with the new body.

Dying in Dundee in November, 1773, Glas was buried in the old " Howff" Cemetery. " Minister of the Congregational Church in this place," reads the epitaph on his tombstone, " he long survived Katherine Black, his beloved wife (interred also in the same grave) also of his children, fifteen in number, many of whom arrived at mature age, and nine lie here beside their parents. His character in the churches of Christ is well known, and will outlive all monumental inscriptions."

It is pleasing to be able to record that the Synod of Angus, which had moved for his deposition, successfully petitioned the General Assembly 12 years later to have that sentence lifted, and his ministerial status recognised, though not in the Church of Scotland ; and that the city of Dundee, in which he had so long made his home, elected him an honorary burgess.

If the movement he launched is to-day a spent force, and the books and pamphlets which poured forth from his pen for more than forty years moulder to dust on the shelves of the reference libraries, his influence lives on in directions he would never have looked for. The Glasite Church itself died because of its narrowness of outlook, its slavish literalism, its harsh and pettifogging discipline and its complete lack of missionary spirit; but, as their own historians have testified, the Congregational and Baptist Churches, the "Relief" denomination among Presbyterians, the " Plymouth " Brethren and other smaller bodies, owe to the pioneer work and preaching of the deposed minister of Tealing much of what is most distinctive alike in their doctrine and in their practice.

In the pages of our Scottish Church history John Glas will live as the first " Voluntary " and the first " Independent " ; and as the man who recalled a generation in danger of being in thrall to the immediate past, to fresh appraisement of what its Church really stood for in the light of the teaching of Christ Himself. That was no mean achievement !

## Chapter VIII

# Those Maidens of the Glen

THERE are few more romantic spots in the Sidlaws than Glen Ogilvy, down which the Glamis Burn flows from the hills above Auchterhouse to join the Dean in the policies of the old Castle.

It was here, according to legend, that William The Lion encountered Gilchrist, son of the second Earl of Angus, outlawed because of the murder of his wife, the King's daughter; and, gratified by his frank confession and genuine contrition, not only pardoned him but bestowed on him the lands of Glen Ogilvy, then a royal estate.

It was here that Viscount Claverhouse — " Bonnie Dundee " — fearless soldier of fortune and scourge of the Covenanters, was born ; here that he spent most of his childhood, and here that he brought his bride, the fair Lady Jean Cochrane, after their marriage in Paisley Abbey. And it was from the Castle of Glen Ogilvy — the largest and most imposing of his three seats — that he rode forth on that last fatal adventure which was to win him immortality at Killiecrankie.

A little over a hundred years ago the Glen was a famous haunt of smugglers — Macleods and Macdonalds from the Highlands and Islands, who came down through the Grampians with their hardy little " shelties " carrying the illicit liquor for which the men and women of Dundee were willing to risk meeting them out on the moors under cover of darkness.

Older than any of these tales, however, is the story by which the Glen will be remembered long after Claverhouse and William The Lion are forgotten, the tale of the Nine Maidens, and of their adventures in the cause of Christ far and wide throughout Scotland.

It has been recorded in the pages of Church History ; it lives in the annals of the saints, and it is enshrined in the homely verses of James Cargill Guthrie[1]—descendant of the martyred Covenanter whose name he bears, and founder of the first free library in Scotland — who was born in 1812, at Airniefoul at the foot of the Glen.

1 James Cargill Guthrie—The Vale of Strathmore: Its Scenes and Legends.    29

"Barbaric darkness shadowing o'er
    Among the Picts in days of yore,
St. Donevald, devoid of lore,
    Lived in the Glen of Ogilvy.

"Beside the forest's mantling shade,
    His daughters nine a temple made,
To shelter rude his aged head
    Within the Glen of Ogilvy.

"Nine maidens were they spotless, fair
    With silver skins, bright golden hair,
Blue-eyed, vermilion-cheeked, nowhere
    Their match in Glen of Ogilvy.

"Yet these fair maids, like muses nine,
    God-like, etherealised, divine,
To perfect some high-souled design
    Within the Glen of Ogilvy.

"Did with the aged hermit toil,
    With their own hands in daily moil,
Hard labouring rude the barren soil
    Around the Glens of Ogilvy."[1]

Austere as their lives were, their diet consisting of one frugal
meal a day — of barley bread and water — their labours
were not limited to the Glen, nor were their interests confined
to the soil.

"A chapel built they rude at Glamis,
    From whence like sound of waving palms,
Arose on high the voice of psalms,
    Nearby the Glen of Ogilvy."[1]

And far and wide throughout Scotland they travelled,
aiding in that rude age, when Pict and Scot still dwelt apart,
and when vast regions of the country had yet to be won for
Christ, in the spread of the Gospel and the establishment
of the Church among the people. The names of three of them
have survived.

*Mazota* was the one who impressed herself most on their
neighbours in the Glen. Many a tale they had to tell of the

1 James Cargill Guthrie—The Vale of Strathmore: Its Scenes and Legends.

power she wielded over animals, the very goats in the valley forbearing to nibble at her father's corn because of the prohibition she had laid on them. Away up on Deeside, St. Maik's Well near the Parish Church of Drumoak, on a haugh beside the river, recalls her name and fame. The Church at Forbes in Aberdeenshire was dedicated to the Nine Maidens, as were so many throughout Scotland ; and in Logie Wood, in the neighbouring parish of Auchendoir, there is a Nine Maidens' Well, one of a score that bear that name.

*Fincana* is commemorated in different parts of Perthshire. She is the *St. Fink*, at whose chapel in the Parish of Bendochy, between Alyth and Rattray, a monthly service is still held in summer time, the hill which bears her name overlooking the road which leads into the Grampians.

*Fyndoca* it is, however, whose shrine is the most romantic of all. It is on the island of Inishail, in Loch Awe, in Argyllshire, that her life and labours are recalled.

"There are few spots" says Dr. Frank Knight,[1] "sweeter, more lovely, or more peaceful. The islet lies, an emerald gem, embosomed in the blue waters of the loch upon which the gigantic mass of Ben Cruachan looks down. The chapel which she built became a sacred spot, and here for centuries the Campbells, the MacArthurs, the MacCalmans, the MacCorkindales and other old races buried their dead, bringing them in galleys from the shores of the nearest lands. On the very summit of Glenary is a spot where of old stood a pilgrim's mark called the Cross of Prostration, where the traveller from the South first gets a glimpse of the green isle of Inishail."

The island lies in the lower part of the loch and on it stood the Parish Church of the district from the time of the Reformation to the year 1736. Its ruins are visible to-day, beside those of a mediaeval convent, the nuns of which were famed alike for " the sanctity of their lives and the purity of their manners."

"The slopes of Innishail," says Seton Gordon,[2] "are golden with flowers that are the descendants of bulbs set in the ground by the delicate hands of the nuns many centuries ago. The daffodils of Innishail are in flower at a time when those of the mainland are still in bud, for the slopes of the isle lie full open to the sun."

When their aged father died the sisters left Glen Ogilvy. Attracted by the fame of St. Bridget, with whose name and

1 Archeological Light on the Early Christianising of Scotland, Vol. 11.
2 Highways and Byways in the West Highlands.

work it will always be associated, they sought a refuge at Abernethy, under the shadow of the Round Tower, where the Earn flows into the Tay. Here, until their deaths, they lived and laboured, the Pictish King whose capital it was giving them a grant of land and an oratory.

When they died they were buried one by one at the foot of a great oak tree and for centuries it was one of Scotland's most famous places of pilgrimage.

> " And to their grave from every land,
>   Came many a sorrowing pilgrim band,
>   The oak to kiss whose branches grand
>     Waved o'er the maids of Ogilvy."

" The oak trees disappeared by natural decay," says Dr. Dugald Butler,[1] " or were destroyed at the Reformation, and the only trace of the existence of the Nine Maidens that may now be found is at the well near Macduff's Cross called the Nine Wells. Dempster, writing in 1622, preserves an interesting account of them, which affords a glimpse of their influence and the veneration with which their memory was surrounded. He tells us that their abode at the oak tree was shown in the memory of our fathers ; that their miracles were engraved on the walls of the ancient oratory at Abernethy, and that these had been lately profaned and abolished by ' the heretics '."

15th June was the traditional day of the pilgrimage, and as late as the 17th century the Kirk Session of Glamis had to pass an ordinance forbidding the local maidens going on pilgrimage to the oak trees of Abernethy.

" In condemning the superstitions," says Dr. Dugald Butler,[1] " it is only just to recall what is the sufficient cause to explain them, and that is the splendour of saintly lives. — It was a time of unrest, and when the Church, through concentration upon secondary and unimportant questions, was failing to discharge its spiritual function, these women workers faced the duties that were being neglected."

> " Nine maidens fair in life were they,"
>   Nine maidens fair in death's last fray,
>   Nine maidens fair in fame alway,
>     The maids of Glen of Ogilvy.[2]

1 Dugald Butler—The Ancient Church and Parish of Abernethy.
2 James Cargill Guthrie—The Vale of Strathmore : Its Scenes and Legends.

# FOR FURTHER READING

GENERAL

WILLIAM MARSHALL—*Historic Scenes in Forfarshire* (1875—William Oliphan & Co.—304 pp.)

WILLIAM MARSHALL—*Historic Scenes in Perthshire* (1880—William Oliphant & Co.—444 pp.)

LAWRENCE MELVILLE—*The Fair Land of Gowrie* (1939—William Culross & Son—240 pp.)

ADAM PHILIP—*The Evangel in Gowrie ; Sketches of Men and Movements* (1911—Oliphant, Anderson and Ferrier—451 pp.)

JAMES CARGILL GUTHRIE—*The Vale of Strathmore : Its Scenes and Legends* (1875—Wm. Paterson, Ed.—524 pp.)

J. G. M'PHERSON—*Strathmore : Past and Present* (1885—S. Cowan & Co.—264 pp.)

---

CHAPTER I—KENNETH MOODY STUART—*Alexander Moody Stuart : A Memoir* (1899—Hodder & Stoughton—330 pp.)

CHAPTER II—FERGUS FERGUSON—*The Life of Rev. Dr. Andrew A. Bonar* (N.D. —John J. Rae, Glasgow—284 pp.)

Ed. MARJORY BONAR—*Andrew A. Bonar, D.D., Diary and Letters* (1893—Hodder & Stoughton—317 pp.)

Ed. MARJORY BONAR—*Reminiscences of Andrew A. Bonar, D.D.* (1895—Hodder & Stoughton—357 pp.)

CHAPTER IV—J. R. MACDUFF—*The Parish of Taxwood and Some of its Older Memories* (1883—David Douglas—238 pp.)

*The Auther of " Morning and Night Watches ": Reminiscences of a Long Life* ; edited by his Daughter (1896—Hodder & Stoughton—400 pp.)

MRS. OLIPHANT—*A Memoir of the Life of John Tulloch, D.D., LL.D.* (1889—3rd Ed.—William Blackwood & Sons—502 pp.)

CHAPTER V—SIR WALTER SCOTT—*Memorials of George Bannatyne MDXLV-MDCVIII* (1829—Ballantyne & Co.—120 pp.)

CHAPTER VI—W. MASON INGLIS—*An Angus Parish in the Eighteenth Century* (1904—John Leng & Co.—200 pp.)

CHAPTER VII—JOHN GLAS—*A Narrative of the Rise and Progress of the Controversy About the National Covenants* (1828—2nd Ed.—Hill & Baxter —355 pp.)

J. T. HORNSBY—*Articles—The Case of Mr. John Glas* (1937—Vol. 6 Part II—pp 116-136) and *John Glas : His Later Life and Work* (Vol. 7—Part II—pp 93-113—Records of the Scottish Church History Society.)

JOHN ROSS—*A History of Congregational Independency in Scotland* (1900 James MacLehose & Sons—282 pp.)

CHAPTER VIII—JOHN STIRTON—*Glamis: A Parish History* (1913—W. Shepherd —254 pp.)

DUGALD BUTLER—*The Ancient Church and Parish of Abernethy* (1897—William Blackwood & Sons—524 pp.)

G. A. FRANK KNIGHT—*Archeological Light on the Early Christianising of Scotland, Vol. 11.* (1933—James Clarke & Co., Ltd.—434 pp.)

# CONTENTS

---

*List of Books Recommended for Further Reading*

THE MUNRO PRESS LTD., PERTH, SCOTLAND.

# IT HAPPENED IN KINTYRE !

*by*
D. P. THOMSON, M.A.

'THE COMING OF ST. COLUMBA'
by William McTaggart, R.S.A.
(By kind permission of the Trustees of
the National Gallery of Scotland)
*Crown copyright reserved*

At the Cauldrons,
Machrihanish

**Price One Shilling**

# IT HAPPENED IN KINTYRE !

KNOWN to the ancient world as *Epidion Akron*, the nose or promontory of the Epidii, Kintyre claims to have been the first locality on the Scottish mainland colonized by man. The scene of many a bloody battle and many a savage siege throughout the centuries, it has been peopled uninterruptedly since long before the dawn of history.

"It's tale," says J. J. Bell, in his *Scotland's Rainbow West*, "is far-reaching, for it was known to Ptolemy, was visited by Agricola, and saw the beginning of the western kingdom of Dalriada, founded in the fifth century by the Scots who came over from Ireland."

Classed for centuries along with Bute, Arran, Islay, and Jura as one of the "Southern Isles" of the Hebrides, it formed, until the reign of Edward I of England, part of the diocese of Sodor (Southern Isles) and Man. Divided from the rest of Argyll by a narrow isthmus at the head of West Loch Tarbert, over which a vessel could easily be dragged, it was the subject of a grim jest in the days of Magnus Barefoot.

Forty-one miles in length this longest peninsula in Britain, "dangling by the very narrowest of necks from the poetic land of the mystic Ossian and the modern Campbell," has been described as "thrusting greedily towards Ireland," from which it is separated by a narrow channel, only twelve miles in width.

Ending in the Mull of Kintyre, where "the roar of the waves dashing against the precipitous sea-wall of the iron-bound shore . . . has been heard at the distance of forty miles," this *Caput Regionis* of Adamnan, St. Columba's biographer, was the *Satiri*, or Land's Heel of the Norse Sagas, in which it figures prominently. Celebrated alike in story and in song, Cuthbert Bede is right in claiming (in his entertaining book, *Glencreggan*) that "it yields to no other part of Scotland in historical interest."

It is not, however, with the general history of Kintyre that we are concerned here, but with its spiritual heritage which is equally rich. "There is a great past for the dwellers here to live up to," said a Dowager Duchess of Argyll long ago, "as to us is left the duty of keeping the torch burning which was lighted by the saints of old, who brought into the darkness of Paganism the glorious light of the Gospel."

It is of that storied and splendid past, and of some of those who have kept the torch burning down the centuries, that this booklet tells, and it is in the hope that it will do something to interest and inspire the coming generation as well as the older that it is given at this time to the public. Of necessity there is much that it leaves untold. Should it meet with a favourable reception I hope to follow it with a second series of tales, for which there is abundant material in hand.

Meanwhile, I would like to thank all those who have assisted me, who came to Kintyre a few months ago as a stranger, in the collection of the material assembled here. Particularly am I indebted to Rev. Angus MacVicar, Minister of the Parish of Southend, for his help and encouragement, to the Librarian of Campbeltown who has put the treasures of that fine collection so fully at my disposal, and to the Editor of the *Campbeltown Courier* who has allowed his files to be used so freely.

D. P. THOMSON.

THE CHURCH OF SCOTLAND OFFICES,
    232 ST. VINCENT STREET, GLASGOW.
        *18th July*, 1949.

## Chapter I

# The Man from Inis-Ainghean

JUST when the first Scots settlers came from Ireland to Kintyre we have no means of knowing. Across that narrow stretch of sea between Antrim and the Mull there must have been traffic of some kind from a very early date. If tradition is to be accepted, close relations between the two shores were established as far back as the first century. Four hundred years later there was founded the Kingdom of Dalriada, with its capital at Dunadd, on the Moss of Crinan, not far from the village of Lochgilphead.

Into this Scots colony, by then firmly established in Lorne, Knapdale and Kintyre, as well as on the islands of Jura and Islay, there came about the year 530 A.D. an Irishman from Connaught, Kiaran by name. The pupil of St. Finnian of Clonard, the friend and colleague of St. Columba—"Son of the Carpenter" (for that is how he was known), and descendant of kings—this was "The Man from Inis-Ainghean," destined to give his name to what is now Campbeltown, but was once Kinlochkerran.

Prior to the coming of St. Kiaran there is no record of any active Christianity in the Western Highlands, although the settlers had probably been baptised in their own country, and here and there, as on Sanda, are to be found chapels dedicated to St. Ninian.

Three miles south of Campbeltown there is a great "limestone cavern" at the foot of high cliffs, difficult of access from whatever angle one approaches it. Barring the entrance are the remains of a substantially built brick wall with a doorway in the centre. It was here in this rocky abode, "the silence of which was broken only by the thunder of the waves on the iron-bound coast," that the pioneer missionary had his headquarters. Here he would spend weeks in solitary prayer and meditation, practising, by day and night, those austerities for which he afterwards became famous. From here he must have made the expeditions by which the Gospel was carried far beyond the bounds of the peninsula.

Known to-day as "The Apostle of Kintyre," there are traces of St. Kiaran's work over a very wide area. In the islands of Arran and Bute, on Colonsay, Luing and Lismore, and as far afield as Barra, Lewis and Caithness, his footprints are to be found. On the mainland of Scotland alone he is said to have founded as many as twenty churches.

"In the neighbourhood of the cave," says Dr. Frank Knight, in his fascinating book, *Archæological Light on the Early Christianising of Scotland*, "is Glen Kerran, with the Kerran Water descending from Kerran Hill, place names that bear witness to the long continued memory of the saint. In the hills behind Clachan, at the mouth of West Loch Tarbet lies Loch Ciaran, a lonely deserted sheet of water on which a crannog has been discovered. Was it to bring the Gospel to the people of this remote lake dwelling that Kiaran toiled over the bogs and heather, and thereby bequeathed his name to this solitary tarn?"

The view from the cave itself is magnificent and far-reaching —northward to the creeks and promontories of the Kintyre Coast as far as Carradale, westward and south to the high peaks of Arran, and the bold outline of Ailsa Craig; and in the far distance beyond —the hills of Carrick and the southern uplands.

Within there is much to arrest the eye—a flat round stone, two feet in diameter, which is said to have served the saint for a seat, and exactly underlying a steady drip of water from the roof a small oval basin scooped out of a block of solid stone. These, it is thought may date back to St. Kiaran's own day.

Cut in the face of the rock at the back of the cave is a cross in a circle. That, too, may be the missionary's work. In Drummond Castle some years ago there was found an ancient missal containing prayers ascribed to St. Kiaran. Earnest in spirit, they are at once simple in style and language.

Shortly before his death at the early age of 33, St. Kiaran returned to his native Ireland  There on an island in the River Shannon he founded the great monastery of Clonmacnois. Aided by the fame he had achieved as a missionary and an ascetic, it became in course of time one of the most famous schools in Western Europe, the burial-place of kings and a favourite resort for pilgrims.

Seven months after his return, Kiaran fell a victim to yellow jaundice, a plague which was then sweeping the country. "The lamp of this island," Columba called him, in a hymn he wrote in Kiaran's honour. "The glory of the nation of the Scots," was Alcuin's verdict.

"Since the coming of Christ into flesh," says the Book of Lismore, "there never hath been one whose charity and mercy was greater, whose labour and fasting and prayer were greater, whose care and watchfulness concerning the Church were greater." Such an one was Kiaran, the Apostle of Kintyre, after whom are called two of the churches which stand to-day in the old town at the head of the loch which once bore his name.

## Chapter II

# McTaggart's Inspiration

IT was the month of June, 1897, and William McTaggart, R.S.A., Scotland's great seascape painter, was paying his annual visit to his native Kintyre.

"Sunburnt and tanned by exposure to the open air," with his "thick, tawny beard," says his biographer,[1] "his West Highland ancestry was written on his face and shone in his eyes"—those "clear, bright eyes of medium grey-blue" that his friends knew so well!

"Of medium height and strongly-built," says Sir James L. Caw, "his every action was instinct with vitality." The reefer-cut, dark blue jacket he affected, and the "easy swing and roll of his carriage," added a sailor-like look which did not belie him.

"Born within sight and sound of the Atlantic, where it flashes and thunders on the sands of Machrihanish, the call of the sea was strong in McTaggart's blood. He loved it in all its moods." . . . "From dawn to sunset, and from calm to storm, he painted every phase of its fascination with insight and mastery. . . . Each of his finer pictures is a realization of some aspect of the sea's mighty magic never before captured by painting."

On this June day McTaggart had reached a crisis in his life. Sprung of a race of small farmers and crofters, and brought up in a deeply religious Free Church home, he had early achieved fame in the chosen branch of his profession. At the age of 24 he had become an Associate of the Royal Scottish Academy. Now, at 62, he had been told by the doctors, in the spring of the year, that the illness from which he was then suffering was Bright's Disease, and that he must never attempt to paint out of doors again. Possessed of many of the natural characteristics of his race —"innate delicacy of feeling, high, flashing temper, quick response to sympathy . . . the deep love of beauty, the swift, spontaneous flow of emotion, and the instinctive feeling for the transitoriness of life, which are so often considered the special qualities of the Celt's inheritance," there must have been moments when McTaggart felt that he had received his death sentence. He was not, however, the man to give in. This "great interpreter of the Scottish scene," as Stanley Cursiter calls him, was about to paint what many regard as his masterpiece—what is certainly one of

1 James L. Caw,
*William McTaggart, R.S.A.* (1917)  3

his boldest canvases and most manifest inspirations.

The 1300th anniversary of the death of St. Columba had just been celebrated at Iona, and the papers had been full of the subject. Stirred by what he had read, and moved by that fact that the venerable minister of Campbeltown, whom he had known as a young man, had taken the closing act of that service—and with memories of his own many visits to Iona, and of what he had painted there—McTaggart decided to commence a picture which would emphasize the connection of his native Kintyre with the coming of the great Irish missionary.    True, it might be his last, but he could have no more fitting theme for a climax.

"The Cauldrons," says Sir James Caw, "usually shored with pebbled beaches, was filled with golden sand as he had never seen it before.  Some seventeen or eighteen miles from the nearest point in Ireland, towards which it looks, the bay was just such a spot as Columba and his followers would look out to beach their frail coracles after crossing the stormy waters of the Moyle."

The landscape of "The Coming of St. Columba," which hangs in the National Gallery of Scotland, and is featured on the cover of this little booklet, was painted there and then, the boats and figures being added later, after the artist had returned home.

"It is a slumberous, opalescent day of early summer . . . the horizon is faint and far-withdrawn. . . . The figures lying upon the daisy-gemmed green knowe, the tall, red-haired man dressed in a rude brownish tunic, and with leathern thongs upon his legs, turning lazily to look seaward, and the white-kerchiefed woman playing with her child, typify the happy, careless heathen Scots; the two white-sailed boats drawing in silently from the sea, the approach of the missionaries of the Cross. . . . Strength of handling and delicacy of perception were never more happily wedded."

Ignoring the persistent traditions that connected the arrival of St. Columba with Southend and with Oronsay, prior to his advent on Iona, McTaggart had come to his own characteristic decision that he would paint him making his first landing where he himself had so often played as a boy.

What matter whether he came to confer with a predecessor already in possession of the field, or to rebuild work that had fallen into ruins?  The great fact, as McTaggart himself put it, was not that Columba landed (whether here or there) but that he came to Scotland!  It is of that fact that we are made so powerfully aware when we stand before the artist's masterpiece.

CHAPTER III

# The White Monks of Saddell

IT was Somerled who planned it—the stately Abbey of Saddell, with its splendid buildings, its shaded cloisters, and its white-robed monks—the only Cistercian House in the Western Highlands of Scotland.

That was in 1160, four years before the old warrior met his death on the battlefield of Renfrew—Thane of Kintyre, Lord of the Isles, Prince of Argyll and "Scourge of the West"—the progenitor of more Highland clans and more distinguished families than any other Scotsman of the age; and it was within the rising walls of the Abbey that his bones were later laid to rest.

> "Heard ye the toll of the great abbey bell?
> Saw ye the monks line the bay of Sadail?
> Saw ye what corse on their shoulders they bore?
> Know ye that Somerled's glory is o'er?"

It was Reginald, his second son, who was responsible for the building of the Abbey—Reginald whose portion of his father's great estate was the whole of Islay and Kintyre, and whose last days were to be spent as a lay brother of Paisley Abbey. According to tradition he sent to Rome for a quantity of consecrated dust and "made the buildings commensurate with the extent to which it could be scattered," a cruciform church on the high right bank of Saddell Water just above the modern village, 136 feet long, and 78 feet across the transepts.

Taking sixty years to complete it became one of the most celebrated ecclesiastical centres of the West, an important place of sepulchre and a favourite resort of pilgrims.

It was the great age of monasticism in Scotland, and the Cistercians or White Monks, a Reformed branch of the Benedictines, were becoming the favourite Scottish order. Introduced by David I, who had come under the spell of their founder, St. Bernard of Clairveaux (whose hymns are sung in all our churches) their first house had been established at Melrose in 1136, to be followed rapidly by others at Newbattle and Dundrennan. Now came Saddell—and later Kinloss, Deer, Culross, Balmerino and Sweetheart.

"Monasticism," says Dr. G. G. Coulton,[1] "was one of the great formative forces in the social life of the Middle Ages, and in the

1 Scottish Abbeys and Social Life     5

twelfth century it did more than anything else to bring Scotland into line with general European civilization. . . . To the very end of the Middle Ages the Cistercians kept something of their superiority over the older branches of the Benedictine Order; and during the century which saw them settled in Scotland that superiority was still very strongly marked. Men believed in their prayers even more than in those of most other monks."

Abjuring linen, and wearing coarse white woollen garments night and day, giving themselves to corporate prayer almost every three hours from dawn to midnight, and combining manual labour with their devotions, the Cistercians built costly and beautiful abbeys which by "the contrast which they presented to the primitive architecture of the Scots increased the reverence which they excited and . . . imparted a new stability and graciousness to social life . . ."

Of the history of Saddell Abbey we know very little. A single incident has come down to us from the early years, and the name of one abbot has been preserved, but that is all.

King Haco of Norway, in one of his expeditions against Scotland, anchored his fleet off Gudey (God's Isle) or Gigha, and there, according to one of the old Norse Chronicles, "an abbot of a monastery of grey friars waited upon him, begging protection for their dwelling and holy church, and this the King granted him in writing." There were no grey friars in that part of Scotland, but the unbleached wool of the Saddell habit must have looked like grey. It is undoubtedly the monks of that Abbey who are referred to. Of the long line of mitred abbots, "whose bones are mouldering beneath the ruins, one solitary name is all that has descended to us, that of Abbot Thomas (1257), celebrated for his continence and his austerity, whose works were long preserved in the library of St. Andrews."

In 1507 the abbey, now uninhabited, was annexed by James IV to the Bishopric of Argyll, and many of its stones were built into the massive old keep that stands to-day on the shore to the south of Saddell House.

Into one of the few remaining fragments of the Church, more than 80 years ago, Colonel Macleod gathered the best of the sculptured stones, and there, among unknown clerics and warriors, lies one of the lairds of Saddell—the inscription on his grave reading: "John Macleod Campbell—who died universally beloved and regretted, 11th April, 1936, aged 47. A succourer of many, life is sweeter because he passed through it." What higher tribute could one ask than that?

CHAPTER IV

# Cornelius Omey—Poineer!

IT was in the year 1526 that Cornelius Omey set out for St. Andrews, the first student from Kintyre of whom we have any record to study at one of the three Pre-Reformation Universities of Scotland.

Founded in 1411, the oldest of our Universities, it was also the most virile. "During the period 1450-1560," says R. G. Cant, its modern historian,[1] "St. Andrews, if no longer the only University in Scotland, retained unquestioned the intellectual primacy of the country. Her masters were figures of considerable eminence not only in the life of Scotland but of Europe as well. Her students continued to win fame and fortune in many fields and countries."

What was true of the University as a whole was even more true of its youngest college, the one towards which Cornelius set his face. "Whatever new ideas were stirring at the time," says Professor Lorimer,[2] "and whatever new books were then in people's hands in any part of Scotland, there was at least one society in St. Andrews where they would be able to find access. . . . St. Leonard's was to some extent in sympathy with whatever new life was to be found in the kingdom, and became a vital element for its development and training."

Founded in 1512 by the masterful Prior Hepburn, as "a College of Poor Clerks," and intended at first for 20 scholars, St. Leonard's was housed in a building of that name which had originally belonged to the Culdees and had been successively a hospital, a pilgrim's hospice, and an almshouse for old women. An appendage of the Priory of St. Andrews, it formed a long courtyard occupying the N.W. corner of the precincts.

Entering between the ages of 15 and 21, most of the students were destined for the Church. Housed two in a room, in buildings that were somewhat makeshift, they wore gown and hood of monastic form, and were subject to a rigid discipline. All conversation had to be in Latin, and students were required to help with the domestic work of the community. One day a week they were allowed to visit the links for sport, but they had to go in company, "dishonest games such as football" being strictly forbidden. Even their allowance for each meal was prescribed for them by their thoughtful founder.

1 The University of St. Andrews
  A Short History

7

2 Life of Patrick Hamilton

The Colleges provided the tutors and the background of community life, but the University prescribed the curriculum. Four years were spent in Arts, leading to the Master's degree, then four more in Divinity. Entering with a knowledge of Latin Grammar, and after passing (in the case of St. Leonard's) a minute examination in character as well as educational attainments, these young men went through a course that began with grammar, rhetoric, and logic, and proceeded by way of music, arithmetic, geometry, and astronomy to the three philosophies—natural, mental, and moral—being permitted after 18 months to go forward to their Bachelor of Arts degree, taken in two parts, *determination* at Christmas, and *responsions* in Lent.

Further than that there is no record of Cornelius Omey having gone, but before he reached that stage an event had taken place which was to leave its mark on every student in the University. It was on the 29th of February, 1528, when he would be nearing the end of his second year, that Patrick Hamilton, the first Scottish martyr of the Reformation, was burned at St. Andrews, and almost certainly the Kintyre man would be there among the watching crowd. It was a spectacle which must have left an ineffaceable impression upon him.

Hamilton himself was a St. Leonard's man, and it was in the Priory and in the College that most of his supporters were to be found. Returning to St. Andrews in January, for a whole month he had had the ear of the University, students and teachers alike flocking to his lectures and disputations. "To drink of St. Leonard's Well" was to become a synonym for belief in the Protestant faith, and the Principal of the College himself, Gavin Logie, one of the most distinguished men in the University, was to go over to the Reformed cause at an early date.

It was impossible that Cornelius Omey should remain indifferent to these influences. First of a long line of Kintyre men to enter the ministry—and to serve the Church at home, in the Colonies and on the mission field—he may well have been also the pioneer of the new faith in the far south-western corner of Argyll. Rector of Kilblaan in Southend at the time of the Reformation in 1560, he was one of a family destined to give notable service to the Church in the years to come. Among the signatories to the National Covenant of 1638 are to be found the names of Donald and Duncan Omey, Ministers respectively of Kilkerran and Kilcolmkill. Both were founder members of the Synod of Argyll, and both knew what it was to suffer for their convictions.

## Chapter V

# "A Nest of Cneaffs"

A NEST of Cneaffs"—knaves, cads, worthless fellows! That was how John, 6th Earl of Rothes, described the Covenanters of Kintyre, when writing to his friend and colleague the Duke of Lauderdale, in the summer of 1665, to report on his progress in disarming the men of the western shires at the mandate of Charles II, whose restoration five years before had inaugurated an era of persecution.

Rothes —that "coarse, illiterate boor, salacious in speech and scandalous in behaviour," as one who knew him well described him; that notorious adulterer, who was "always either sick or drunk," and to whom "extortion appears to have been the only object, and brutality the only method." "Nest of cneaffs," indeed! And who was he to speak?

It was of the men who opposed him in the field that Rothes was writing, the men whose convictions he despised, and whose lives were a standing reproach to his own. Some of them, like "The Captain of Skipness," were natives of Kintyre. Others, like "Hakate" and "Hilabeth," had come with the second Lowland Plantation about the year 1650, and already they had given evidence of the part they were to play in the land of their adoption, and of the contribution they were to make to its development.

Lord Neil Campbell belonged to this "Nest of Cneaffs"— second son of the great Marquis of Argyll, who had been the first victim of the persecution, losing his head at Grassmarket in Edinburgh, on 27th May, 1661. A man of a very different stamp from his brother, Archibald, the 9th Earl, he had sat in the Synod of Argyll as a representative from the Lowland Church at Lochhead, as Campbeltown was then known.

Colonel Robert Halkett was another—a ruling elder in the same Lowland congregation, who had commanded a regiment of French guards raised by Lord Kintyre, in 1642, and who was to suffer fines on several occasions for attendance at conventicles, finally going to prison for 2 years along with his friend William Ralston, at the instigation of this very Rothes.

William Ralston himself might be described as the pioneer of the Lowland plantation. The principal heritor in the Parish of Beith, in Ayrshire, from which his friend and fellow elder, John

9

Cunningham ("Hilabeth") also came; his ancestors had fought with gallantry at Flodden and Pinke. Given the lands of Saddell Abbey and Castle, with the latter for a residence, he had undertaken to have that stronghold put in order by 1652. Rebuilt by the Bishop of Argyll in 1508 it had been burned by the Earl of Sussex in 1558, and had long lain in ruins.

In 1653 Ralston had held the castle of Lochhead against the Royalists. In Presbytery and Synod, as in Kirk Session, he was known as a man of insight, and of wise and sagacious counsel. Losing his Saddell holdings when arrested in 1665, and spending two grim years in prison, he later obtained some of the best lands in Campbeltown and Southend parishes. Buried at the old cemetery of Kilcolmkill, a walled tomb marks his resting-place. Many of his descendants are still in the district, and the typewritten history of his family can be consulted in Campbeltown Library.

Most outstanding of all, however, in this goodly company was Colonel James Wallace, the hero of Rullion Green. Of the stock that gave Scotland its most romantic hero, he had sold his family estate of Auchens in the Parish of Dundonald, in Ayrshire, to come with the Lowland Plantation to Kintyre. An old campaigner of the Civil Wars, and a former Governor of Belfast, he had been taken prisoner both at Kilsyth and at Dunbar. "A man of piety and purity, whose patriotism and love of justice impelled him to the side of the persecuted," he had been made Lieut.-Colonel of the Scots Guards when that regiment was first formed. In the Lowland congregation at Lochhead he was known as one of its most devoted elders.

"A good man and a skilled soldier," says Dr. Alexander Smellie,[1] "we can see him still in his long cloak, with his montero, or huntsman's cap, drawn well over his brow, and his beard very rough." "He was," says Woodrow, the historian of the Covenant,[2] "the most faithful, compassionate, diligent, and indefatigable elder in the work of the Lord that ever I knew at home or abroad; and as for his care, solicitude and concernedness in the work and people of God, I may say the care of all the churches lay more upon him than upon hundreds of us."

Driven into exile after the Battle of Rullion Green, where the Army had to confess of the poor, ill-armed peasants he led that day that "they never saw men fight more gallantly or endure more," he settled eventually at Rotterdam, and there, many years later, he died.

"Nest of Cneaffs," indeed? To such evil uses will men put words!

CHAPTER VI

# The Passing of "The Thatched House"

IT was in Kirk Street, in Campbeltown, that the old building
stood, and it was in the year 1706 that it gave place to a more
pretentious structure. Popularly known as "The Thatched
House," and referred to in a list of buildings in the burgh which
is bound up with the earliest records of the Town Council, as
"The Preaching House," this was the first home of the Lowland
congregation of Campbeltown, with which the great Marquis of
Argyle associated himself as a ruling elder after its formation
in 1655.

It was not the first body of Lowlanders to be constituted as
a separate congregation in the peninsula. "The assembly considering that there is a number of Lowland gentlemen and others
come to reside in Kintyre," reads a Minute of the Synod of Argyll,
dated 19th May, 1652, "and that they are scattered through
severall parishs of the same, think it fite that in the maine tyme,
until parishs be formally distinguished and bounded, and a settled
ministrie be gotten for these boundes, that these be not left without
all order and discipline. Doth therefore ordaine a session to be
erected, and that sessione to be called the session of Sadall, and
this to be until the Synod's further consideratioune of the mater."

Just one year later a strong Committee was appointed to visit
the Presbytery of Kintyre and to carry through the settlement of
Mr. James Gardiner as first Minister of the "Inglish congregation
of Kintyre," as it was then known. For some considerable time
he and Dugald Darroch, Minister of the Highland Charge of
Kilkerran, had the whole of Kintyre on their hands, and their
Kirk Sessions were required to sit jointly every six weeks "for
the bearing down of sin and the good of the whole country."

Then, in 1655, the Lowlanders of Kintyre—the English-
speaking settlers who had been compelled to travel the long
distance to Saddell—got a Minister of their own in Campbeltown.
It was on Edward Keith, son of the Sheriff of Montrose, and
member of a famous Scottish family closely identified with the
Episcopal and Jacobite causes, strangely enough, that their choice
fell. About the new Minister himself there could be no doubt
at all, for he came with the personal recommendation of the great
Samuel Rutherford under whom he had studied at St. Andrews.

Built by the congregation itself, with the help of the Marquis no doubt, the first Lowland Church was a simple and homely structure, and the site on which it stood is occupied to-day by the Kirk Street Hall.

Deprived of his charge for 10 years for failure to conform during the stormy days of the Covenanting struggle, Edward Keith was restored to his people in 1672, dying in harness in 1681, after a ministry of twenty-six years.

For 13 years the Church remained vacant, and then in 1694 the congregation called Mr. James Boes, who had already won fame as a schoolmaster of quite outstanding quality. It was in the 12th year of his ministry that the old kirk gave place to a new. "In 1706" reads the Minute preserved in the archives of the Longrow congregation, "the Thatched House became too little as well as ruinous, and therefore it was judged expedient to pull it down and build a slate house on the ground where it stood. This was accordingly done."

With the old Church went the old bell, which is now preserved among the treasures of Inveraray Castle. "Gloria Deo soli; Michael Burgherhuys me fecit 1638," reads the Latin inscription on it, and the date is a significant one, being that of the year in which the National Covenant was signed and the "Fifty Years' Struggle" began. On it also are the arms of Charles I and those of Neil Campbell, first Bishop of Argyll and the Isles, and for a time Minister of the Highland Church at Kilkerran.

At Limecraigs House, on the way between Campbeltown and Kildalloig, there lived at this time Elizabeth Tollemache, Dowager Duchess of Argyll, a woman of great strength of character and a staunch Presbyterian. Identified with the Lowland congregation, she was said to have been the largest single subscriber to the building of the new church. In addition to that donation she gifted for use in the new building sacramental vessels of solid silver. These included a baptismal laver and basin of exquisite workmanship which are still preserved and used in Castlehill Church, although not both for their original purpose.

Measuring about twenty inches in diameter, the basin has three flat rims, each a little lower than the other, and on each there is an nscription. On the inner rim there are just three phrases, printed in bold capitals:

THE BAPTIZEM OF WATER   THE BAPTIZEM OF THE SPIRIT
THE BAPTIZEM OF BLOOD.

It is a striking and thought-provoking conjunction, especially for the times in which we are living.

## Chapter VII

# Migration to the Longrow

FROM the time Rev. James Boes died the Lowland congregation of Campbeltown was in trouble. It was with his passing on 14th February, 1749, that controversy began, the Duke of Argyll claiming, to the disgust and surprise of the people, that his was the right of appointing a successor. To add fuel to the flames, the man of his choice was a Highlander, for more than one reason by no means acceptable to the people.

The Vacancy that occurred on Mr. M'Alpine's death was filled by the appointment of one who had come to Campbeltown as an Assistant Master in the Grammar School, had married the daughter of the Highland Minister, and had become that worthy man's assistant. So strong was the opposition to his nomination that only three members of the Lowland congregation could be found to sign the "Call," one being the Duke of Argyll's Chamberlain.

Rev. George Robertson, however, had made up his mind that there was to be no turning back. Refusing an annual payment for life offered him equal to the difference between his existing emoluments and the stipend to which he would be entitled if settled, he was equally decided when the Duke, at a later date, suggested his transfer to another and more lucrative charge.

It was in 1763 that Mr. Robertson's settlement took place, and exactly four years later the majority of his congregation left him. It was to a new denomination—the Presbytery of Relief—that they applied for recognition, for the necessary "supply of sermon," and for liberty to "moderate in a call."

Six years before that denomination had come into being, originating in a protest against the deposition from his church at Carnock, in Fife, of Rev. Thomas Gillespie, a man of high character and stainless reputation, who had incurred the General Assembly's displeasure for his refusal to take part in the forced settlement of a minister in a neighbouring congregation.

With them into the Relief Church, numbering then only seven causes throughout the country, the Lowland elders and members carried the Register of Baptisms and other historic documents, by which they sought to establish their continuity with the Covenanters of the 17th century. Their first problem was a building; the next to find a minister. The Relief Church had no Divinity

Hall, and in both matters they were to be left very much to their own resources.

It was in the year 1766 that they began to raise funds, the heads of families pledging themselves "to purchase seats in the proposed meeting-house—and to pay for each sitting such yearly rent as might be deemed necessary for the maintainance of ordinances"; for that was the common method by which Relief and Secession Churches were then built and their ministry provided for.

The next step was to choose thirteen "Managers," giving them "power to purchase ground and to procure materials for carrying on the building to completion." Armed with this authority, the Managers made up their minds that they would do their own contracting; and having bought a piece of land they cast about for materials with which to build.

First, they had trouble about the stones, being interdicted by the Duke's Chamberlain from using the common quarry. Opening a quarry of their own, three miles out, and below the seamark, they were then charged with spoiling the grass over which they had to carry the stones! Finally, obtaining permission to take material from Davaar Island, they were refused permission to employ carts or horses. It was at this juncture that the patience of the men showed signs of giving out. Not so the women, however!

"Shame on ye!" cried a heroine, on the outskirts of the meeting called to deal with this new situation. "Shame on ye to be turned back by this bogle; let the men quarry the stanes, and the women will carry them!" That settled it—there was no thought of turning back! One old worthy, however, did recall, more than half a century later, "the elder women of the congregation preparing bands of cloth to protect the hands of those who bore the burdens, as well as to dress their bruises, and alleviate the inflammation of their blistered palms."

In due time the Church was built—a vessel going to Ardnacross, four miles away, to get sand; another to Cumbrae for freestone; and a third all the way to Norway to obtain timber. Then came the call to the first minister, a certain Mr. James Pinkerton, Licentiate of the Church of Scotland. It was the beginning of a long history, the end of which is not yet.

To-day, at the far end of Campbeltown's main thoroughfare, the Longrow, almost on the same spot, stands the successor of this first building—the handsome Italian campanile of which catches the eye of every traveller approaching this famous harbour by sea. Its strong congregation belongs once more to the Church of Scotland.

## CHAPTER VIII

# John Smith's Successor

IT was in the manse he had built for himself on the glebe lands at Kilchousland that Dr. John Smith, Minister of the Highland Charge of Campbeltown, lay dying. That was in the month of June, in the year 1807.

Born at Croft Brackley, in Glen Orchy, just sixty years before, and licensed by the Presbytery of Kintyre after completing his course at Edinburgh University, he had begun his ministry in charge of the Mission at Tarbert; going from there in 1775 to the Parish of Kilbrandon and Kilchattan in Nether Lorne. Four years later he came powerfully under the influence of the Evangelical Revival which had been sweeping the country in the latter part of the 18th century. Translating Alleine's *Alarm To The Unconverted* into Gaelic, he had the joy of seeing it lead to a widespread religious awakening.

Presented to the charge of Campbeltown by John, Duke of Argyll, and admitted there in April, 1781, John Smith was awarded the D.D. of Edinburgh University six years later. A noted Celtic scholar and poet, and an authority on Ossian, he was, before the age of forty, regarded as one of the most outstanding ministers in the Highlands. His metrical version of the Psalms in Gaelic passed quickly through thirty editions, becoming a favourite in Argyll and the Isles, and a revision of the Paraphrases followed quickly. Of his share in the Revised Gaelic Bible a leading authority has said, "We do not know any Gaelic work, long or short, which can at all be compared with it."

It was this remarkable man, long since recognised as the greatest Highland minister of his day, who now lay dying in the manse at Kilchousland, and it is to his successor's account of what happened that we instinctively turn.

"The effect of Dr. John Smith's ministry," he wrote, when himself in old age, "remains even to this present day. He was the means of introducing family worship very generally into the parish, and of awakening strong religious affections in the minds of the people so that it might truly be called a time of revival."

"Dr. Smith, when on his death-bed," he continues, "asked all his elders to come to him. He told them that he had not many weeks to live, that it was in vain for them to attempt to have a temporary assistant, and that they must look out immediately for a successor. Being asked if there was anyone he could recommend, he at once suggested that they should apply for me, and he authorised them to state to the resident heritors that such was his dying advice to them."

The elders were deeply moved by the dying man's request, and they had no hesitation as to how to act. Immediately after the funeral, which was the largest and most impressive ever seen in Campbeltown, application was made to the Duke of Argyll.

The man on whom the choice thus fell was Norman Macleod, a son of the Manse of Morven, and the second of a long line of distinguished preachers and leaders which that family has given to the Church of Scotland. Known far and wide as *Caraid nan Gaidheal*—"The Friend of the Gael"—he was to become Dean of the Chapel Royal in Edinburgh, and Chaplain to Queen Victoria, and in that capacity was to officiate at Blair Atholl on the occasion of her first visit to Scotland, in 1862.

It was at the age of 23 that Norman Macleod began his great ministry in Campbeltown. Three years later he was married, the first child of that union becoming the famous and beloved "Norman Macleod of the Barony," perhaps the best known parish minister Scotland has ever had. It is his grandson, Dr. George Macleod, who is to-day leading the Iona Community, and who by his personality and preaching has so influenced the youth of Scotland.

In 1825 Norman Macleod, senior, was translated to the Parish of Campsie in Stirlingshire, the first minister to go from Campbeltown to another charge since the Reformation. "I preached my farewell sermon," he says in the reminiscences written in his old age, "and could I have known beforehand the scene which I then witnessed, and the feelings that I myself experienced, I do believe that no inducement could have tempted me to leave them."

Of the second Norman, born at the Manse in Kirk Street, on June 3rd, 1812, his brother and biographer wrote, "When a boy he was sent to the Burgh School where he gained an insight into character which served not only to give him sympathy with all ranks of life, but afforded him a fund of amusing memories which never lost their freshness. Not a few of his boyish companions are portrayed in *The Old Lieutenant*. Among the numerous souvenirs he used to keep, and which were found after his death in his sanctum at Glasgow, were little books and other trifles which he had got as a boy from these early associates."

So great a hold does Campbeltown have upon its sons!

CHAPTER IX

# The Arrest of Mr. James Haldane

WHEN Mr. James Haldane set out from Edinburgh on the morning of 9th June, 1800, he had no thought of going to Kintyre. Accompanied by his friend, John Campbell —the one a retired Naval Officer and the other an ironmonger—he was embarking on his fourth summer campaign as an itinerant evangelist. Born in London in 1764, and educated at the Grammar School of Dundee, he had, along with his brother, Robert, the well-known proprietor of Airthrey, founded the "Society For The Propagation of the Gospel at Home." They and their lay evangelists were covering Scotland with a network of evangelistic agencies.

The route taken by the two evangelists in this summer tour of 1800, was S.W. by Peebles and Biggar to Ayr, Stranraer and Portpatrick; then North by Sanquhar to Cumbrae and Arran.

"Dignified in manner, commanding in speech, fearless in courage, unhesitating in action," James Haldane commanded attention wherever he went, his open air meetings being attended always by hundreds and often by thousands.

"On reaching the West side of Arran," writes his colleague, who kept a journal of the tour, "we observed a long neck of land stretching towards the northern coast of Ireland. On enquiry we found it was Kintyre. As our Parish extended to wherever there were human beings, and hearing that there was not one Gospel preacher in the whole range of seventy miles, except in the chief town, we determined to pay it a visit."

The crossing was made in the late afternoon, and at 10 o'clock the preachers were scrambling over the rocks near Carradale, trying to reach the Inn. A day or two later they were in Campbeltown, having met with varied receptions on the way.

It was after they left Campbeltown that they met with really serious opposition. Friends had advised them to send a messenger ahead announcing four sermons a day in the different villages, and this they had done. But the country ministers were hostile, and at their instigation the local J.P.'s. took upon themselves to stop the field preachers. In extenuation let it be said that the General Assembly had issued a warning against these very men, as "opposed to the Establishment of the land."

It was a retired Army Officer who first attempted to stop them, but Mr. James Haldane was not a man to be trifled with. The magistrates he said, were exceeding their powers; he would continue to preach as advertised! Repeating his prohibition, the Major said he would be at the next place of meeting before them. There, when the evangelist arrived, they found him sitting on horseback, on the outskirts of the crowd, attired in a scarlet hunting coat. After the meeting he attempted to carry out his mission but, "as often as his eye encountered Mr. Haldane's unflinching glance his courage seemed to fail, and he again and again faltered and passed on."

It was at Clachan that the evangelists met their fate, after Mr. Haldane had preached under somewhat menacing circumstances at Whitehouse. Faced by a warrant for their arrest, they learned that volunteers were waiting to take them both before the Sheriff of Argyll at Lochgilphead. There was nothing to be done but submit.

Reaching Tarbert that night, the procession set out at 7 in the morning up the shores of Loch Fyne. The Sheriff, however, finding that both his prisoners had taken the oath of allegiance, and were prepared to take it again on the spot, could not but refuse to sanction what was, after all, an illegal proceeding.

Back through the villages at which they had intended preaching went the evangelists, greater crowds than ever greeting them, and Mr. Haldane speaking with "an eloquence, a fervour and an animation which seemed to have acquired redoubled force from the circumstances in which he had been placed." When he next met the fox-hunting Major it was in the precincts of Holyrood reserved for debtors.

At Clachan, where the arrest had been made, a little church was established, one of the lairds who had fallen out with the minister giving a piece of ground for the purpose. Among the first converts and adherents were the sergeant of the guard and the beadle of the Parish Kirk. Forbidden to attend the ministrations of a Haldane preacher, the latter had been converted listening through a hole in the wall.

The last minister of the little congregation lies buried in the old kirkyard. "Dugald McGregor, Minister of the Gospel at Clachan, 1857—His children," one reads on the simple tombstone. The little church itself, after serving as a Free Kirk Preaching Station, passed through many vicissitudes. To-day its old oak beams are to be seen behind the counter of the village Post Office.

CHAPTER X

# The Three and the '43

THERE are three churches in Campbeltown which owe their origin to what is known as "The Disruption"—the popular movement led by men like Thomas Chalmers, by means of which the Free Church of Scotland came into being. They are Lorne Street—now in the Church of Scotland, Lochend United Free Church, and the Free Church of Campbeltown.

The ministers of the Church of Scotland in Campbeltown in 1843 were Duncan McNab and Hector McNeill, the one in the Highland Charge and the other in the Lowland. The former was a man of outstanding ability, a noted preacher, universally liked and respected. Tall and handsome, "courtly in his manners and kindly in disposition," McNeill was an able man with strong local connections, whose standing was equally good. The affairs of the two charges were administered by a joint Kirk Session.

In the course of "The Ten Years Conflict"—the period immediately before the Disruption, when the issues between Church and State, and party and party, were being argued and fought out in every parish it became clear which way the majority in Campbeltown was likely to go.

When the fateful day came there were two Campbeltown names appended to the historic documents then signed, the Act of Separation and the Deed of Demission. One was that of Rev. Hector McNeill—the other that of John Grant, elder, of the firm of Grant & Kelly, Distillers. The name of Rev. Duncan McNab, Minister of the Highland Charge, can be seen inserted, as it was later, immediately above that of his colleague. In the Public Library of Campbeltown there is an "Act of Demission by Elders of the Free Church of Scotland Appointed by the General Assembly at Edinburgh at 26th May, 1843." dated "Parish of Campbeltown, 27th June, 1843," and bearing 22 signatures. That left only seven elders who did not "come out"!

On the Sunday following the Disruption, 28th May, never-to-be-forgotten scenes were enacted in both churches, special sermons being preached appropriate to the occasion, and congregations rising instead of sitting for the closing Psalm in each case.

"I witnessed," Duncan McNab told the first meeting of the new Free Church Presbytery of Kintyre, "an outburst of anguish from 3,000 of my fellow-countrymen when robust men forgot their manhood, wept like children, and wrung their hands as they gathered their Bibles and walked away in silence."

The Free Church congregations then formed held their services for some time, the one in the Secession Church of Campbeltown, whose building they were loaned, the other in the courtyard of Grant & Kelly's Distillery, roofed over and seated for the purpose. Later both acquired buildings of their own—large, square, barn-like structures near the present Lorne Street Church, the Gaelic building seating 1249, and the English one 839. With the min-isters there had "come out" from the Church of Scotland nearly the whole body of the day school teachers of the district—that meant the erection of new schools as well as new churches.

In 1867 the two congregations, collegiate until then, decided to go their own ways, and the following year the Free Church General Assembly approved the separation. In 1900 there was a fresh division—a minority disapproving of the proposed Union with the United Presbyterians by which the United Free Church came into being. It was Lorne Street which suffered most. For the three years following the House of Lords decision in that case (from 1904-7) the congregation lost their building. It was some time later that the present Free Church was erected.

In 1929 came another parting of the ways, when Lochend Church, representing the "Lowland Free" of older days, decided not to enter the Union with the Church of Scotland consummated that year. In Campbeltown to-day these three congregations represent the "Disruption tradition" of more than 100 years ago. Their ministers and congregations are on the friendliest of footings, and in all good causes they have long since learned to co-operate happily.

"Perhaps the most extraordinary fact connected with the Dis-ruption in Campbeltown," says Colonel McTaggart, in his story of the Lowland Congregation, "was the comparatively rapid recovery of the two Parish Churches. . . . During Dr. Russell's long and very successful ministry the Highland Church was again filled, and the congregation regained its old position as the largest in Campbeltown. . . .25 years after the Disruption the Castlehill Church was crowded. . . . The two Parish Churches were, I believe, chiefly recruited from what we would now call 'the lapsed masses.' That was specially true of the Highland Church—the enormous personal influence for good which Dr. Russell exercised over the poorer classes of the town being operative there."

## CHAPTER XI

# John MacVicar's Youngest Son

A SEVENTH son, and one of a family of twelve, Donald MacVicar was born, like his father before him, at Dunglass, in the parish of Southend. That was on the eve of St. Andrew's Day, 29th November, 1831.

Mentally and physically a powerful man, noted for his strength, his courage, his outspokenness, and his utter abhorrence of all quackery, formality and sham, John MacVicar was unswerving in his devotion to truth, a lover of his Bible in both the English and the Gaelic versions, and a friend of the poor and the oppressed.

Like her husband a native of Southend, Janet McTavish was "a woman of rare energy and marked executive ability, possessing a large measure of common sense, a strong will, untiring perseverance, and tremendous force of character, not unmixed with pawky humour."[1] Well fitted to be the mother of a pioneering family and enjoying good health all her life, she was to survive to the ripe age of 92, "with faculties unimpaired and cheeks withered, but still rosy."

Donald was not quite four—"a quiet little fellow, grave and absurdly fat, who could only prattle Gaelic"—when the family emigrated to Canada, travelling on the good ship *Platina*. It was at Chatham, in Ontario, that the MacVicars settled, where two generations later they, the McCovvies, the McKerseys and other Southend families were to be found. "You can scarcely go to any place in Ontario," wrote a correspondent at the turn of the century, "but you will meet someone from Kintyre."

Twenty-six years were to elapse before Donald set foot in Campbeltown again. In the interval he had gone from a log cabin school, by way of Gale's Academy, Toronto, to old Knox College in the same city. Now, at 31, he was minister of Coté Street Presbyterian Church, Montreal, the largest and finest congregation of the day in that city; and on this, his first return visit to the homeland he was renewing old associations in Kintyre.

Out walking on the Saturday afternoon near Campbeltown, he overtook an old woman on the road. Did she by any chance know anything of a man called John MacVicar, and what had become of him? "I ken him weel," was the quick reply; "he went to Ameriky long ago. It was a sad, sad day when he left. I can still see the

1 Life and Work of
Donald Harvey MacVicar                21

crowd gathered on the quay. They stood greetin' and wringing their hands as the ship moved off . . . he was awfu' kind to the poor; and they kenned they would never see him again."

It was then that Donald introduced himself, telling her of his last good-bye to the father he loved so well on the day he set out for Toronto, and letting her know that she could hear him preach next day in the Free Kirk of Campbeltown. When she realized who it was, and that she was actually talking to John MacVicar's youngest son, "she turned her tearful eyes on him with a look never to be forgotten," and the waiting group at the church door on Sunday morning at the close of the service was evidence of the way in which she had spread the news.

It was at the end of that year, 1862, that Coté Street Church was visited by a great spiritual awakening, and that the minister himself entered into a new and deeper experience of divine grace and power. To realise just what that meant one must turn to the glowing pages in which Donald MacVicar is described in that five million copy best-seller, Ralph Connor's *The Man from Glengarry*. He it is who is (a little prematurely) "the recently appointed college professor . . . with a reputation for doctrinal preaching."

"He would not let them escape," says the novelist, in the chapter headed, "The Revival," —"behind all refuges and through all subterfuges he made his message follow them, searching their deepest hearts. And then, with his face illumined, as if with divine fire he made his final appeal. . . . And all over the church women were weeping, and strong men were sitting trembling and pale." And that, the reader will remember, was the beginning of a great movement—"the mighty sweeping of that religious up-heaval," says Ralph Connor in his own autobiography,[1] "that tamed the fighting, drinking, lusting Glengarry men into the finest rivermen that plied their adventurous trade on the Ottawa and the St. Lawrence."

Professor of Divinity in 1868, and Principal of his Church's College in Montreal five years later, Donald Harvey MacVicar (by this time D.D. of Toronto and LL.D. of Montreal) was Moderator of the Canadian Assembly when still only 50. Dying in harness twenty-one years later his funeral was one of the largest ever seen in Canada. A man of strong personality, and with qualities which would have fitted him for leadership anywhere, he is recognized to-day as one of the greatest teachers and organizers Canada has had. "Truth was for him," said a colleague who knew him well, "not merely a beautiful theory with which the mind might dally; it was a guiding light by which life is inspired."

1 Postscript to Adventure

## Chapter XII

# Floodtide in the Peninsula

IT was in the winter of 1859-60 that the whole peninsula of Kintyre was swept by a wave of religious revival to which there has been no parallel since. Coming to Scotland by way of North America and Northern Ireland a few months before, it is as "The '59 Revival" that this movement lives in history.

"It appears from information obtained," says a long and fascinating report on the work, engrossed in the Kirk Session Minutes of Longrow Church, "that for some time prior to September there was a conviction resting on the minds of the Christian portion of the community that a Revival in religion was most desirable. This conviction was strengthend by the details reaching us from other quarters—respecting the revelation of the Lord's arm in the conversion of sinners. According to the testimony of your Congregational Missionary not a few people in the humble walks of life, previously careless, were evincing some concern."

It was just at that time that two things happened, the conjunction of which was to act as a spark does to timber dried and ready-laid. One was the meeting of the Free Church Synod of Argyll, held in Campbeltown that September, at which glowing and moving reports were given by some of the brethren present as to what they had seen in Ireland. The other was the arrival in the town of two young men of the Glasgow City Mission, who had already seen the beginnings of the movement in that city.

"After coming here," wrote one of them to his friends, "we felt anxious to do some good, so we sent the town bell through, calling a meeting in a school. It was filled. Next evening it was crowded, inside and out. On Monday evening our meeting was to commence at 8 o'clock, but a few minutes past seven it was packed full, and hundreds standing around the school." A night or so later the larger of the two Free Churches was made available.

"Such a crowded place of meeting I never saw in Campbeltown," wrote a father to his son in Glasgow. "Upwards of two thousand attended, the crowd filling the porches, and hanging on the windows and dykes of the church, and wherever any glimpse or sound could be got of the meeting." [1]

Soon almost every church in the town was open, and before long all were crowded. "Hundreds," said the *Argyleshire Herald*, before the work had been in progress more than a month, "come from the different parts of the country all round even from a distance of 10, 15 and 20 miles. Towards evening the various roads leading into the town are thronged."

Within a few weeks similar reports were coming in from every part of Kintyre and from Gigha, "where the island has become an island of prayer, and though the weather has been exceedingly wet and stormy, people come from all parts to these meetings," to Kilberry in Knapdale, where, by way of contrast to the strong crying and tears, and the sudden downstrikings that were so prevalent, a correspondent writes: "We have been cheered by instances coming to our knowledge of various individuals among us who have silently undergone a change of a very decided kind." [1]

Meanwhile, in Campbeltown, the work went on unabated, the Highland Church of Dr. Russell being open all night the whole winter. "Conversions are taking place," said the *Argyleshire Herald* of 12th November, "of such a nature that even gainsayers are silent. Some who doubted of the work are now its hearty promoters."

"The parties impressed with the truth," says the Longrow Session Report from which we first quoted, "belonged to all classes of society—people who even in the judgment of a suspecting charity had been for years living devout lives and efficient and zealous Sabbath School teachers. In many instances, however, the sovereignty of God's grace was most markedly exemplified in the impressions that were produced on the minds of the most ignorant, depraved and dissipated persons in the community."

Into this work in his native Kintyre no one threw himself more wholeheartedly from the start than Mr. John Colville, Yr., of Burnside, later to be so well known throughout the country as an evangelist. Thirty-two years of age at the time, he had been Dux Medallist of Campbeltown Grammar School and a brilliant student in both Arts and Theology. Early manifesting a power of dealing with the awakened and the anxious such as few possessed, he was the heart of the movement as long as it lasted, and in it he found his lifework, hundreds being led to Christ through his special ministry all over Great Britain in the years that followed."

"His clear mind, warm heart, and open hand," said Dr. Russell, "could be traced in every local missionary enterprise. If Mr. Colville travelled much and left his spiritual footprints in many places throughout Scotland and England, there is no place in which these footprints are so sharply cut, or in which time will take so long to obliterate them, as in his native Campbeltown."

1 Wynd Journal (1859)

CHAPTER XIII

# Nephew and Namesake

IT was James Curdie's claim to distinction that he had taught a future Prime Minister of Great Britain. Born at Kilmory in Arran, a farmer's son, Curdie had gone south after taking his training at the Universities of Glasgow and Edinburgh, and in John Pothicarry's School, at Blackheath, Benjamin Disraeli, the future Lord Beaconsfield, had been among his pupils. In Gigha to-day there is preserved in one of the village homes a table from Disraeli's house, bought at the disposal of the old minister's effects.

Presented to the living of Gigha and Cara by John, Duke of Argyll, James Curdie was 37 years of age when he came to his island parish. There, for just over half a century he remained, performing his duties faithfully, winning the esteem of his people, dying unmarried, and leaving as his principal literary legacy the *Statistical Account of the Parish.*

It was to James Curdie's manse, first as an Irvine Royal Academy schoolboy and later as a student of Glasgow University, that the nephew who was to make his name known came to spend the long summer vacations. It was there in Gigha that he became such a lover of the Gael and of the Gaelic—"a Highlander of the Highlanders," loving his people with a love that never grew cold.

Born in Ardrossan in 1830, three years after his uncle's settlement in Gigha, James Curdie Russell lived to become "The Father of the Church of Scotland," and the most influential minister in the Highlands, "half a century ahead of his own generation in his passion for social reform." "When he spoke in the General Assembly," said one who knew that Court well, "he was one of the few whose utterances not only commanded the attention, but stirred the enthusiasm of the House."

Summoned to the Glasgow Manse of Norman Macleod, Sen. —"Caraid Nan Gaed-heal" for his breakfast, on a cold winter's morning in the year 1854, young James Russell found himself selected for a task that might well have daunted the heart of the stoutest. Called to the Highland Charge of Campbeltown at a time when, for all practical purposes, the congregation had been reduced to the merest handful, he left it the largest church in the Highlands. An arresting figure wherever he was encountered, and a preacher "whose voice was vibrant with the emotion of his

25

message and full of the charm of the Gaelic intonation," he knew every man, woman, and child in the town by sight, and on the street he had a greeting for each.

Partly with his own hands, and largely if not wholly at his own expense, he laid a wooden floor in a church that had known only bare earth. Championing the cause of temperance in a town boasting its twenty distilleries, introducing an English service to the worship of a Gaelic congregation, promoting the Volunteer movement, and fostering the growth of a Free Breakfast Mission and a Boys' and Girls' Religious Society, James Curdie Russell did it all with a tact, a firmness, and an absence of bitterness and personal feeling that won for him the esteem, and retained the friendship, of men who could not share either his outlook or his enthusiasms.

Compelled at an early age to seek relief from his charge on health grounds, he gave himself, when he had regained his powers, to the Convenership of the Highlands and Islands Committee of his Church with a devotion and a thoroughness that left no corner of the North or West, however remote, unvisited. Given his D.D. by Glasgow University in 1881, Dr. Russell was Moderator of the General Assembly of the Church of Scotland in 1902, and in that capacity he was present at the Coronation of King Edward VII in Westminster Abbey. When shortly afterwards, by an Order in Council, precedence was given to the Moderator of the General Assembly of the Church of Scotland after the Lord Chancellor of England, and before even the members of the Royal Family, it was said freely that the striking personality and dignified bearing, the intellectual keenness and gracious and kindly manner, of Campbeltown's senior minister must have had not a little to do with the decision.

"One of the most beautiful memories we cherish of him," said Dr. Norman Maclean, preaching in St. Cuthbert's Church in Edinburgh on the Sunday after Dr. Russell's death, "is his standing at the Communion Table at the close of a service in connection with St. Columba, pronouncing the benediction in a way that made us feel the fluttering of angels' wings." That was in Iona Abbey, on the occasion of the 1300th anniversary of the death of the great Irish missionary, at the first Protestant service to be held in the building since the Reformation.

To-day in the little Church at Gigha their portraits hang side by side in the Session House—James Curdie, Minister there for fifty years, and the nephew who bore his name, and by the fame and worth of whose work the eventide of his life was gladdened.

## CHAPTER XIV

# For Lands Afar

IT was the morning of 23rd July, 1883, and the dream of Robert Johnston's heart was about to be realized. Son of the farmer of Langa, near Kilchenzie, and a graduate in both Arts and Divinity, he was that day to be set apart as a missionary of his Church to Jamaica.

"Let me ask you," said Rev. John Thomson, his minister, at the Ordination Service that afternoon, "to begin your work with a high idea of its greatness and grandeur. No work that a man can do on this globe can for a moment be compared to it."

Robert Johnston never forgot these words. Settled at New Broughton among the hills of Manchester, in the beautiful orange-growing country of Jamaica, he gave himself without stint for more than fifty years to the children of the slaves. Chairman of the Manchester School Board, and Moderator on three occasions of the Synod, the supreme Court of his Church, he exercised a deep and lasting influence on the whole life of the island.

"He was," said his colleagues, looking back on his life-work in 1946, "a man who by his saintly character, by the depth of his scholarship, by the winsomeness of his personality, by his abundant labours as Minister of the Gospel, as Theological Tutor and Educationalist, and as Founder—and for long years Superintendent —of the Woodlands Industrial Home for Destitute Boys, made an indelible impression on the Presbyterian Church, and set a standard of character and service that has been an inspiration and a challenge."

Six years later, on another July day, there was a second Missionary Ordination Service in Longrow Church. This time it was Peter L. Hunter, son of the Sunday School Superintendent, who was being set apart for South Africa. Going out in 1889 he was settled first at Sulenkama, but it was at Mount Ayliff, in East Griqualand, under the shadow of the Drakensburg Mountains, that the work of his life was done. Going to a tribe 10,000 strong that was wholly pagan, at the request of its Chief, Jojo, P. L. Hunter had the satisfaction of leaving behind him, at his great mission station of Gillespie, in 1935 when he retired, a Christian congregation nearly 1000 strong, with more than that number of children thronging its day schools.

Trained in a Campbeltown bank, his records were said to be models of what mission books should be. One of the moving spirits in the creation of the Bantu Presbyterian Church of South Africa, he was for many years Convener of its Business Committee, and was among the first to be elected Moderator of its General Assembly.

Campbeltown, when it welcomed them home together at a memorable missionary meeting in the Longrow Church, on the evening of 1st October, 1906, had good reason to be proud of those two sons of Kintyre, and of the work they had already done for the dark-skinned races of the world.

To South Africa also went Duncan W. Semple from the little United Free Church at Carradale, and to the Cayman Islands first—and later to Jamaica—went Robert C. Young, son of the U.F. Minister of Southend, two of whose sisters were missionaries in India, as their mother had been before them. To India also, though under different auspices, went the Misses Colville from the Lowland congregation at Castlehill.

"Few people have been so much loved and valued by people differing widely in environment, outlook and occupation," said those who knew her best in India of Isobel McLaren Young, who worked first at Bombay and later at Poona. "She was one of those who love so much that they have only to *see* a need, and at once they will be engaged in some activity to meet it."

To Manchuria in 1908, as a pioneer medical missionary, went Dr. Jeanie Andrew, who had taken her M.B., Ch.B. at Glasgow University with distinction in surgery, and had served for some time on the staff of both the Royal Infirmary and the Maternity Hospital in that city. It was at Kaiyuan, the big market town 70 miles north of Moukden, that her hospital work out east was done, and it was there, in 1915, a year after she had been compelled to retire through ill-health, that Dr. Jean M'Minn, another Campbeltown woman, succeeded her.

"Kaiyuan," the post-war Commission the Church of Scotland despatched to the Far East in 1945 was able to report, "has carried on right through, and its work has increased in extent. For the courage, resource and Christian stedfastness of its women Superintendent, Dr. Shih Yu Ju, Dr. Leo, of Moukden had the highest praise. 'She has been worth a whole group of men,' he said."

Quite evidently Dr. Jeanie Andrew and Dr. M'Minn had not laboured in vain! Here in Manchuria—as in South Africa, in India, and in Jamaica—Kintyre's contribution had counted in the most vital way possible.

CHAPTER XV

# Drumlemble in the News

IT was in the spring of 1897 that Drumlemble found itself in the news. The first announcement of what was happening was a modest paragraph in the local newspapers. The last was a pamphlet printed by authority of the General Assembly of the Free Church of Scotland and circulated throughout the country. By that time it was clear that Drumlemble had made history!

It all arose through the appointment of a new student assistant. "The Session," reads a Minute of Lorne Street Church, of 28th September, 1896, "unanimously appoint Mr. Alexander Frazer to be assistant in this congregation in place of Mr. ———, who is leaving for College."

"My chief work in Lorne Street," says Frazer himself, looking back across an interval of more than 50 years, "was a Sunday morning service in the Church and a district meeting in the evening, with a Bible Class for young people on a week-night in a village called Drumlemble in the Laggan of Kintyre. My class was made up largely of young farmers and farm lads and lassies and young miners. The subject I tried to expound was the Shorter Catechism.

"I resolved to finish my last four weeks with a series of evangelistic meetings. Much to my surprise, I have to confess, a young farmer well-known as a successful, as well as an honourable youth, remained behind seeking help. I, being Highland, and conservative in spiritual matters, did not make too much of his anxiety, but he came boldly out. His decision very naturally created a good deal of interest. His influence was great, and his witness courageous. Crowds began to gather. . . . No outward signs were asked for. It was the old method of dealing with seekers individually . . . Space was at a premium when brakes from Campbeltown began to arrive, and the ministers rendered noble help. I remember one man praying, 'Be pleased, Lord, to set the Laggan on fire.' To a considerable extent that actually happened."

"By the end of the first week," says that fascinating chronicle, *Revivals in The Highlands*, "the work came to be all the talk in mine, field and home. The miners began to come in. With the exception of two or three, every miner in the village, which was formerly a Sabbath-breaking, godless place, was enlisted. The coal pit that used to ring with vile song and savage blasphemy now resounded with 'songs and hymns and spiritual psalms.' The day's work, done in the darkness, began with prayer and ended with song."

"As the month was nearing its end," says Mr. Frazer, "there were pressing requests to carry on, but I had everything arranged for leaving for home at the set time. Campbeltown made a strong plea for a campaign. I had a Sunday before leaving on the following Tuesday, and a meeting was arranged."

"The Victoria Hall, the largest in Campbeltown," we read elsewhere, "was requisitioned, and on Sabbath, 11th April, a beginning was made. The meeting was crowded, there being over 2000 present, and during the four following weeks the work went on in the large hall of the Y.M.C.A. Institute, which was packed each night with an eager throng."[1]

"The success the Mission has attained," said the *Campbeltown Courier*, "is phenomenal. It has been productive of a widespread religious awakening in town greater than attended the efforts of the celebrated evangelist, Mr. Moody."

"So great has been the ingathering," reads a Minute of Lorne St. Session, "that at the first Communion which is being held during the Revival, 55 have joined the Church's membership, the other churches in town also sharing the blessing."

"Three things were noteworthy," says one record,[1] "the place and power of prayer, the depth and tenderness of the Spirit's working, and the striking results in lives of Christian devotion and obedience. Farmers told of the wonderful transformation wrought in the ploughmen's bothies. Men surrendered the work they could not reconcile with the dictates of an enlightened Christian conscience." When on evangelistic tour in Canada, South Africa and Australia more than 40 years later, Frazer met the fruits of that month's work.

"At Drumlemble, a mining district about 4 miles from Campbeltown, with a population of 400," said a public appeal for funds, issued shortly afterwards, "the people have long felt the need of a hall for religious purposes, especially since the Spring of 1897, when a remarkable religious revival took place. The sessions of the five Presbyterian churches in Campbeltown have agreed to unite in erecting a hall . . ."

The money was forthcoming, and the hall was built. Bearing the date 1899, it stands to-day on the main road to Machrihanish, serving the needs of a wide district, a permanent memorial of the Revival.

1 "Revivals in the Highlands"

## Chapter XVI

# The Cave Picture of Davaar Island

TUCKED away among a score of other news items in the *Campbeltown Courier* of 20th August, 1887, was a small paragraph headed "A Curious Painting".

"Visitors to Davaar Island recently," it read, "were surprised to find on the rocky wall of one of the caves on the south-west side of the island what is supposed to be a reproduction of Munkacsky's famous "Christ on Calvary", The picture is life-size, and considering the rough nature of the surface is said to be exceedingly well done. The novel painting was viewed by several parties who visited the island on the Merchant's Holiday on Thursday last."

Joined to the shore by a great sandbank known as the Dhorlin, which is bare at low tide, the Island of Davaar is a conspicuous landmark in Campbeltown Loch, serving as a natural breakwater to the harbour, and rendering it particularly safe for shipping. Its proximity to the town naturally makes it a favourite resort for visitors. On the Sunday following the announcement we have quoted they streamed across the breakwater in hundreds.

"Nothing could be more suitable," the *Courier* informed its readers a week later, "for the contemplation of such a subject than the semi-darkness and rocky grandeur of the large cavern in which the picture is placed. It is hoped that some effort will be made to preserve it from defect, either by the damp of the cavern or the action of unscrupulous or mischievous persons; for there can be no doubt that if properly preserved the painting will be one of the chief attractions and curiosities of the district in future years."

"The anxiety to have a sight of the painting," the paper told its readers in the same edition, "has been so great that many people have suffered great inconvenience in order to reach the island. The air is filled with conjecture as to the identity of the artist."

The mystery was about to be solved! In its next week's issue the *Courier* announced to the public that Mr. Archibald Mackinnon had acknowledged the work to be his, and that photos of the artist at work were to be seen in various local shops. "It is," he was reported as saying, "a subject which I have long had at heart. Early on the morning of the first day I began to paint I awoke from a dream in which I thought I beheld the body of our Saviour on the Cross shortly after His passion."

More than fifty years passed by, and in the interval thousands had crossed to Davaar Island to see for themselves what had come to be known as "The Cave Painting". It was in the summer of 1934 that the suggestion was made, emanating, it is said, with Rev. Dr. Wylie Blue, himself a native of Campbeltown, that the artist should be invited to visit his native place and touch up his famous painting.

Publicity being given to this suggestion, the *Bulletin* published a photograph and the artist, then living in retirement at Nantwich, in Cheshire, intimated that he was willing to come if the way could be made clear. At a meeting of the Town Council it was decided that the necessary expenses including his journey North, should be met out of the "Common Good" of the town, rooms were secured for him, and it was arranged that he should arrive on his 84th birthday.

Hundreds lined the pier that afternoon as the ship drew in, included in the crowd being the Provost, Magistrates, and leading citizens of the town. It was 35 years since the old man had been in Campbeltown, and it was obvious that he was deeply touched. The incident was extensively publicised in the press of the country and every cinema news reel in Britain carried pictures of the return of the artist, many of them showing the old man at work in the cave itself.

"The greatest of all human tragedies, and the most appealing of divine triumphs," said the *Courier*, "depicted thus on the rock face, it is now being preserved for generations yet unborn." The artist himself stated that he thought he had been able to treat his work in a way that gave it much more hope of permanence.

On Wednesday, 6th June, 1934, an inaugural ceremony was held at the Cave. Among those taking part were the Provost, Magistrates, and Town Council of Campbeltown, the Moderator of the Presbytery of Kintyre, and Father Webb, the Roman Catholic priest. A public subscription was raised for the benefit of the artist, and two of his pictures, "Campbeltown Fair in the Main Street, 1880" and "St. John's Night in Campbeltown" hang to-day on the walls of the local museum.

In the intervening years the stream of visitors to the Cave has continued. As to the merits of the painting itself, and the motives which inspired it, there have been the most varied estimates.

About one thing alone there can be no room for doubt. In a world of changing values the Cross of Christ retains its power, and it will never lose its challenge. It is the subject of this picture that draws men; not its execution.

PICKERING & INGLIS LTD., GLASGOW

# FOR FURTHER READING

THE following books are suggested for further reading. Most of them can be obtained at the Campbeltown Library. They are arranged in the same order as the stories in this booklet.

---

G. A. FRANK KNIGHT. 'Archaeological Light on the Early Christianizing of Scotland.' (1933. James Clarke & Co., Ltd. 2 vols., 880 pages).

T. P. WHITE. 'Archaeological Sketches in Scotland: District of Kintyre.' (1873. Wm. Blackwood & Sons, Ltd. 192 pages).

CUTHBERT BEDE. 'Argyll's Highlands.' (1902. John Mackay. 307 pages).

CUTHBERT BEDE. 'Glencreggan: or A Highland Home in Kintyre.' (1861. Longman, Green, Longman & Roberts. 2 vols., 729 pages).

JAMES L. CAW. 'William McTaggart, R.S.A.: A Biography and an Appreciation. (1917. James Maclehose & Sons. 302 pages).

G. G. COULTON. 'Scottish Abbeys and Social Life.' (1933. Cambridge University Press. 293 pages).

R. G. CANT. 'The University of St. Andrews: A Short History.' (1946. Oliver & Boyd. 156 pages).

ANDREW McKERRAL. 'Kintyre in the Seventeenth Century.' (1948. Oliver & Boyd. 189 pages).

ED. DUNCAN C. MACTAVISH. 'Minutes of the Synod of Argyll (1639-1651). (1943. Scottish History Society. 254 pages); and 'Minutes of the Synod of Argyll (1652-1661).' (1944. Scottish History Society. 278 pages).

JOHN WILLCOCK. 'The Great Marquess: Life and Times of Archibald, 8th Earl and 1st (and only) Marquess of Argyll.' (1903. Oliphant, Anderson & Ferrier. 396 pages).

JOHN WILLCOCK. 'A Scots Earl in Covenanting Times: Being Life and Times of Archibald, 9th Earl of Argyll (1629-1685).' (1907. Andrew Elliot. 448 pages).

C. VICTOR A. MACECHERN. 'The Book of Old Castlehill.' (1921. T. & A. Constable. 100 pages).

'Memorial Volume of the Centenary Services of the United Presbyterian Church, Campbeltown.' (1868. Alex. McEwing. 67 pages).

DONALD MACLEOD. 'Memoir of Norman Macleod, D.D.' (1876. Daldy, Isbister & Co. 2 vols., 794 pages).

ALEXANDER HALDANE. 'Lives of Robert and James Haldane.' (1855. W. P. Kennedy. 658 pages).

JOHN McQUEEN. 'After Fifty Years: A Historical Sketch of the Free Church in Campbeltown.' (1893. Campbeltown Courier. 80 pages).

JOHN H. MACVICAR. 'Life and Work of Donald Harvey MacVicar.' (1904. Westminster Co., Toronto. 351 pages).

RALPH CONNOR. 'The Man from Glengarry: A Tale of Western Canada.' (1901. Hodder & Stoughton. 440 pages).

M. A. COLVILLE. 'John Colville, Yr., of Burnside, Campbeltown, Evangelist: A Memoir of his Life and Work.' (1888. Andrew Elliot 389 pages).

---

*There are also a large number of interesting and valuable pamphlets in the Campbeltown Library.*

# CONTENTS

Chapter                                                        Page

*List of Books Recommended for Further Reading*

# KINTYRE
## THROUGH THE CENTURIES

By D. P. THOMSON, M.A.

# KINTYRE THROUGH THE CENTURIES

FROM the founding of the Kingdom of Dalriada, early in the sixth century, to the present day the peninsula of Kintyre has played a part in Scottish history out of all proportion to its size or population. Colonised by the hardy Scots from Ireland, who were later to give their name to the whole country, it formed a convenient stepping-stone for successive relays of Irish missionaries who crossed the narrow intervening sea to play their part in the evangelisation of both Highlands and Lowlands. Its strategic position between the Clyde and the Atlantic made it a bargaining counter of great value in the long drawn-out struggle between Scotland and Norway in the Middle Ages, and its remoteness appealed to Robert Bruce, when a hunted fugitive in the years immediately preceding Bannockburn.

Overrun, harried and pillaged by successive invading armies during the Covenanting period, when the star of "the Great Montrose" was still in the ascendant, it became—as the possession of his great rival, the head of the powerful Campbell family—the scene of the most successful "plantation" these islands of ours have witnessed in their history. To-day it presents the most striking contrast to the situation across the water in Ulster. Within its narrow confines for 300 years the two races —Highland and Lowland, English-speaking and Gaelic—have mingled and blended as they have done perhaps in no other part of Scotland.

Boasting one of the only two coal pits in the Highlands, once celebrated for its distilleries, and famous still for its dairy farms and as the centre of an important fishing industry, its hardy sons have penetrated to almost every part of the world. Wherever they have gone they have carried with them, in addition to the spirit of enterprise and initiative, a love of their own little corner of Argyllshire that has left its traces here and there across the map of the world. There is, for example, a Campbellton on the shores of Chaleur Bay, New Brunswick, and another in New South Wales, while out on the Uganda Railway, as it winds its way inland from Mombasa to the heart of Africa, a station called Mackinnon Road perpetuates the name of one of Kintyre's most famous sons.

This is not a history of the peninsula; that has yet to be written. Nor is it a history of the Church in Kintyre, the materials for which may hardly be said to exist. What is attempted here is rather a series of pictures, setting forth, chiefly through the medium of biography, some of the things most distinctive of the religious life of the peninsula, and of the contribution that its people have made to the onward march of the Kingdom of God throughout the world.

In these pages I have tried to hold the balance between those who came as strangers to labour in Kintyre and those who went from it to take their share in the extension of Christ's Kingdom elsewhere. In order to give the work a certain unity I have begun and ended with Sanda. Emboldened by the kindly reception given to my earlier booklet, *It Happened In Kintyre*, I have ventured on this sequel. Should the demand warrant it, there is material in hand for a third series of studies.

I am again indebted to many friends for their help—among others to the Editor of the *Campbeltown Courier*, and the Librarian of Campbeltown, both of whom have so readily placed material at my disposal; to Mr. Angus MacVicar, the well-known novelist, whose books have made Kintyre known to so many; and my friend and colleague, Mr. Robert Marshall, who has designed the cover.

D. P. THOMSON.

THE CHURCH OF SCOTLAND OFFICES,
    232 St. Vincent Street, Glasgow, C.2,
        29th October, 1949.

## Chapter I

# A Base of Operations

THREE miles off the headland of Dunaverty, on the south coast of Kintyre, lies the little island of Sanda, about a mile and a half in length and less than four miles in circumference. Once the home of seventeen families, it has to-day a population of less than a dozen. The most southerly isle in the Hebrides, it occupied for centuries a position of great strategic importance, and as such it figures frequently in the old Norse Sagas.

"It is certain," says Sheriff McMaster Campbell, in his fascinating brochure, *The Island and House of Sanda*, "that, from the time of Magnus to the time of Haco, Sanda was continuously utilised as a Norse harbour. . . . Its situation as a base of operations against the neighbouring coast was an ideal one. It is not too much to suppose that from 1093 A.D. to 1263 A.D., Sanda occupied a key position in the Norse dominion over Western Scotland corresponding pretty nearly with the importance of Gibraltar to British interests in the Mediterranean."

That is a big claim, but it is justified. When at the Battle of Largs in 1263 A.D., the Norse power in Scotland was finally broken it was on Sanda that King Haco fell back with his shattered fleet, before rounding the Mull of Kintyre to Gigha, and sailing North to his death in Orkney. It was on Sanda that Edward Bruce kept watch on the mainland, while his brother Robert lay in hiding at Rathlin, during the decisive period of the struggle for Scottish national independence at the beginning of the 14th century.

Long before the days of Haco or Bruce, however—and centuries before even the first Scandanavian attack on the Hebrides— Sanda had become a base, Sheriff McMaster Campbell would have us believe, for operations more significant and far-reaching than any of these.

"Here," says Father McCana, who visited Sanda at the end of the 16th century, "is a chapel sacred to St. Ninian, towards whose cell in Galloway the whole island faces." Now Ninian, who landed on the shores of the Solway in 397 A.D., was the pioneer apostle of our Scottish Christianity, and it is the Sheriff's belief— and one that other antiquarians and Church historians share— that the great missionary himself once sought to make Sanda his base, and from this point to attack the western seaboard of Scotland for Christ.

"Sanda," says the Sheriff, "was extremely easy of access from Whithorn, the home of the Saint." Travel in these days was most easily undertaken by sea, and "with favourable winds the passage should be accomplished within three hours." It was the first point at which fresh water could be obtained, sailing North, and "it is natural to suppose that Ninian would reckon on Sanda as a convenient base for his projected mission to the Picts. The circumstance that he effected no other settlement in Argyllshire does not negate his landing on Sanda; rather does it demonstrate that the opposition, at this particular point, of the pagan priesthood, was of such a formidable character that other avenues of approach, less difficult of entry, had perforce to be sought, and the line of Ninian's mission journey carried him in consequence through the eastern rather than the western division of Scotland."

That was about the year 400 A.D., long before the Scots established their western kingdom of Dalriada, and more than 160 years before St. Columba landed on Iona. On the mainland of Kintyre, just above Campbeltown, there is a McRingan's Point, known in the 18th century as McNinian's Point. "There can be no question," says the Sheriff, "that it commemorates a landing by the Saint which, though it failed in its momentous object, is further evidence of the solicitude of St. Ninian for the welfare of the Picts in the West which impelled him to found a cause on the lonely island of Sanda."

On Sanda itself, in addition to the Chapel, there was a St. Ninian's Well—long a favourite resort of pilgrims—and there is still a very ancient St. Ninian's Cross, "a pillar of rude bumpish type without a vestige of ornament," for which "the claim may safely be made that it is among the very earliest Christian remains in Scotland." From the 12th century till long after the Reformation the island was an appendage of the Priory of Whithorn, and on it the monks maintained, in addition to the little church whose walls are still standing, a hospice as a place of retreat.

"Filling," says the Sheriff, "the high place it did later in the Columban cycle, the particular glory of Sanda will remain the well-authenticated circumstance that of all the territory of Scottish Dalriada, this unpretentious islet—less than half the size of Iona —divides with Bute the distinction of having sheltered the evangelist who first proclaimed the Christian message in Scotland —St. Ninian of Candida Casa."

## CHAPTER II

# The Footprints of St. Brendan

IT is in the north-east corner of the Kintyre peninsula that one comes on the footprints of "Brendan the Voyager," the story of whose fabulous wanderings was the favourite adventure book of the Middle Ages, known everywhere in Western Europe.

Six miles south of Skipness is a sandy bay called Brian-Puirt-Brendan's Port—while in the little village itself to-day, with its declining population, the only place of worship is St. Brendan's Church, the parish kirk itself being some two and a half miles to the south. Less than a mile beyond Skipness is the ruined Church of St. Brannan, while between Kintyre and Arran—27 miles in length and famed for its fine herring—flows Kilbrannan Sound, on the other side of which, high above Shiskine, this greatest of the "Twelve Apostles of Ireland" had his Scottish headquarters.

"To any ship approaching from Ireland round the Mull of Kintyre," says Dr. Frank Knight,[1] "the sight of that monastery with its high, white-washed enclosing wall, planted on the southern slope of Arran amid the dark heather of the hill, must have spoken of peace, Christian grace and security. From this centre Brendan sent forth his evangelists."

Far and wide they travelled—those intrepid missionary companions of the great Irish voyager. There is a Kilbrannan in Islay and a Culbrandon on the lonely Garvelloch Islands. On Tiree, on Barra, and on Uist traces of this evangelist are to be found. The parish embracing the islands of Seil and Luing off the Oban coast is Kilbrandon. In far-off St. Kilda is the site of a chapel called St. Brengan's. In Ross there is a "hill of the follower of Brendan." Birnie in Moray and Kilbirnie in Ayrshire are but variations of the same name, and in the latter place St. Brendan's Fair was held for centuries on the 16th of May. Glenbranter was once Glenbrandane, and this day the people of Bute are familiarly known as "Brandanes."

Up the Sound that bears his name, shortly after his arrival in Scotland, Brendan must have sailed to Skipness. There on the Kintyre coast, close to the ruined church, is a creek called Brann-a-Phuirt, the place at which he probably landed to do for northern Kintyre what Kieran had done for the south.

[1] Archæological Light on the Early Christianising of Scotland.

It was in early manhood that St. Brendan made his famous voyages. Born in County Kerry about the year 484, he set out with 14 chosen companions in three frail coracles of skins to search for the "Isle of Promise" in the West, the existence of which had been revealed to him in a vision.

For five years they journeyed, crossing the Arctic Ocean with its spouting whales, reaching Iceland with its scalding geysers and flaming volcano, where demons from the fiery pit (swarthy Eskimos!) hurled stones at them, seeing islands of crystal columns towering to the very skies (icebergs), and enveloped at times in thick clouds—recognisable to-day as the fogs of Newfoundland and Labrador. At last they reached the "Land of Promise," thought by some to have been America or the West Indies, and by others to have been Madeira.

The fame of Brendan's supposed discoveries spread over the entire world, influencing the Arab cartographers of the 12th century, stimulating the voyage of Prince Henry, the Portugese "Navigator," and firing the imagination of Christopher Columbus, in the maps of whose day "Brendan's Country" is placed to the west of the Cape Verde Islands. It was from these voyages that Brendan returned to become in middle age one of the apostles of Northern Britain.

"Christ never had a more intrepid missionary," says Dr. Frank Knight, "than this sailor-evangelist, who has bequeathed such a noble memory of heroism and devotion as he carried the Gospel over Arctic and tropical seas, through bare northern archipelagoes, or through Scotland's dense forests."

Such was the man who came to Kintyre about the middle of the 6th century, founding in later life the great Irish monastery of Clonfert, and dying in his 94th year on the island of Inisquin on Lough Carib. "A very human touch" says one of his biographers," is related of his passing. The great voyager who had faced countless dangers, and had crossed many stormy seas, feared the last crossing of all.

"To his sister Briga, on his deathbed, he said, 'Pray for me in my departure.' 'What do you fear?' she asked him. 'I fear that I shall journey alone,' was the memorable reply, 'and that the way will be dark; I fear the unknown country, the presence of the King, and the sentence of the Judge.'" It was left to that gracious woman to bring him the assurance with which one of the greatest of all Scotsmen, David Livingstone, was, centuries later, to comfort himself as he too neared the river: "Lo, I am with you alway, even unto the end."

CHAPTER III

# Death of a King

ONLY one King is known to have died in Kintyre, and he
was a Cornishman. Slain by Norse raiders on the eastern
coast of the peninsula, some two miles north of Campbeltown, Constantine lives in history as the first martyr of the
Christian faith in Scotland. The old ruined kirk of Kilchousland,
which marks the scene of his death, is his memorial, and in the
modern Parish Church of Govan, tucked away among the busy
shipyards on the banks of the Clyde, the interested visitor will
be shown its greatest treasure—his sarcophagus.

The son of Padarn (or Paternus) whom he succeeded on the
throne of Dammonia, a territory which comprised the modern
Devon and Cornwall, Constantine is pilloried in the pages of
Gildas' famous *De Excidio Britannica* as an adulterer, a perjurer
and a murderer, his iniquity being said to have reached its climax
in the slaying of his own two sons within the walls of a church.
Either through the working of conscience, or deep sorrow over
the death of his wife, the conversion of this ruthless man came
about while he was engaged in stag hunting. Repenting of his
disorderly life, he determined to renounce the world, and retired
to a hermit's cell on the seashore, later becoming an evangelist.

It was in his own royal territory that Constantine began his
missionary work, in the parish of Cornwall that to-day bears
his name. From there he went to Menevia, to sit for a time at
the feet of St. David, the Apostle of Wales, who, living a life of
the utmost austerity, was to become the spiritual father of so great
a host of monks and missionaries, and the beauty of whose
character in that rude age "compelled the veneration of kings
and princes" says Dr. Frank Knight,[1] "some of whom even surrendered their thrones and entered his monastery as lowly
disciples."

From Wales Constantine crossed to Ireland, where for seven
years he toiled as a lay brother in the monastery of Rathen, having
successfully disguised his rank. One day, however, he was overheard talking aloud: "Is this King Constantine of Cornwall, who
wore helmet and bore shield," he was asking himself, "who
drudges thus at a handmill grinding corn? It is the same, and not
the same," he mused, and as it happened a monk overheard him,

[1] Archæological Light on the Early Christianising of Scotland.

5

and hastened to the Abbot with the news. That prelate summoned him to his presence and insisted that he should be placed among the students, and later ordained.

Leaving Ireland, Constantine crossed to Scotland, where on the banks of the Clyde, at what we now know as Govan, he established a monastery and built a church on the little hill beside the ferry. "No trace of the original building—doubtless of wood —or of its immediate successors now exists," says Dr. T. B. Stewart Thomson, in his *Guide to Govan Old Parish Church.* "On the same site a Norman stone church was built in 1136— dedicated to St. Constantine . . Govan was the mother church of Glasgow south of the Clyde, and it has been instrumental in erecting no fewer than 34 daughter churches. . . . The present church, built by Dr. John Macleod, was begun in 1884. . . . A the time of its erection it was the most imporatnt church built in Scotland since the Reformation."

Constantine had long desired to die a martyr's death—perhaps in atonement for the abuses of his earlier life—and in the end his prayer was granted. Engaged in a missionary expedition to Argyll he was preaching one day near the shore in the "island of Kintyre," when he was set on by a band of savage pagans, who landed just below the little church of Kilchousland and raided the little Christian settlement that had sprung up there. Cutting off the hand of Constantine's servant they then attacked the missionary himself, hewing off his arm, wounding him terribly, and leaving him for dead. Calling his people round him the dying man commended his soul to God, and gave them his last messages.

It was to the church at Govan which he had founded that his remains were reverently conveyed for interment, and it was there, in 1855, at the roots of some very old elm trees, that his sarcophagus was found, the striking decoration with which it is adorned having, in all probability, been added at the time the later Norman Church was built.

"There can surely," says Dr. Frank Knight,[1] "be few more romantic careers than that of this aged saint. A king in his own rights; a candidate for the supreme sovereignty of Britain; a brutal murderer; a foul traitor and tyrant; a changed and converted penitent; a humble monk; a missionary of the Cross; a founder of churches; a far-traveller as an evangelist; a noble martyr for Christ—is there not in the career of this man something that exalts the Gospel, and emphasises its power to redeem and sanctify the vilest of human beings?"

[1] Archæological Light on the Early Christianising of Scotland.

CHAPTER IV

# Crusay—The Elusive

IN the year 1935 the Encyclopaedia Brittanica Co. Ltd.,
published a massive work entitled: *The March of Man: A
Chronological Record of Peoples and Events from Prehistoric
Times to the Present Day*. With it went an historical atlas, and
there, at Map 33, Dr. Harvey Thomson, a well-known member of
the Kintyre Antiquarian Society, made a memorable discovery.
Two miles north of Grogport, on the coast of the peninsula
he knew so well, was marked an ancient Monastery of Crossaig.
Authority on ancient churches that he was, it was a foundation
of which he had never heard even a whisper!

"When some time later I visited Crossaig," he tells us,[1] "I at
once discovered what would appear to be the ruins of such a
building ideally situated in Crossaig Glen, some thirty yards
to the north of Crossaig Water, and not far from where this
water enters the Sound of Kilbrannan.

"The ruins" he continues, "lie to the south of the farm steading
of North Crossaig, and consist of a large collection of dark, ancient
looking stones, which rise to the height of a few feet and form
an elevated plateau, the south and east portions of which are
particularly distinct. My visit quite convinced me that the map
was correct, and that an old monastery did once exist here, some
of the modern farm buildings now doubtless occupying part of
the former site."

Then began a long search for confirmatory details. In an old
book, dated 1796, entitled: *Geographical Illustrations of Scottish
History*, Dr. Harvey Thomson eventually found what he was
looking for. "Crusay Monastery in the Western Isles (Keith—
*Scottish Bishops*—p. 239)" the entry reads, "Q., if not rather in
Kintire, frequently reckoned an island, where there is now a
small haven called Crusay."

That reference was most illuminating, and later, through the
help of a friend, in Spottiswood's *Religious Houses*, the Doctor
found Crusay listed among the Augustinian monasteries of the
Western Isles, as having been founded by St. Columba. Finally,
in a 17th century MS. in Edinburgh University Library, the
following entry was discovered: "Crusai. In Ins. occid. Ordo.
S. Augustini, Fundator S. Columba." Proof positive this

[1] Ancient Churches and Chapels of Kintyre.

seemed to be—there was evidently a monastery of Crusay, and its reputed founder was St. Columba!

The quest, however, was not quite over! One authority remained to be consulted—Dr. Archibald B. Scott, of Helmsdale, the historian of the Early Scottish Church. That worthy man, it transpired, had himself visited Crossaig some thirty years before. Impressed by what he had seen, he had pondered the matter deeply. Crusay, he had come to the conclusion, was an early monastic settlement of the Celtic type, here on the Kintyre coast, at the foot of the Crossaig Glen. It had been followed in the 12th century by a building of the Roman type, neither of them a large community. The establishment, he judged, had persisted more or less till the 15th century. As for its reputed founder—that was in all probability not St. Columba, but his nephew Colmonela, after whom the ancient parish of Kilcalmonell had been called. (Crossaig was, till the 18th century, part of that parish).

Born in 555, in Co. Tyrone, where his mother, Mor, Columba's sister, had fled for refuge in time of war, Colmonela had lived with his famous uncle for some time at Iona, later becoming himself a founder of churches. The beautiful parish and village of Colmonell, in the Stinchar Valley in Carrick, recall his labours in South Ayrshire, while on a hill above Clachan, which Dr. Frank Knight thinks[1] may have been the site of his original cell in the district, "is a curious conical tumulus, with an upright slab, three feet high, sculptured with a fragmentary cross. It is a spot from which a noble view can be obtained of Gigha, Islay and Jura, revealing thus the love of the beautiful which was such a characteristic of these early Celtic saints."

When Colmonela went to Crossaig, or how long he remained in the monastery he founded there, we have no means of knowing. "No doubt," says Dr. Thomson, "its isolated situation on the east coast of Kintyre, before the advent of the motor car, the sparseness of the population, and the disappearance of any local records, have contributed to that all but complete oblivion into which this very Ancient Monastery of 'Crusay' in Kintyre has fallen. Even if we discover but little of its long and fateful story, we may, at least, be very sure that for centuries through the misty ages of the olden times, many generations of pious workers were well content to devote their lives and their labours to the service of God in this hallowed spot, by the banks of Crossaig Water, in the 'Island of Kintyre.'"

Archæological Light on the Early Christianising of Scotland.

## Chapter V

# Under Paisley's Sway

FOR nearly four hundred years—from the middle of the twelfth to the middle of the sixteenth century—a large part of Kintyre was, for all practical purposes, under the domination of the monks of Paisley Abbey—that great Cluniac House, whose possessions extended over so much of south-western Scotland.

It was with Reginald, Lord of the Isles, that this surprising relationship began. Not content with founding the Abbeys of Saddell and Iona, this second son of Somerled decided to endow in a most unusual way the monastic establishment which his father's great rival, Walter Fitzalan, Lord High Steward of Scotland, had founded on the banks of the River Cart, in 1163, in the heart of his newly-acquired wide domains in Renfrewshire.

"It may have been," says Dr. Cameron Lees, the historian of the Abbey,[1] "the circumstances of his father's death at Renfrew[2] in the neighbourhood of the newly-founded monastery, that led him to take an interest in the Paisley ecclesiastics. . . ."

"The account of the transaction between the Abbey and the Island Lord given in the charter," Dr. Lees continues, "is very curious. . . . Reginald bestows on the convent, for the first year, eight cows and two pennies from every house in his dominions from which smoke proceeds; and in every succeeding year, one penny; while his wife, Fonia, gives a tenth of all the goods which God has given her, 'both those which she retains for her own use, and those which she sends by sea or land for sale.'

"Unless the tax is promptly paid by his heirs, he tells them they shall have his curse—a threat which to a highlander was of fearful import. He charges them to be always at peace with the brotherhood at Paisley; he beseeches his allies, and commands his men, that wherever the monks or their men should go by land or sea they should hold them by the hand, and aid them in all their transactions. If his heirs ill-treat them, they are to have his malediction; if his men, they are to be punished with death. This he swears by the most sacred oath an isleman could take.

"For these good offices towards the priory he is made a brother, and Fonia is made a sister of the House of Paisley, and of the whole Order of Clugny (to which Paisley belonged) sharing in

---

[1] J. Cameron Lees—The Abbey of Paisley from its Foundation till its Dissolution          [2] In 1140 A.D.

9

their prayers and the 'rites of the divine service.'" It was on Iona, however, that Reginald was buried, and there, in the Reilig Oran, a stone inscribed with a sword, a small cross and a treasure-box (significant and striking symbols!) is the one thought to mark his last resting-place.

In succeeding years the Highland possessions of Paisley Abbey steadily increased. Angus, Lord of the Isles, one of Reginald's successors, bestowing upon the monks "the church of St. Querani (Kieran) in Kentyr"; and "Dugald, the son of Syfyn," giving them "the church of St. Colmanel, with the chapel of St. Columba, near his castle of Schypnincnhe, for the welfare of himself and his wives, and desiring that his body should be interred at Paisley."

Confirmation of these and similar gifts is to be found in a Bull of Pope Clement IV, dating from the reign of Alexander III, specifying among other possessions of the Abbey, "¹the churches of Kykkeran, of St. Colmanel, of Scybynche, with chapels, lands and pertinents," and going on to say: "We forbid anyone to dare to build chapel or oratory within the bounds of your parishes without your consent . . . ."

What that meant for Kintyre it is difficult for us to realise. "The little village church," says Dr. Taylor Innes², "preserving the memory of some early teacher of the faith, with its modest parsonage, where were wont to be found the consolations of religion, refuge and help for the needy, and encouragement for all on the road to heaven, was left in the hands of a stipendary vicar, an underling of the monastery, ground down to the lowest stipend that would support life, whose little soul was buried in his cloister, or showed its living activity only in disputing about his needful support with his master in the Abbey, while his hungry sheep looked up, and were not fed."

"The consequences of this system," says Dr. Cameron Lees, "might have been foreseen . . . It was one of the chief causes which brought about the destruction of the (Roman) Church. . . The tithes and property which it had obtained for the support of a resident clergy were swallowed up by the monks. The parochial system of the country was destroyed. . . . The advantages conferred by the monasteries were of small account compared with the mischief of degrading the parish clergy."

¹ Archæological Light on the Early Christianising of Scotland.
² Sketches of Early Scottish History

## Chapter VI

# "My Lord Marquess"

THERE has only been one Marquess of Argyll, for his father and his son were but Earls, while later heads of the family became Dukes. Owner of the whole of Kintyre during one of the most troubled periods of Scottish history, the fortunes of its church and its people were for nearly quarter of a century closely identified with his own. It was in 1607, the year of his birth—and just 47 years after the Scottish Reformation —that the peninsula came into the possession of the Campbell family in the person of his father; and it was in 1638—the year of the National Covenant—that Archibald succeeded to the title.

Slight and wiry, "with high forehead, long aquiline nose, small dark-blue eyes, slightly arched eyebrows," and reddish-fair hair, this 8th Earl and 1st (and only) Marquis of Argyll was a man as noted for his spirit of devotion as he was for craft of statesmanship.

"Very piouse," says Woodrow, the historian, "he rose at five and was still in privat till eight. Besides family worship, and private prayer morning and evening, he still prayed with his lady morning and evening. . . . He never went abroad, though but for one night, but he took his write-book, standish (ink-stand) and the English notes, Bible, and Neuman's Concordance with him."

"My Lord has brought me a friend from the Highlands of Argyle," wrote Samuel Rutherford, the great Covenanting leader, in the hour of his own deepest need, "My Lord of Lorn, who hath done as much for me as was in the compass of his power. I shall pray for him and his house while I live. It is his honour to open his mouth in the streets for his wronged and oppressed Master, Jesus Christ."

That was in 1636. Two years later, in November of 1638, after the signing of the National Covenant, there was held in Glasgow the famous General Assembly over which Alexander Henderson presided. There Argyll came out boldly as a Covenanter, the Moderator referring in his closing speech to "the comfort and strength given by his presence and counsel."

"The Earl of Argyll," wrote Hamilton, who was Lord High Commissioner that year, to the King in London, "is the only man now called up as a true patriot, a loyal subject, a faithful counsellor, and, above all, rightly set for the preservation of the purity of religion." For a young man of 31 he had certainly travelled far! After that his rise was rapid, and in 1641 he was created a Marquis.

Given a commission against the rebel Earls of Athol and Angus in 1640, and against Huntly in 1644, Argyll did not show to advantage as a soldier, and it was the people of Kintyre who had to suffer when surprised in his own country by his great rival, the Marquis of Montrose, he was compelled to flee for his life, later being disastrously defeated at Inverlochy.

When the sack of Dunaverty Castle ended the power of the Macdonalds in Kintyre in 1647, Argyll's estates were restored to him again, and it was he who, on the 1st of January, 1651, placed the Crown of Scotland on the head of Charles II at Scone, and who later installed him on his throne. Now at the height of his power, Argyll attempted what for him was the impossible.

"Sabbath night after supper," says Woodrow[1], from whom we have already quoted, "he went in with the King to his closet, and there used a great deal of freedom with him, and they came that length as to pray and mourn together till two or three in the morning. When at that time he came home to his Lady . . . he said he had never had such a sweet night in the world, and told her all; what liberty they had in prayer, and how much concerned the King was. She said plainly, they were 'crocodile tears' and that night would cost him his head."

The Marchioness was right—it did! Argyll and the King never met again, and when that nobleman went South after the Restoration to pay his homage, it was on the Sovereign's direct orders that he was seized and thrown into prison.

"The greatest subject the King had," said Robert Baillie, "it was not thought safe he should live"; and so, on 27th May, 1661, after a summary trial, accompanied through the streets of Edinburgh by fellow peers in mourning, by the Magistrates of the city, and by a great concourse of the people, the Marquis was led out to the Grassmarket to be beheaded.

" I could die like a Roman," he is reported to have said, "but I choose to die as a Christian." Nothing so much became this owner of wide acres as the way in which he met his fate—the first Martyr of the Covenant, reading his last, carefully-prepared speech from the scaffold, and praying with his dying breath that the King might be given good and faithful counsellors.

[1] Analecta

CHAPTER VII

# The " Relief" Expedition

AT the end of the 18th century there were in Scotland four Presbyterian denominations of some size and importance, the largest by far being the Church of Scotland itself, with a minister and congregation in every parish. Next, far behind in point of numbers, came the two Secession bodies, the Burgher and Anti-Burgher Churches. Smaller than either of these, but known for its tolerance, its catholicity, and its modernity of outlook, was the Relief Church—the first Presbyterian body to open its pulpit to all ministers of Christ and its Communion Table to all believers; the first to espouse the cause of Foreign Missions and to oppose the Slave Trade; the first to introduce a Hymn Book into its public worship. That was a record of which any church might well be proud!

It was in the early summer of 1796 that the Synod of Relief decided on the bold step of launching a "Mission to the Highlands." Certainly the times seemed propitious for such a move. Over the whole country, within the space of a few months, there had swept a great wave of missionary enthusiasm. Societies for the prosecution of aggressive work at home and abroad had been formed in every part of Scotland. Their coffers were full of money, and their prayer meetings were crowded. It seemed as if a new era had dawned, and it was only natural that a church like "The Relief" should wish to take advantage of this swelling tide.

It was on 18th May, 1796, that a resolution was passed by the Synod to appoint a committee to draw up a scheme for sending evangelical ministers, or probationers "to the Highlands."

It was just a year later that the two missionaries appointed set out on their journey. One was Daniel McNaught, Relief Minister at Dumbarton, himself a native of Southend and formerly a joiner in Campbeltown. The other was Neil Douglas, from Dundee, a firebrand whose extreme political views were later to get him into trouble, and to whose diary we are indebted for some account of this venture.

In Campbeltown itself the Relief Church had its only congregation in the Highlands, numbering some two thousand souls out of a population of nine thousand. In the neighbouring parish of Southend, a Relief Church was in process of being constituted, Daniel McNaught being appointed by the Relief Presbytery of Glasgow to preach there on the first and second Sundays in June, and to take part in the laying of the foundation stone of the new building.

"Preached at Southend" writes Neil Douglas,[1] "as appointed, the first Sabbath of August, when the number of people who attended was supposed to be about a thousand. The people were very attentive, and some of them, to appearance, much affected. . . . The walls of the church were nigh finished when I was there, and all the necessary materials collected and prepared. This is the second church erected in the Highlands in connection with the Relief."

"The first Wednesday of August," he continues, "I preached, according to intimation, at [2]Kilwhinny, where there is burying ground and the ruins of an old chapel, from John 14. 6—*I am the way*. The first discourse was in Gaelic, the other in English. The number of people who attended was computed to be about fifteen hundred, some thought two thousand. It was allowed to be the largest concourse of people met to hear a sermon on a week-day ever met in that country. . . . Many seemed to hear with more than ordinary concern." To this day, it is worth noting, Longrow—the old "Relief" congregation in Campbeltown, —is strongly represented in that area.

At Killean, a month earlier, there had been a memorable gathering. "The number of people who attended were thought to be not fewer than fifteen hundred, some of them from a considerable distance, chiefly men, by reason of the badness of the morning. . . . So heavy and constant was the rain as to make it scarcely possible to read the verses that were expounded. Yet the people stood with great composure all the time, many of them to all appearance deeply affected. . . . The tears of many flowed visibly . . . and their deep sighs and moans might easily be heard. . . . They stood like statues under the heavy rain, while deep concern seemed painted in every look, and every eye was fixed on the speaker."

Kintyre, it was clear from this and similar experiences on that mission, was hungry for the Gospel in these days, and was ready to make a response at once immediate and overwhelming.

---

[1] Journal of a Mission to Part of the Highlands of Scotland in Summer and Harvest, 1797.
[2] Kilchenzie

## Chapter VIII

# The Provost's Brother

A N outstanding figure in the life of Campbeltown for many
years in the middle of the 19th century, was John Beith,
Jun., for long Provost of the Burgh. Treasurer from the
time of the Disruption of the united congregations of the Free
Church—Highland and Lowland—he was largely responsible for
the erection of what is now Lorne Street Church. More conspicuous by far, however, were the services rendered to the
Church in Scotland by his brother, Alexander.

Born in Campbeltown on 13th January, 1799, the third of a family
of eight, Alexander Beith entered Glasgow University when only
twelve years old, and in his journal there is a graphic description
of his journey to the great city, most of it on foot. Licensed by
the Presbytery of Kintyre on 7th February, 1821, he preached
his first sermons in his native Campbeltown the following Sunday,
in both Gaelic and English. Minister successively at Oban, at
Hope Street, Glasgow, at Kilbrandon and at Glenelg, he was
inducted to the East Church of Stirling on 26th September, 1839.
It was in that town that his name was to be made and his work
was to be done.

Realising the tendency of the people to gravitate downwards
from the heights of the old town, Dr. Beith (as he later became) was
instrumental in the erection of a new place of worship—now
the North Church in Murray Place. It was opened in 1842,
and he became its first minister. These, however, were the days
of what came to be known as "The Ten Years Conflict"—the
period immediately preceding the Disruption of 1843. A warm
supporter of Dr. Thomas Chalmers and the Evangelical Party
which he led, Dr. Beith left no one in doubt as to where he stood.
A signatory to both the Act of Separation and the Deed of Demission, he was in the historic march to Tanfield Hall on the day
of the Disruption, and on the following Saturday night drove
back to Stirling in the stagecoach not knowing how many of his
people would follow him in the newly-constituted Free Church
of Scotland.

His supporters, who were not few, had taken the Corn Exchange,
seating 1,200, for the next day's services, and on the Sunday
morning it was filled to overflowing. Compelled to pay for the

church they had to vacate as well as to erect a new place of worship, Dr. Beith and his people went about their work with a will, and in April, 1844, their building was opened. Eight years later they vacated it for a second—what is now the South Church, Stirling. Long after Dr. Beith's death they moved again—this time to the Peter Memorial Church further west.

An author with many works to his credit, and an active leader in the work of the Free Church throughout the country, Dr. Beith was elected Moderator of its General Assembly in 1858, the year of the famous Cardross Case. The father of a family of fourteen, one of his daughters married Rev. J. Rennie Caird, for some years Minister of Lochend Church, Campbeltown.[1]

Under his ministry in Stirling in the early 60's sat two High School boys, already firm friends, and destined both to become world famous. One was Henry Drummond, the "St. Francis of our Scottish Presbyterianism," the most celebrated religious writer of his day—whose books are still being reprinted—and the most successful evangelist to students this country has ever known. The other was Dr. John Watson, of Sefton Park Church, Liverpool, better known by his pen-name of Ian Maclaren, whose family had but lately come to the town.

" I shall always remember the figure of Dr. Beith," says the author of *The Bonnie Brier Bush*, "moving through this town with a certain dignity which I think we of the younger generation of clergy have not been able always to sustain, and preaching in the pulpit with a note of authority which the pulpit now very seldom has."

It was in Dr. Beith's old age, and after his retirement to Edinburgh, that he was involved in the most famous episode of his life. William Robertson Smith, the great Old Testament scholar was on his trial for heresy, and the veteran minister of Stirling, who recalled so vividly the case of John Macleod Campbell, fifty years before, was anxious to prevent a like catastrophe.

"Authoritative decisions," said the speech read by his M.P. son, by permission, in his father's absence, "which are dictated by motives of expediency, however good the object may be, ultimately avail nothing. In the case of Professor Smith an extreme sentence would ere long appear indefensible and therefore not be for the truth but against it." "The Assembly," read his closing motion, "leaves the ultimate decision to future enquiry, in the spirit of patience, humility, and brotherly charity."

Taken in its context that is an utterance which deserves to ring down the corridor of history!

[1] And later of Middle Free Church, Paisley.

CHAPTER IX

# Founder of British East Africa

ABOVE the entrance to No. 23 Argyle Street, Campbeltown, is a plaque inserted in the wall. There, in clear white lettering on a dark blue background, one reads: "In this house lived Sir William Mackinnon, Baronet, the Founder of British East Africa; a Leader who added fleets to the Commerce and great territories to the Dominions of his Country. His life guided by Christian Charity and Courage is proudly remembered in this his native town. Born 1823. Died 1893. In Thy fear will I worship toward Thy Holy Temple. Psalm V. Erected by his friend Lord Lorn. 1894."

That, it would appear, is the only memorial in his native place to Campbeltown's most famous son. In the great East African port of Mombasa, however, a colossal statue of Sir William dominates the main square of the city. It was in Africa that his greatest work was done.

Born on 31st March, 1823, in comparatively humble circumstances, and brought up in a home "where religion was the ruling impulse," young Mackinnon went from Glasgow, where he had refused the offer of a partnership in the Portuguese East India merchant's office in which his training had been finished, to join his old schoolfellow, Robert Mackenzie, in one of the smaller towns on the Ganges in India. That was in 1846. Nine years later their successful coasting trade led them to Calcutta, where the firm of Mackenzie, Mackinnon & Co. still flourishes.

In 1856 they launched their shipping venture, beginning with a single vessel plying between Calcutta and Rangoon, and becoming, as the British East India Steam Navigation Co., with its 100 vessels, long before Sir William's death, one of the largest maritime concerns in the world. "Look out for a little Scotsman called Mackinnon," said Sir Bartle Frere to Sir Lewis Pelly, in 1862, when sending him to the Persian Gulf. "You will find that he is the mainspring of all the British interest there."

It was the opening of the Suez Canal that brought the little Scotsman to Africa, and in 1873 his steamers began their regular service from Aden to Zanzibar, linking up with those from India to Britain. "So satisfied was the Sultan of Zanzibar with the benefits accruing to his dominion," says Sheriff Macmaster Campbell in his monograph,[1] "and so firmly was he impressed by the integrity and the capacity of Sir William, that he made him one of the most extraordinary offers ever made by a reigning prince to the subject of another realm"—virtual sovereignty for 70 years over all his territories on the mainland of Africa.

Foreign Office coldness prevented the acceptance of that offer, but in 1888 the Imperial British East Africa Company came into being with Mackinnon as Chairman, and men like Sir John Kirk and Sir Thomas Fowell Buxton as his associates, to take advantage of another concession almost as great.

The published aims of the new Company included the abolition of the slave trade, the prohibition of commercial monopolies, equal treatment for men of all nations, complete religious liberty, and regulations governing the administration of justice whereby careful regard was to be had to the customs or laws of the class or nation to which persons belonged.

"The foundation of British East Africa," says the Government *Handbook of Kenya Colony and Kenya Protectorate*, "is due to the Company, and more particularly to its Chairman, Sir William Mackinnon." "No other trading corporation," says McGregor Ross, in his *Kenya from Within*, "has ever commanded the vigorous and practical support of missionary circles in Great Britain that was accorded to this Company. It set, in some respects, a higher standard in its treatment of native peoples than the British Government subsequently maintained."

Proprietor of the estates of Loup and Balinakill in his native Kintyre, most generous donor of his day to the work of the Free Church of Scotland, and helper of causes and individuals innumerable, Sir William Mackinnon, as he became in 1893, was the founder of the East Africa Scottish Mission, out of which came the Church of Scotland Kenya Mission, which recently celebrated its jubilee, with 14,000 African communicants and its flourishing schools, hospitals and churches. A few years before that, in saving the work of the Church Missionary Society in Uganda from extinction, he had averted what the *Times* foresaw as a national disaster and had saved Uganda for the British Crown.

"His record," said the *Scotsman*, at the time of his death, in June, 1893, "is one of which any man might be proud. He has done more for his country and mankind than those who have fought great battles and won them. His victories were those of peace, and they have indeed been great and beneficent. His name was known and his influence was felt in almost every part of the world."

[1] Sheriff Macmaster Campbell—*Sir William Mackinnon, Bt.*

## CHAPTER X

# The Bond of Brotherhood

NOTHING has been more characteristic of the church life of Campbeltown than the happy relations prevailing between ministers and congregations of different denominations. Beneath their real differences of outlook and tradition they have not been slow to discover an underlying unity of origin, of loyalty and of purpose.

It was on the 8th of June, 1808, that Rev. Norman Macleod—the celebrated *Caràid nan Gaidheal*—was ordained and inducted as Minister of the Highland Charge of Campbeltown, and from the beginning he had his difficulties. Welcomed with enthusiasm by a vast crowd of hearers of all classes, he was received with marked coldness by his brother Presbyters. When the relatives who had come to take part in his settlement returned home he accompanied them as far as Glen Saddell. Referring to this long afterwards he said:—

"When I parted from my friends I shall never forget the feeling of despondency, amounting almost to despair with which I returned to Campbeltown. . . . I had all the people on my side, and from none of them did I meet with greater sympathy than from the members of the Relief congregation, with the ministers and elders of that numerous and most respectable body."

Now the "Relief" might well have been regarded as the opposition church. It was to all intents and purposes a rival congregation. It belonged to another denomination. It had originated less than 50 years before in a breakaway from the local Church of Scotland! Yet a few years later it made one of the most striking gestures of friendliness and goodwill of which there is any record in the ecclesiastical annals of Scotland.

It came about in this way. The stipend of the Highland Charge of Campbeltown was small, and the new minister, now married, found himself saddled with increasing family responsibilities. When he was offered by the Duke of Hamilton and his brother, who were the patrons, the more attractive and better paid living of Kilmory in Arran, the temptation was a very real one. It was at this point that the Campbeltown Relief Church stepped in.

"The leading members of the Gaelic congregation," says Dr. Macleod's biographer,[1] "proposed to increase the stipend, and it is a most interesting fact, demonstrative of the Christian goodwill and kindly feeling that existed in Campbeltown at that time, that the managers of the Relief congregation offered to contribute a sum equal to what his own congregation gave." To that action, so far as we know, there is no parallel anywhere.

It was the privilege of the little Secession Church, in the aftermath of the Disruption of 1843, to show a like friendly spirit to the new English Free Church—comprising those who had left the Lowland Church of Scotland congregation in Campbeltown. For many months, until they were able to erect a building of their own, the members of that Church were accommodated in the Secession Meeting House, the hours of worship being so arranged as to suit both congregations.

Sixty years later it was the turn of the "Auld Kirk" to show kindness to a sister congregation in need. Dispossessed for a time of their premises, a result of the House of Lords' decision of 1905, Lorne Street United Free Church (as it had become) was befriended in many ways in her time of trial, not least by the Minister of the Highland Church of Campbeltown.

"On the walls of what we still lovingly call 'The Study,'" says Mrs. Hector Mackinnon in the biography of her husband, which gives so vivid a picture of the years he spent in Kintyre,[2] "hangs an illuminated address in the following terms :—

"At Campbeltown, the twenty-ninth day of March, 1905, which day the Kirk Session of the Lorne Street Congregation of the United Free Church met and was constituted; *Inter Alia*. It was cordially and unanimously agreed to, that in view of the approaching translation of the Reverend Hector Mackinnon, M.A., Minister of the Highland Parish Church of Campbeltown to the Parish Church of Shettleston, the session place on record their warm appreciation of the kindly sympathy and help which Mr. Mackinnon, from his own pulpit, and from that of Lorne Street and elsewhere, has so opportunely rendered to Lorne Street congregation in their time of special difficulty and trial as a congregation of the United Free Church of Scotland, and that they express their earnest prayer that his work may be as richly owned of God in his new pastorate as it has been in his former spheres of labour."

The same kindly spirit of friendly co-operation is manifest in Campbeltown to-day.

[1] John N. Macleod—*Memorials of Rev. Norman Macleod, Sen.*
[2] *Hector Mackinnon: A Memoir.*

## CHAPTER XI

# Its Native Air

IN Cuthbert Bede's *Glencreggan*, that racy account of things seen and heard in Kintyre ninety years ago, there is a graphic account of an open-air service at which the writer was present in the parish of Killean.

"I was an accidental witness to a novel and very impressive open-air service at Barr," says Bede, "given by the minister of the Free Church at Killean, on a Sunday evening, chiefly for the benefit of those who were unable to attend his (or any other) church. His preaching was in Gaelic, and was therefore altogether a dead letter to me. It was given *ore rotunda*, with great energy and action, and he engaged the devout attention of his hearers.

"The spot in which they were assembled was a field to the rear of the village, where the ground sloped towards the sea and the river. They sat before the preacher upon the green grass rising in so many tiers with the rise of the hillside, and picturesquely grouped. In front was a row of old crones, muffled in plaids, with their white mutches tied down by a black ribbon, and their parchment faces wrinkled and scarred by age and exposure. Among the women the long blue cloaks like bathing gowns, with thick woollen petticoats of dark blue or red stripes, predominated.

"A few of the lassies wore their pretty loose jackets of light pink, but had no other covering for the head than their own veils of hair. Their elders had nothing more than a cap or a plaid wrapped nun-like round their heads to protect them from the sharp evening air. The only bonnet wearers were the men, whose were the blue bonnets of Scotland. Here and there was a plaid, and though tartans were sadly deficient, yet, altogether there was more of the Scottish element in the dresses than I had seen on any other occasion.

"The minister sheltered by a few trees stood before his congregation with an open Bible in his hand. The sun was setting over the Atlantic and flooding the scene with a holy halo of golden light. The sea was close at hand within sight and hearing, its breakers rolling up on the shore with monotonous regularity, and the only sounds to be heard besides the preacher's voice, were the occasional plaintive cries of the gulls, and the crow of the moor-fowl, mingled with the deep diapason of the waves. The scene insensibly carried back the thoughts to the days of the Covenanters."

Convenanting conventicles there had been in Kintyre, perhaps near that very spot, and open-air Communions of which the memories linger to this day.

"A few Sundays after his admission," says the biographer of Norman Macleod, Minister of the Highland Church of Campbeltown, "the time for the administration of the Lord's Supper came on. At a meeting of Presbytery, held shortly before, all the members present refused to assist him on that solemn occasion, except on condition that there should not be a service in the open-air." Knowing how his predecessor, the great Dr. John Smith, had administered the Sacrament in the open field, he would not consent to this prohibition.

"The whole congregation to a man, remembering the efforts of Dr. Smith, determined to support him.[1]. . . On Sabbath morning, crowds came from the neighbouring parishes, and . . . it was calculated that there could not be fewer than four thousand hearers when the sermon was concluded. The minister and elders, followed by the mass of intending communicants, passed into the church by the front door, in the most quiet and deeply solemn manner, singing the 24th Psalm."

"Never to the day of my death," said Norman Macleod, referring to this service in after years, "can I forget that solemn hour."

When Christianity returns to the open-air it is going back to its native air. It was a fitting thing, then, that the Presbytery of Kintyre, meeting in Campbeltown on 26th April, 1921, should have decided to celebrate the 1,400th anniversary of the birth of St. Columba with a service at Southend, where, according to tradition, the great missionary first set foot on Scottish soil.

"When the day arrived," says the Minister of Southend, "long before the hour appointed for the ceremony, all the roads leading to the sacred and historic spot of Keil were thronged with people . . . some of whom had come a distance of 30 miles. The service was held on the site of the first Columban Church, on the rising ground west of the old Churchyard of Keil-Colm-Kil, on the spot locally known as St. Columba's footmarks."

That service has now become an annual event, and on a June Sunday evening, as many as 1,000 people may gather, "Singing, the grand old Psalms of David and lifting up their hearts in gratitude to God for the blessing of the eternal Gospel."

[1] John N. Macleod—*Memorials of Rev. Norman Macleod, Sen.*

CHAPTER XII

# The Romance of Willow Creek

IN the year 1821 the joint population of the three country parishes of Kintyre—Killean, Saddell, and Southend—was over 7,000. By 1851 it had fallen to 5,000, and by 1881 to less than 3,500. From all these rural areas there had been, during that period, a steady stream of emigration to the Colonies and to America.

It was in the year 1739, according to Professor J. P. Maclean of Cleveland, that the first Kintyre settlement in the United States took place, in the State of North Carolina. It was in Illinois, however, in what was then the Far West, on the borders of Boone and Winnebago Counties, that the largest Kintyre Colony in the world was to grow up, in a district appropriately named Argyle.

The first to arrive in this area from the home country was James Armour, a shoemaker from Ottawa, U.S.A. There in North Illinois, in what had been until a few months before the hunting-grounds of the Winnebago Indians, the ashes of whose camp fires were still to be seen on the ground when he took possession, this intrepid Scotsman staked out his claim to a lot of timber and prairie land.

In the summer of 1836 came John Greenlees—Greenlee, as he came to be known—and his wife. The first to take up permanent residence, they were the real founders of this Argyle in the Far West, and their daughter Ellen was the first child to be born in the colony. From the Campbeltown and Southend districts, belonging almost wholly to the distinctively Lowland stock of Kintyre, came then in rapid succession the Reids, Pickens, Howies, Ralstons, Andrews, and McEacherns. By 1841 there were 17 Kintyre families resident in this district.

It was in the homes of John Greenlee and Andrew Giffen that the first services were held, a little log schoolhouse being built in 1842 to serve as classroom and place of worship. Two years later there followed the first log church, and it was in that primitive building, with its walnut pews and latched doors, and its box pulpit painted white, that the Willow Creek Presbyterian Church was formally constituted in December, 1844, the first Communion Service being held on Sunday, 13th January, 1845.

23

Sailing direct from Campbeltown to New York in June of 1842, the good ship *Gleaner* had brought a large contingent of settlers bound for Argyle, and in 1850 there was a further big influx. Built on the same principle as their "Relief" churches at home in Kintyre—by the selling of seats in perpetuity to pay the cost, the first log building stood till 1850, its timber having been brought from Chicago on the return journey by the members who were fortunate enough to own horse transport.

1850 saw the building of a brick church, and 27 years later the present handsome structure was raised at a cost of $12,500.

In the 100 years of its history the Church has had some 20 ministers. "I do not think," said Rev. M. L. Pearson, whose term of service was the longest of all, "that any minister's education is complete until he has had a pastorate in the Willow Creek Church. The Scotch people," he went on to say, recalling his own ministry in the district," are appreciative, but they are not demonstrative."

That was at the 75th Anniversary Celebration, when tribute was paid by the representative of Freeport Presbytery to Willow Creek's well-earned reputation for loyalty to Presbyterian tenets and forms of worship. Passed at that gathering was a resolution which showed how true this Scottish Colony was to the traditions of the homeland.

"Resolved," it read, "that the six hundred people assembled in Willow Creek Presbyterian Church, at Argyle, Illinois, in celebration of the Seventy-fifth Anniversary of its history, do hereby respectfully and earnestly petition the Constitutional Convention of the State of Illinois to replace the Bible to its rightful place in our public schools, that it may continue to exercise its beneficent influence upon the foundation stones of public life." The phraseology may be that of America, but the spirit is that of Kintyre.

Early in 1945, the Church celebrated its Centenary. During that first 100 years there had been only 35 elders in this congregation of 700 members. Five of these bore the name of Greenlee, four that of Ralston; Howie, Picken, Giffen, Andrew, Montgomery and McEachern were others conspicuous on the list. A few months before the new minister, Rev. Robert C. Hubbard, the present incumbent, had introduced, for the first time in Argyle, Illinois, the wearing of the Geneva gown. Willow Creek, it was clear, was entering its second century's history true to the old Kintyre traditions, and strong in the loyalty of the old Kintyre families.

## Chapter XIII

# Women Who Helped

NO one will ever know how much the churches in Kintyre owe to their women folk. By their presence and their prayers, their character and their influence, their giving and their self-sacrifice, they have enriched the life and work of the fellowship beyond all power to estimate.

Near the hamlet of Whitehouse there are two little burial grounds. In one of these lie the remains of Miss Lucy Campbell, of Gowanbank, Campbeltown, a woman to whom the whole peninsula owes a real debt of gratitude. In her lifetime she built two schools in the Dalintober district—one for poor boys and the other for poor girls—endowing them at her own expense. To the Female School of Industry she left in her will the sum of £600; for the support of a parochial missionary, £300; for Sabbath Schools, £300; for the poor of the parish, £500; and to the Female Benevolent Society, £600.

Miss Campbell died in 1843. Sixty-three years later the *Campbeltown Courier* drew the attention of its readers to some of the many benefits they owed to this "Lady Bountiful." The list was an impressive one, and is well worth quoting :—

"*Orphan Hospital, Edinburgh,* £1,150. One child per annum may be sent.

"*Blind Asylum, Glasgow,* £2,300. Takes any number of scholars or inmates from any part of Kintyre. To be supplied with all necessities at the expense of the institution, except clothing.

"*Deaf and Dumb Institution, Glasgow,* £1,725. Takes patients and scholars from the parish of Campbeltown at all times free, and to any number.

"*Eye Infirmary, Glasgow,* £575. Takes patients at all times, and to any number free.

"*Royal Infirmary, Glasgow.* Takes patients to the number of 40 annually, free of all expense whatever.

"*Magdalene's Hospital, Glasgow,* £1,150. A girl may be sent at any time if there happens to be a vacancy."

"Presentation in these cases," one reads, was to be "by the Minister and Kirk Session."

The women of other churches were not one whit behind!

In the year 1880 Lochend Church, Campbeltown, received the gift of a suite of halls for Sunday School and missionary work. No plaque commemorates the donor, but it is well-known that Miss Helen Love of Hawthorn, herself an enthusiastic worker in the congregation, gave and raised the money which made this addition of premises possible. It is nearly twenty years since Miss Love died, but the room in which she taught is still known as "Miss Love's Room," and the pew in which she sat as "Miss Love's Pew."

It is of her married sister, Mrs. Peter Mackinnon, that Emma Powell writes in a biography of her grandmother, Mrs. D. L. Moody[1]: "The New Year of 1874 ushered in, among many of other blessings, a new and wonderful friendship for the entire Moody family, that of the Peter Mackinnons whom they first met in Edinburgh. Often throughout the following pages their names will appear. The last gift of Mrs. Mackinnon to Emma Revell (Mrs. Moody) was a leather volume called: *Recollections of 1874, Part I, Work in Scotland; Part II, Work in Ireland.* It is an invaluable record of all the details of the Moodys' sojourn in the British Isles."

That little book by a Campbeltown woman, with its unforgettable thumb-nail sketches of the great Revival, has been used by all subsequent biographers of the American evangelist, and is recognised to-day as one of the most valuable source books we have on the religious life of the period.

At the foot of New Quay Head, where it joins the esplanade, is a fountain surmounted by a lion with its right paw upraised. Held by that paw for many years, until displaced by an accident, was a metal shield on which these words were inscribed:—

"Erected by the fishermen of Campbeltown in affectionate remembrance of their friend, Katherine Mary Elizabeth Campbell, of Kildalloig, who died 22nd August, 1906. Aged 31 years."

On the day her body was taken south for burial "20 of the fishermen she loved so well, and in whose lives she had taken so deep an interest," mustered at the door of her home to carry the coffin to the pier, flags of the town were flown at half-mast as the cortege approached, and the streets were lined by the weeping poor.

This may be Kintyre's only monument to women's work and worth, but Katherine Campbell was but one of the many who have loved, toiled and served, inspired by the "Man of Galilee."

[1] Emma Powell—*Heavenly Destiny: The Life Story of Mrs. D. L. Moody.*

CHAPTER XIV

# In Lonely Splendour

IT was the month of June, 1921, in Oban, eight years before the union of the Church of Scotland and the United Free Church. A conference of the ministers and missionaries of both of these in Argyll and the Isles was being held, the Chairman being the Very Rev. Principal Martin, of New College, Edinburgh. Out of the depths of what was manifestly his own rich experience, the minister of the island parish of Gigha had just spoken, his quiet humour and deep feeling, his soft voice and almost mesmeric charm, bringing everyone present under his spell.

"Who is that man?" the Chairman asked at the close of the session. He was told. "That is a most remarkable man," said the United Free Church leader, to his Church of Scotland friend who had supplied the answer, "Are there any more such in your Church among the Isles?" He was told that there were none—that Donald Macfarlane stood alone—this tall fair-haired Celt, with his blue eyes and noble forehead; this born sailor whose skill in handling a boat was only equalled by his courage; this builder of churches and physician of souls, who was in such demand for Ordination and Communion Services.

Born at his father's manse of Killean, on the western coast of Kintyre, and educated at the local school in Cleit, Donald Macfarlane had gone to Glasgow University at the age of 13, so small in stature that his gown trailed behind him. Four years later he had graduated in Arts, and on 13th December, 1882, when still only 21 years old, he had been ordained at Morven on the west coast, as Minister of that famous parish, in succession to the two Macleods—Norman[1] and John, father and son—whose joint ministry had covered a period of more than 100 years.

It was not an easy task that young Macfarlane undertook. The names of his predecessors were known from end to end of Scotland. Both had been Moderators of the General Assembly of their Church.[2] Their story had been given to the world by Norman Macleod in *Reminiscences of a Highland Parish*.

It was at Morven that Macfarlane passed through the spiritual crisis of his life, the problem of his personal faith and of his relation to his calling emerging for him there in its acutest form. It was his mother's faith and prayers, her unfailing trust and

[1] Father of the Campbeltown Minister.    [2] Of the Barony Church, Glasgow.

quiet commonsense, that helped to carry him through. Thrown from a dogcart at this period he had suffered serious injury. "In the silence of his enforced retreat," says his biographer,[1] "the light of heaven broke . . . The Cross supplied his need. It drew his gaze away from self. It centred it upon another."

From Morven, Macfarlane went to the island of Gigha, just off the Kintyre coast. From the study window there he could see his father's manse in Killean, across the narrow intervening stretch of water. There his ministry of consolation proved to be one of the many fruits of the experience through which he himself had come. There, too, he believed his most fruitful work was done. "When Mr. Macfarlane came among us," said one of his parishioners afterwards, "we were an ignorant people; he has taught us almost everything we know."[1]

Macfarlane was a Church builder, and in the Parish of Morven he left behind him two new places of worship—at Ferenish and Keil. He died at Gigha the day before his 62nd birthday, just as the new church he had planned for the island was about to be built. It stands there to-day as his memorial. Within it is a beautiful stained-glass window which his friends raised to his memory. In the background it shows the boat in which Columba sailed from Ireland. In the foreground the pioneer missionary is kneeling on the shore in the attitude of prayer. The inscription is a simple and moving one.

"He was utterly unlike any minister of religion whom I had ever met," wrote Dr. Norman Maclean,[1] recalling his first encounter with Macfarlane, in a Hebridean Hotel, "the first morning he arrived he awoke me with his singing. . . . For me he opened a door into a new world. . . . The way he read and prayed showed me he had entered into the secret place of the Most High. . . . This man, who seemed to my eyes the ideal minister, allowed no wall to separate him from his fellow Christians. He had a good word for them all."

"The sound of his name," wrote another,[1] "is music to my heart, and the music is often there. . . . In common with so many of my brethren in the Church of Scotland, his thought, his teaching, and his spirit so interfused my own as to become at last an indestructible part of my being. . . . Here was a man who lived for the smile of One Face. . . . Had he lived in Galilee when Jesus lived with flesh, I doubt not, but that the Master of them that know would have companied with this man."

[1] Sydney Smith—"Donald Macfarlane of Gigha and Cara."

CHAPTER XV

# Carradale's Contribution

THE little village of Carradale, halfway up the eastern side of Kintyre, is one of the beauty spots of Scotland. With its sandy bays and white-washed cottages, its tree-lined roads and rock-cuttings, its picturesque harbour and rhododendron-covered hills, it looks across the Kilbrannan Sound to Arran, only four miles away.

To Carradale, late in the 1890's, came Samuel Mackenzie, Evangelist, to conduct a fortnight's Mission in what was then the little Free Church in the village. So manifest was the interest, and so evident the blessing attending the preaching of the Word, that the evangelist stayed a full month in the district.

Among those who came under religious impression at this time was the 13-year-old son of Richard Semple—farmer, elder, lay preacher, and active worker in the Free Church. It was the lambing season, and although young Duncan had not left school, he was just marking time till he should be fourteen, and many a day that he might have been at work in the classroom he was to be found instead on the hill with his father.

"What are you going to be, Duncan?" said the father one morning as they stood together on the slopes of Beinn Bhreac, the highest hill in the district, right in the heart of the pensinsula, "A farmer?" "No," said the boy immediately, "A missionary!" It was the first hint he had given of such a thought, and they sat down together in silence for a few minutes on a nearby stone. It was a day for long thoughts and far views. Below them spread the western isles; Ireland could be seen on the horizon.

"That," said the father, "will mean going back to school for some years—and hard work." Duncan said he knew it would. When they made their way back home down the hill, both knew instinctively that the matter was settled.

Five years later Duncan Semple went up to Glasgow, to begin his course of study at the University, and in due time he graduated and finished his course in Divinity. Then, in 1912, he sailed for South Africa, an ordained missionary of the United Free Church of Scotland, Carradale's first contribution to the work of the Church among the heathen.

For 37 years now Duncan Semple has served with distinction

in the South African Mission Field—as Chaplain and Tutor in Theology at Lovedale and at Fort Hare, the two great educational institutions in Cape Colony; and as District Missionary at Emgwali, at Sulenkama, at Cunningham, and at Blythswood, where, combining the work of farm manager with his other duties he was able to make the station's extensive acres pay their way and yield a profit. Always and everywhere a leader of his people in the improvement both of housing and of stock, his strength has been given to the building up of a strong African Church, and to the creation of homes in which the Bible and family worship would have their proper place. Moderator of the Bantu Presbyterian Church of South Africa in 1941, he is to-day the senior Church of Scotland missionary in active service in the whole of Africa. It is a record of which Carradale may well be proud!

Brought up in the home of another elder of that congregation, was Helen Cook—not yet born when Samuel Mackenzie came to Carradale. Leaving home at the age of 21 to train as a nurse in the Glasgow Royal Infirmary, and going on to take her C.M.B. at Edinburgh, she worked for some time in the West Lothian village of Winchburgh as district nurse.

It was while she was undergoing her training that Helen Cook came under religious impression, influenced as she was by the life and witness of a cousin who was going out to Brazil as a missionary. Some years later she herself offered for that field, but it was to Peru that she eventually went under the auspices of the Evangelical Union of South America, the first six months of her missionary service being spent in the city of Arequipa.

From Arequipa Helen Cook went to the little Quecha village of Pitumarca, 12,000 feet above sea level, and close to the old Inca capital of Cuzco. It was there—among Indians sunk in sin and superstition—illiterate, downtrodden and drunken, but warmhearted and lovable people, that her work was done until her marriage, in 1933, to Rev. William Creighton of the Irish Baptist Mission to South America.

After that her life lay more in the towns—among the Aymara Indians of Peru, at Puno, on the shores of Lake Titicaca, close to the Bolivian frontier; then on the coast of Southern Peru; and finally, for three years, before her return to Ireland, at Rosario in the Argentine Republic. The mother of five children, her husband is still at work in the Lake Titicaca district.

## CHAPTER XVI

# The Invasion of Largie Castle

APPROACHED by an avenue which leaves the main Tarbert to Campbeltown Road just before the hamlet of Tayinloan is reached, Largie Castle belongs to a branch of the famous Macdonald family which has played so notable a part in the history of Kintyre. Built in the first half of the 19th century, in what has been described as the "French baronial" style, its battlements command a magnificent view of the islands. Immediately below lie Gigha and Cara, the latter still part of the Largie estate; beyond are Jura and Islay.

To Largie Castle in the middle of August, 1949—by motor-bicycle, by special bus and shooting-brake, and on foot, to the number of about fifty—came the members of the Church of Scotland Summer Training School in Kintyre, a very miscellaneous company. Down in the entrance hall of the castle, which served as refectory and office, they mingled and talked—ministers, divinity and other students, day-school teachers and landed proprietors, young men and women from office and bank, from shop and factory; some from as far away as Aberdeenshire and the Solway, and even from Italy and Africa, others from Kintyre itself.

A quite unusual type of Summer School this was—capable of being mounted on a seven-ton lorry and completely mobile, so far as its equipment was concerned; staffed, both in kitchen and classroom, entirely by voluntary workers who shared to the full in the life of the fellowship; combining in the most realistic way possible theoretical and practical training; and making its facilities available both for those on holiday and for those who were at their daily work in Campbeltown, some eighteen miles away.

For several days the "School" had been located in the Parish of Southend, where visits had been paid to lonely lighthouse keepers and to dwellers in remote glens, and where lectures had been given, and Bible study and meetings held, in the picturesque St. Columba Church. For a week it had been centred in Carradale, special Sunday afternoon services being held on the Sunday afternoon there at beautiful Port Righ Bay and within the ivy-clad ruins of Saddell Abbey. Now it had come to the west coast of the peninsula, that the area from Whitehouse to Kilchenzie might be visited as that from Skipness to Peninver had been, few homes however remote being missed.

It was one of the aims of this Summer Training School that the people of the districts in which it was held might have the opportunity of meeting some of these young folk from all over Scotland and from beyond the seas, many of whom had been taking part in July in the Summer Seaside work of the Church, and of hearing from them something of what they were doing, and of what they had discovered. It was also the intention that they should have the chance of seeing for themselves, on their own doorstep and by their firesides, some of the new literature which the Church was producing for old and young alike.

Within the castle itself was activity and variety in abundance. On the floors of the upstairs rooms were stretched palliasses which had once been intended for the needs of air-raid victims, serving—with a handful of army blankets and a pillow to each—as beds for the trainees. In the cosy dining room gathered for study each forenoon and evening those whose period it was indoors (next day they might be out visiting) while down in the kitchen went forward a schedule which provided for the manifold needs of this company from "1st Breakfast" at 6.45 (for those beginning work in Campbeltown at 8) to "last Supper," for those coming in from late visitation, just before midnight.

An unforgettable experience this was, destined to leave its mark on many lives. Already from that Summer School with its fun and its fellowship, its deep commerce of mind with mind and heart with heart, its open air and indoor meetings, and its visitation of home, farm and tourist hotel, have gone three young men to whom the call came in August, to begin their preparation for the ministry; while others have returned to their homes and daily work with a new vision of possibilities, a new sense of loyalty to Christ and His Church, and a new realisation of the meaning of Christian discipleship.

It was after the main body had left Largie that the rearguard crossed one afternoon to the little island of Sanda,[1] embarking at Dunaverty Bay under the shadow of the famous rock. And it was by a son of Kintyre who had given his life to missionary work in far-off Africa that the address was given, two hours later, at the little service held in the home of one of the lighthouse keepers on that lonely island. How the heart of St. Ninian would have rejoiced! It was the fitting climax to a Summer School full of promise for the future of the Church in Scotland.

[1] See Chapter I.

# FOR FURTHER READING

IN addition to book named in *It Happened In Kintyre*, the following are suggested for further reading. They are arranged in the same order as the stories in this booklet.

---

H. CAMERON GILLIES. 'The Place Names of Argyll.' (1906. David Nutt, London. 273 pages).

Sheriff J. MACMASTER CAMPBELL. 'The Island and House of Sanda.' (1924. *Campbeltown Courier*. 37 pages.)

T. HARVEY THOMSON. 'The Ancient Churches and Chapels of Kintyre.' (*Campbeltown Courier*. 71 pages).

ARCHIBALD B. SCOTT. 'St. Ninian: Apostle of the Britons and Picts.' A Research Study for the First Founding of the Church in Britain. (1916. David Nutt. 132 pages).

T. B. STEWART THOMSON. 'A Guide to Govan Old Parish Church, Glasgow.' (Henry Munro Ltd. 24 pages).

J. CAMERON LEES. 'The Abbey of Paisley from its Foundation till its Dissolution.' (1878. Alex. Gardner. 525 pages).

A. R. HOWELL. 'Paisley Abbey: Its History, Architecture and Art.' (Alex. Gardner. 173 pages).

ALEXANDER SMELLIE. 'Men of the Covenant.' (1903. Andrew Melrose. 433 pages).

GAVIN STRUTHERS. 'The Rise, Progress and Principles of the Relief Church.' (1843. A. Fullerton & Co. 573 pages.)

NEIL DOUGLAS. 'Journal of a Mission to Part of the Highlands of Scotland in Summer and Harvest, 1797—By Appointment of the Synod of Relief.' (1799. Thomas Turnbull, Edinburgh. 189 pages).

A. McLAREN YOUNG. 'Southern Kintyre in History.' (1898. David M. Small. 85 pages).

'Kenya 1898-1948: The Jubilee Book of the Church of Scotland Mission, Kenya Colony.' (1948. Church of Scotland Foreign Mission Committee. 48 pages).

JOHN M. MACLEOD. 'Memorials of the Rev. Norman Macleod, Sen., D.D., of St. Columba's Church, Glasgow.' (1898. David Douglas. 303 pages).

M J. MACKINNON; 'Hector Mackinnon: A Memoir.' (1914. Marshall Bros. 234 pages).

'Centenary Brochure of St. Columba's Church, Stirling.' (1943. Jamieson & Munro, Ltd. 72 pages).

ED. HORACE BUTLER WARD. 'The Diamond Jubilee of the Willow Creek Presbyterian Church of Argyle, Illinois.' (1920. Daily News Publishing Co., Benoit, Wis., U.S.A.

ED. R. C. HUBBARD and MONTELLE M. BOYD. 'The Centennial Anniversary of the Willow Creek Presbyterian Church of Argyle, Illinois.' (1920. Willow Creek Church. 106 pages).

Various.—'The Statistical Account of Argyllshire.' (1845. Wm. Blackwood & Sons, Ltd. 728 pages).

EMMA MOODY POWELL. 'Heavenly Destiny: The Life Story of Mrs. D. L. Moody.' (1943. Moody Press, Chicago. 343 pages).

"J. M." (JESSIE MACKINNON). 'Recollections of D. L. Moody and his Work in Britain, 1874-1892.' (1905. Printed for Private Circulation. 290 pages).

SYDNEY SMITH. 'Donald Macfarlane of Gigha and Cara: A Biographical Sketch.' (1925. James Clarke & Co., Ltd. 141 pages).

# *CONTENTS*

*List of Books Recommended for Further Reading*

## Price One Shilling

Pickering & Inglis Ltd., Glasgow